PRIME TIME
LAW ENFORCEMENT

PRIME TIME
LAW ENFORCEMENT

Crime Show Viewing and Attitudes Toward the Criminal Justice System

James M. Carlson

PRAEGER SPECIAL STUDIES • PRAEGER SCIENTIFIC

New York • Philadelphia • Eastbourne, UK
Toronto • Hong Kong • Tokyo • Sydney

Library of Congress Cataloging in Publication Data

Carlson, James M.
  Prime time law enforcement.

  Bibliography: p.
  Includes index.
  1. Crime in television. 2. Political
socialization. 3. Criminal justice, Administration
of--Social aspects--United States. I. Title.
PN1992.8.D48C37 1985   302.2′345   85-9420
ISBN 0-03-003538-4 (alk. paper)

Published in 1985 by Praeger Publishers
CBS Educational and Professional Publishing, a Division of CBS Inc.
521 Fifth Avenue, New York, NY 10175 USA

© 1985 by Praeger Publishers

56789 052 987654321

Printed in the United States of America on acid-free paper

INTERNATIONAL OFFICES

Orders from outside the United States should be sent to the appropriate address listed below. Orders from areas not
listed below should be placed through CBS International Publishing, 383 Madison Ave., New York, NY 10175 USA

Australia, New Zealand
Holt Saunders, Pty, Ltd., 9 Waltham St., Artarmon, N.S.W. 2064, Sydney, Australia

Canada
Holt, Rinehart & Winston of Canada, 55 Horner Ave., Toronto, Ontario, Canada M8Z 4X6

Europe, the Middle East, & Africa
Holt Saunders, Ltd., 1 St. Anne's Road, Eastbourne, East Sussex, England BN21 3UN

Japan
Holt Saunders, Ltd., Ichibancho Central Building, 22-1 Ichibancho, 3rd Floor, Chiyodaku, Tokyo, Japan

Hong Kong, Southeast Asia
Holt Saunders Asia, Ltd., 10 Fl, Intercontinental Plaza, 94 Granville Road, Tsim Sha Tsui East, Kowloon,
Hong Kong

**Manuscript submissions should be sent to the Editorial Director, Praeger Publishers, 521 Fifth Avenue,
New York, NY 10175 USA**

For my wife Harriet and
my daughter Erica

PREFACE AND ACKNOWLEDGMENTS

The influence of television has never been a major topic for research on political socialization. Early studies of voting behavior and a major study of media effects published at about the time interest in political socialization was developing led researchers to assume that the mass media has "limited effects" on political orientations. It is only recently that there has been a renewal of interest in mass media effects on politically relevant attitudes. This renewed interest has led to a set of findings that indicate that television may have a greater influence on electoral politics than previously thought. I argue in this book that television deserves renewed attention as an agent of political socialization. The results of my research show that a particularly popular form of television entertainment—crime dramas—cultivate conceptions of the nature of crime, law, and the criminal justice system.

The central ideas of this book are drawn from two quite distinct literatures. The political socialization literature gives scant attention to television but has focused on fundamental questions concerning the stability of political systems. The literature on mass media has been less concerned with the political substance of television's messages than the conditions under which effects occur. I think the research reported in this book reflects the benefits of a multidisciplinary perspective.

I have many people to thank for help in completing this project. Two students assistants, Lynn Mullins and Cheryl Morrissey, worked closely with me in the initial stages of the study. They watched many hours of crime shows and also helped collect and code the questionnaire data. A third assistant, Patricia McLaughlin, became involved in the project later and helped with the analysis of the data. Access to the student sample was facilitated by the cooperation of school superintendents, principals, and teachers. I am grateful for their help. Funding for the project was provided by the Providence College Committee on Aid for Faculty Research.

I incurred many debts from colleagues at the writing stage of the project. Initially some of the data were presented in papers delivered at conventions. I am grateful for the comments offered by Norman Luttbeg and Edie Goldenberg on my paper on civil liberties. Ethan

Katsh read several papers and chapters and was particularly encouraging and helpful. Robert Trudeau offered useful suggestions at different points in the project.

I am especially grateful to Mark S. Hyde and Bruce McKeown who read the entire manuscript. Few scholars are blessed with associates who are both good friends and good critics. Finally, I want to thank Grace Petrarca for typing and proofreading the manuscript. Her patience and tolerance contributed greatly to the reduction of anxiety throughout the project.

Portions of Chapter 8 appeared in "Crime Show Viewing by Pre-adults: The Impact on Attitudes Toward Civil Liberties," *Communication Research*, Vol. 10, No. 4 (October 1983): 529-552 and are reprinted by permission.

CONTENTS

LIST OF TABLES

PRIME TIME
LAW ENFORCEMENT

I

TELEVISION AND SOCIALIZATION

INTRODUCTION

Television entertainment plays an important role in the development of conceptions of law, legal compliance, and criminal justice.
Perhaps it is not surprising that the most pervasive medium in American culture makes measurable contributions to conceptions of reality,
but there has been very little research on the influence of entertainment programming on attitudes that are relevant to social control and
the persistence of the political system. Television, unlike other agents
of socialization except the family, is present virtually at birth. Its influence is present long before a child enters school or gains access to
media that require literacy. To the extent that Americans lead relatively secluded lives and do not experience many aspects of contem-
porary life, television provides a window to the world; it is the one
agent of socialization all Americans have in common. If television has
become such an important member of American families (the average
American watches over seven hours per day) and a major source of our
conceptions of reality, it is important to determine what it is teaching
to whom.

The messages transmitted through television are not accurate reflections of reality, nor are they neutral with regard to social and political values. Recent research has made it clear that there is a "television
reality" that is quite distinct from the "real world." Television programming does not accurately reflect the real world because those who

1

transmit the images are constrained by a wide variety of factors including societal values, the need to maximize audience size, organizational procedures, and personal values.[1]

Despite the great deal of attention given to the possible antisocial consequences of television viewing in recent years there is increasing evidence that the medium presents programming that encourages values that are supportive of the status quo. It seems especially likely that American television programming plays a system-supportive role; the major networks are owned and operated by those who have a vested interest in current economic and political arrangements. Indeed the historical role of the mass media has always been to promote stability. George Gerbner and Larry Gross remind us that:

> Throughout history, once a ruling class has established its rule, the primary function of its cultural media has been the legitimation and maintenance of its authority. Folk tales and other traditional dramatic teaching stories have always reinforced established authority, teaching that when society's rules are broken, retribution is visited upon the violators. The importance of the existing order is always implicit in such stories.[2]

It may be the case that the same type of programming satisfies two requirements of those who control television entertainment. The entire industry is aimed at developing programming that will attract an audience for advertising. To the extent that audiences share values that are system supportive, successful programs will likely be those that reflect viewpoints that contribute to the maintenance of the social and political order.

This book represents a shift in attention away from the antisocial effects of television programming and provides some evidence that television entertainment, specifically police-crime shows, promotes social stability and control by reinforcing the perceived legitimacy of current power arrangements. Television entertainment has not been considered an important source of political values until very recently. The beliefs that television has "limited effects" on politically relevant issues and a narrow focus on explicitly "political" messages (news and documentaries) have obscured the role of electronic media in sociopolitical learning.

ORIGINS OF SUPPORT FOR THE SYSTEM

Political scientists have given a great deal of attention to the concept of support for the political system. Systems-persistence theory developed by David Easton includes a concept of support defined as "any kind of favorable orientation that prepares a person to act in behalf of or in opposition to a political object."[3] Easton identified three general objects of support: political authorities, the political regime, and the political community. Each of the three objects, according to Easton, must receive diffuse support from most of the people most of the time to prevent or at least reduce stress on the political system.

The political regime refers to the "rules of the game" in the political system. Political scientists usually operationalize orientations toward the regime in terms of the extent to which citizens are knowledgeable about legal rules and the extent to which they willingly comply with the law. Support for the regime also implies that citizens support the basic form of government. In the United States this means that citizens support the basic principles of democracy, as embodied in the Constitution, and take a limited participatory role.

Political authorities refer to the persons who occupy the roles in the regime whether it is the "cop on the beat" or the president of the United States. Support for authorities rests on the assumption that they occupy their roles legitimately; they attained their positions by adhering to the rules of the game. Support for authorities is usually operationalized in terms of respect for such objects as police officers, the president, and other elected or appointed officials.

The political community refers to the implicit sense that groups of people have that they should share in governing, be governed together, and be subject to the same rules of the game. A sense of community implies a generalized trust in one's fellow citizens—an agreement in the case of the United States that collective decisions should be supported. Oftentimes political community is measured in terms of attachments to symbols such as the flag. Basically a strong sense of community implies that individuals feel secure and comfortable with those who surround them.

Socialization is the important mechanism that develops diffuse support for the objects of the political system. A large number of studies have shown that children develop support for authorities, the regime, and the community at an early age. Children at a surprisingly young age develop positive orientations toward the president and police officers.[4] They learn the rules of the game and the requirements of citizenship, as well as develop attachments to the community.

The basic system-supportive orientations are learned from the major agents of socialization. The agents that have received the most attention are the family and the school, but it is usually acknowledged that other agents such as peer groups, churches, and the mass media have at least some influence.

A number of learning models have been put forward to explain how system-supportive attitudes and behavior are developed,[5] but among political scientists it is probably a correct generalization to state that research has been dominated at least implicitly by the "primacy principle" and the "structuring principle." The primacy principle reflects the influence of early psychoanalytic theory on socialization research. It quite simply states that "what is learned early in life is learned best; the orientations that are developed in childhood endure and are relatively unchanged as individuals mature."[6] The structuring principle, which is related to the primacy principle, states that what is learned early in life are very general orientations toward authority, rules, etc. and these general orientations "structure" the acquisition of more specific attitudes later in the life cycle.[7] For example a child may develop a generalized understanding of the norm of compliance in the family. Later this understanding that "rules are to be obeyed" is applied to specific situations facing adults. In recent years scholars have given increased attention to adult socialization, but the belief that childhood is a critical period still dominates.

Given the dominance of the primacy and structuring principles, it is not surprising that the family and school have received the most attention from students of socialization. Focus has been on the transference of positive images of parents as authority figures to authority figures such as policemen and the president.[8] Attention has been given to the relationship between the norm of obedience developed in school and compliance with the law. Agents other than the family and school have been seen as playing a role in the reinforcement of orientations that were developed early in life.

The mass media have been viewed as having limited influence on political socialization. Consequently the role of television has received very little attention from scholars. In a recent review of studies dealing with mass media and political socialization, Chaffee remarked that there is a great deal of confusion over the place of mass media in the learning of political attitudes.[9] The confusion and the paucity of studies relating mass media to political learning can be partially attributed to Joseph Klapper's very influential book, *The Effects of Mass Communication*.[10] The argument put forth by Klapper, whose book appeared at about the same time interest in political socialization was spawned, was consistent with earlier studies that demonstrated that the mass media tend to reinforce existing attitudes rather than develop or change them. Scholars interested in political socialization accepted the argument that people tend to "select" and "accept" only those messages that support their preconceived views. Based on that assumption, investigations of the impact of the mass media were limited to the acquisition of politically relevant information and knowledge. More specifically the questions that have been asked in most studies of the influence of the mass media on political socialization are: Which media are attended?, How much is consumed?, and How is consumption related to knowledge of and interest in politics? Since political knowledge (information relevant to system stability) has been the primary dependent variable studied, it is not surprising that the media that have received the most attention are newspapers, newsmagazines, and television news.

It is the purpose of this book to show that television entertainment, not just the news, plays an important role in the reinforcement and development of orientations related to support for the social and political order. The effects of television on evaluative orientations are not as limited as Klapper and others would have us believe.

TELEVISION AND SUPPORT FOR THE SYSTEM

Earlier perspectives on the role of television in the process of political socialization have for the most part been narrow and limited. When the view that the mass media acted like a "hypodermic needle," powerfully inculcating political viewpoints, was discredited in favor of a "limited effects" viewpoint students of socialization, like others who were interested in mass media effects, moved from one theoretical extreme to another. Additionally it appears that analysts have almost always assumed that entertainment programming is not relevant to political system stability and social control. A more constructive approach would not begin with the assumption of extreme or limited effects. Nor is it useful to assume that there are no politically relevant messages in entertainment programs.

It is necessary to give careful attention to the conditions under which television might have some influence on system-relevant orientations. It seems clear that the family and school play major roles in the socialization of system-supportive attitudes. If that is the case, then it is left to the mass media and perhaps other agents to reinforce existing orientations or influence those who are "undersocialized" or for some reason have developed unconventional orientations.

A great deal of social psychological research indicates that individuals will try to maintain cognitive consistency. It follows that people will attempt to attend those messages that reinforce or at least do not overtly conflict with existing attitudes; the concept of selective perception flows naturally from cognitive consistency theories. If people choose the television programs they view, they are unlikely to choose those that will make them uncomfortable.

Aside from the drive to avoid messages that conflict with one's own viewpoint, there are other reasons why television might be expected to have little influence on system-supportive attitudes. Learning theorists tell us that learning is most likely to take place if the subject is actively involved in the process. Compared to messages transmitted through the print media, the consumption of messages from electronic media requires the expenditure of little effort. The conclusion most often drawn is that messages that are read are more likely to be accepted than those that are "viewed." To summarize, television as a teacher would seem to have two major disadvantages: Its attendance involves passivity, and it is possible for a subject to select those messages that produce the least amount of cognitive discomfort.

Given its apparent weaknesses as a teacher, under what conditions might television be effective as a medium for socializing system-relevant values? Cognitive-consistency theories tell us that messages that conflict with our existing values make us most uncomfortable when they deal with a subject matter that is salient or very important to us. In other words we are more likely to avoid or not attend messages that conflict with important values. If the message challenges beliefs or values that are not important or we are relatively unaware of or are distracted from an inconsistency, then we are less likely to avoid the message, and hence more likely to be influenced by it. Advertisers know that television advertising may be effective because the type of hand soap or deodorant people use may be relatively unimportant to them.[11]

Learning theorists also tell us that the repetition of messages enhances learning. In addition messages that are vivid and long in duration are most likely to be accepted, especially if the source of the message is seen as credible. An analysis of police-crime programming undertaken in a later chapter will show that the system-relevant messages being transmitted are vivid and repetitious. Credibility may not be at issue because few viewers may be aware that television entertainment carries a message.

With regard to the passivity of television viewing, there is some evidence that activity is not a necessary element in learning when other conditions are present.[1][2] The very fact that television viewing is a passive experience, where viewers are not highly aroused and defensive may contribute to its effectiveness as an agent of socialization. Viewers may not discriminate except in very general ways between programs, but if messages are consistent, persistent, vivid, and fail to challenge deeply held values then large number of hours of passive attendance may lead to acceptance.

To summarize, television entertainment may be an effective agent of socialization precisely because the messages transmitted do not challenge deeply held values and because the average viewer attends many repetitions of essentially the same message. Because viewers do not expect to be persuaded by television entertainment, credibility is not an issue and messages may be accepted with little resistance. Therefore, selective perception and passivity of television viewing do not necessarily reduce the influence of the medium on political learning.

MAINSTREAMING

This book is intended to show that television entertainment can influence system-relevant values in some circumstances. The problem becomes one of specifying the nature of the messages being transmitted and the segments of the audience that are most likely to be influenced or socialized.

In the past 15 years George Gerbner and his associates at the Annenberg School of Communications at the University of Pennsylvania have developed an approach to analyzing television's effects called "cultivation analysis."[1][3] They have argued that there is a strong relationship between heavy television viewing and the cultivation of a television-biased conception of reality. Television, they have shown, presents a distorted image of reality, which is reflected in the viewpoints of heavy viewers; heavy viewers of television tend to give "television answers" in response to a wide variety of survey questions. Gerbner and his associates avoid the term "effects" and instead prefer to argue that the process is one of "cultivation" of a point of view and is directly related to the number of hours television is viewed.

The process of cultivation analysis begins with a content analysis of television entertainment to determine the characteristics of "television reality." It is followed by the development of a series of survey questions that measure views of the world (reality vs. television reality). Finally, television viewing is related to viewer perceptions of reality. Perhaps the most consistent finding of cultivation analysis has been that heavy viewers see the world as a threatening or scary place. Heavy viewing has also been found to cultivate distorted perceptions of sex roles, occupational roles, crime rates, and political figures. Given some of the major criticisms of research on "television's effects," cultivation analysis appears to be a promising approach.

Critics of the approach have pointed out that correlations between television viewing and television answers to questionnaire items are small. Furthermore the correlations are often reduced substantially when simultaneous controls for social background characteristics are applied.[14] These criticisms have led to further specification of the conditions under which television viewing is likely to cultivate a television point of view. This increased specification has important theoretical implications for socialization research.

Content analyses have generally revealed that television programming tends to portray and support a mainstream, system-supportive point of view.[15] As noted earlier the television industry is controlled by people and groups who hold mainstream values and have a stake in maintaining the status quo. Furthermore, programming that does not challenge mainstream values has been found to attract the largest number of viewers, which, of course, is the goal of the industry. Gerbner and his associates have theorized that if the messages that are transmitted through television entertainment are essentially supportive of the social and political mainstream, then they are likely simply to reinforce the views of those who already hold mainstream viewpoints. In other words, television viewing should produce little change in the viewpoints of those who are already supportive of the status quo. However, those individuals who for some reason are undersocialized (do not adhere closely to the mainstream point of view), and are heavy viewers of television, are the most likely to be subject to "cultivation." Television has the effect of homogenizing viewpoints of audiences. Those who are predisposed to a point of view that is outside of the mainstream, but are heavy viewers of television are likely to develop mainstream views.

To analyze the process of mainstreaming it is necessary to: (1) specify the television mainstream, (2) determine which groups are predisposed to accept mainstream values, and (3) examine the effects of heavy television viewing on those groups who are not predisposed to accept mainstream values to determine the extent of cultivation. The general hypothesis is that heavy television viewing has its greatest effect on those who do not support mainstream values. Television reinforces the views of those who are "well socialized."

Contrary to the assumption that television has limited effects on political learning, a good case can be made for the expectation that television can be influential. Television entertainment probably affects the political values of those whose values are outside of the mainstream, despite the fact that television viewing is a passive activity. Selective perception is likely less of a factor than it would be for other media or television news.

AN OVERVIEW OF THE BOOK'S OBJECTIVES

This study was undertaken in order to take a close look at the effects of one kind of television entertainment programming, police-crime shows, on the reinforcement and development of attitudes related to the criminal justice system and social control. It was not undertaken without an awareness of the complexities of theory and method that plague the study of socialization. The data are limited because only a single geographical area is represented, but the substantive questions faced are important and I believe that some theoretical advancement is accomplished.

What follows is a conscious application of cultivation analysis and a theory of mainstreaming processes to questions regarding socialization posed by Greenstein: (1) Who (2) learns what (3) from whom (4) under what circumstances (5) with what effects?[16] The resulting analysis hopefully will reduce some of the confusion concerning the place of television in the learning of political attitudes.[17]

An analysis of mainstreaming involves three steps. First, it is necessary to determine the nature of the television mainstream, usually through content analysis; second, survey data is used to determine which groups adhere to mainstream values; and third, statistical analysis is undertaken relating heavy television viewing to mainstream values of groups that are predisposed to values outside of the mainstream.

Chapters 2 through 5 outline the necessary elements for the analysis of mainstreaming. The research design is described in Chapter 2. The discussion includes the process of drawing the sample and some of its limitations. Attention is given to how, through content analysis conducted by others, the television mainstream with regard to law enforcement is determined. The development of an Index of Crime Show Viewing is described, as well as the measures of the major dependent variables in the study: Knowledge of Criminal Legal Processes, Support for the Legal System and Compliance, Support for Civil Liberties, Images of Police, Fear of Crime, Trust in People, and Political Cynicism. The measurement of some of the variables that may influence or condition the process of cultivation is also described.

Chapter 3 involves a review of studies that have included content analyses of television's portrayal of the criminal justice. The studies are summarized in an attempt to determine the television mainstream. Chapter 4 focuses on mainstream views regarding law enforcement in a sample of adolescents. Chapter 5 considers the groups that might be most susceptible to mainstreaming and the conditions that may enhance learning from television entertainment.

Although the format may vary somewhat, Chapters 6 through 10 take the same approach. First, the relationship between crime show viewing and the dependent variable(s) is examined with statistical controls applied; second, an analysis of conditional relationships is undertaken focusing on individual characteristics, family characteristics, and finally on contextual factors. Chapters 6, 7, and 8 deal with orientations relevant to support for the regime: knowledge of criminal legal processes, support for the legal system, and support for civil liberties. Chapter 9 deals with support for authorities, the police. Chapter 10 focusses on perceptions of the crime rate and trust in people, two orientations that are related to support for the community.

In the final chapter relationships between perceptions of crime and support for the legal system are examined. A model is presented that relates law enforcement attitudes to more general support for the political system.

NOTES

1. Muriel G. Cantor, *Prime-Time Television: Content and Control* (Beverly Hills: Sage, 1980).

2. George Gerbner and Larry Gross, "The Scary World of TV's Heavy Viewer," *Psychology Today* (April 1976): 89-91.

3. Quoted in Austin Sarat, "Support for the Legal System," *American Politics Quarterly* 3 (February 1975): 3-24.

4. Fred Greenstein, *Children and Politics* (New Haven: Yale University Press, 1965).

5. Sheilah R. Koeppen, "Children and Compliance: A Comparative Analysis of Socialization Studies," *Law and Society Review* 4 (May 1970): 545-64.

6. Donald D. Searing, Joel T. Schwartz, and Oldin E. Lind, "The Structuring Principle: Political Socialization and Belief Systems," *American Political Science Review* 67 (June 1973): 415-32.

7. Ibid.

8. David Easton and Jack Dennis, *Children and the Political System* (New York: McGraw-Hill, 1969).

9. Stephen Chaffee, et al., "Mass Communication in Political Socialization" in *Handbook of Political Socialization*, ed. Stanley Renshon (New York: Free Press, 1977), pp. 223-58.

10. Joseph Klapper, *The Effects of Mass Communications* (Glencoe: Free Press, 1960).

11. Herbert E. Krugman, "The Impact of Television Advertising: Learning Without Involvement," *Public Opinion Quarterly* 29 (Fall 1965): 349-56.

12. Herbert E. Krugman and Eugene L. Hartley, "Passive Learning from Television," *Public Opinion Quarterly* 34 (Winter 1970): 184-90.

13. George Garbner and Larry Gross, "Living with Television: The Violence Profile," *Journal of Communication* 26 (Spring 1976): 172-99.

14. See Michael Hughes, "The Fruits of Cultivation Analysis: A Reexamination of Some Effects of Television Watching," *Public Opinion Quarterly* 44 (Spring 1980): 287-302.

15. Russell H. Weigel and Richard Jessor, "Television and Adolescent Conventionality: An Exploratory Study," *Public Opinion Quarterly* 37 (Spring 1973): 79-90.

16. Greenstein, *Children and Politics*, p. 12.

17. Chaffee, "Mass Communication in Political Socialization."

2

RESEARCH PROCEDURE:
PARTICIPANTS AND
MEASUREMENTS

IDENTIFYING MAINSTREAMING OF ATTITUDES

This study was undertaken to explore the linkages between viewing television police-crime shows and the cultivation of attitudes toward the criminal justice system, the legal system, and ultimately the sociopolitical order in general. In developing a theoretical framework, a set of procedures, and operationalizations I have drawn on earlier research. The theoretical framework comes primarily from George Gerbner and his associates at the Annenberg School of Communications. In a long series of studies Gerbner and his associates have demonstrated that television presents a distorted view of the world and that heavy viewers are more likely to acquire the television viewpoint than light viewers. Content analyses of television programming have shown that the industry tends to promote "mainstream" or system-supportive values, and survey studies have shown that heavy viewing is associated with these viewpoints.[1] The general findings of cultivation analyses have shown that television tends to homogenize viewpoints, providing support for the status quo. However, cultivation of the television viewpoint is conditional; people who are predisposed to hold mainstream values are likely to have their views reinforced rather than changed by heavy television viewing. Those who are likely to hold viewpoints that are outside of the mainstream are more susceptible to cultivation by heavy television viewing. In other words, relationships between heavy crime show viewing and holding television viewpoints on law enforcement should be strongest among people who are not ordinarily predisposed to support television's version of reality.

In formulating a research design to determine whether mainstreaming occurs with respect to police-crime shows and attitudes concerning law enforcement, attention was given to the collection of several types of information. First, it was necessary to determine how crime and law enforcement are portrayed in television entertainment programming. This is accomplished through a systematic analysis of the content of crime-police shows. Second, data are required concerning television viewing habits and attitudes concerning law enforcement. Specifically, a measurement of crime show viewing is needed, as well as measurements of viewpoints on law enforcement presented by television programming. It is also necessary to collect data on background characteristics and group membership to determine who is predisposed to hold a mainstream or television point of view. The data on individual viewing habits, attitudes, and personal characteristics were collected through a survey of adolescents.

With the information acquired from content analyses and the survey of adolescents it is possible to examine the association between heavy crime show viewing and attitudes toward law enforcement. More importantly, the research design used in this study produced the data necessary to compare the effects of heavy crime show viewing on groups who are not predisposed to support mainstream values to those who are more supportive of the status quo. The remainder of this chapter is given to descriptions of the research design, measurements, and data collection.

THE TELEVISION MAINSTREAM

The analysis of mainstreaming of law enforcement attitudes requires that the nature of television reality regarding crime, police, the law, and legal machinery be determined. For the purposes of this study, it is important to examine messages transmitted by crime shows to determine: Whether or not they are plentiful and accurate sources of information regarding legal processes, the rights of accused, and criminal procedures; Whether or not the norm of compliance is encouraged. Is the legitimacy of the legal system affirmed?; Whether or not explicit support is given to constitutionally guaranteed civil liberties. Are the rights of accused supported or are they portrayed as an obstacle to effective law enforcement?; Whether or not police are portrayed as effective, honest, or repressive; Whether or not the environment in which we reside is portrayed as safe or dangerous. Is victimization portrayed as likely?; Finally, whether or not the system is portrayed as generally corrupt or worthy of support.

Fortunately, the content of crime show programming has been systematically and thoroughly analyzed in a number of previous studies. Studies by Lichter and Lichter, Dominick, Arons and Katsh, as well as Gerbner et al. have included analyses of the aspects of crime show programming of particular interest in this study.[2] These studies will be reviewed in detail in Chapter 3.

THE SAMPLE

The survey data used in this study were collected in the spring of 1980 from 619 sixth through twelfth graders from eight public and private schools in the Providence, Rhode Island metropolitan area. Schools were chosen to guarantee representation of public and private school students from urban and suburban areas. In order to secure the cooperation of schools, principals were contacted and the purpose of the study was outlined. In most instances principals were able to grant permission for the survey, but in some cases the superintendent was consulted. Ultimately, only two schools refused to grant access, but several superintendents asked that the participation of their schools remain confidential.*

The principals determined access to classrooms, so students in the sample cannot be considered representative of their respective schools. In most instances we asked to survey classes that satisfied schoolwide requirements, so that the sample would include a cross section of the student body. Paper and pencil questionnaires were completed in the classrooms.

Because the sampling process was guided by convenience of location and opportunity, care must be taken in the generalization of results. It must also be noted that the Providence metropolitan area is

---

*See (M. Kent Jennings and Lawrence E. Fox, "The Conduct of Socio-Political Research in Schools: Strategies and Problems of Access," *The School Review* 76 [December 1968]: 428-44) for a discussion of the problems in surveying students in schools. Aside from the desire on the part of some school officials to keep their schools' participation confidential, there were some objections to the questionnaire. Fortunately, none of the objections related to questions that were critical to the study. A compromise was worked out for a question concerning grades; it was possible to obtain only a rough estimate of academic achievement.

not representative of the rest of the country; an unusually high proportion of students are Catholic and attend parochial schools. Scholars have expressed concern that studies conducted in a single community may produce findings that cannot be applied elsewhere. However, the vast majority of analyses of media effects have been conducted in single communities. As long as the focus is on relationships between variables and not the magnitude of scores, and appropriate statistical controls for population characteristics that might interact with media effects are applied, then a sample such as the one used in this study is adequate. Characteristics of the sample are given in Table 2.1.

Adolescents were sampled for a number of reasons. First, students in grades 6 through 12 are moving through a developmental period

Table 2.1 Characteristics of the Sample

	Percentage	
Sex		
Male	48.1%	(298)
Female	51.9%	(321)
Grade		
Sixth	14.4%	(89)
Seventh	18.9%	(117)
Eighth	23.4%	(145)
Ninth	12.3%	(76)
Tenth	9.4%	(58)
Eleventh	10.8%	(67)
Twelfth	10.0%	(62)
Head of Household Occupation		
Professional/Managerial	21.2%	(131)
Technical, Sales, Administrative	23.3%	(144)
Service/Clerical	14.1%	(87)
Craftsmen/Foremen/Skilled laborers	18.6%	(115)
Service workers	10.0%	(62)
Unskilled labor	11.9%	(74)
Other	1.0%	(6)
School		
Public	57.7%	(357)
Private	42.3%	(262)
Residence		
Urban	52.3%	(324)
Suburban	47.7%	(295)

when influence of the family and school begins to decline as competition from other agents such as peer groups and the mass media increases. Second, a range of grades was sampled so as to include subjects who may be at different stages of cognitive development. Finally, since this is a study of socialization processes, adolescents are a theoretically interesting group to study.

CRIME SHOW VIEWING: AN INDEX

The major independent variable in this study is an index of crime show viewing. A simple content analysis of prime time programs was conducted to identify crime shows. Three coders viewed all regularly scheduled prime time series during the last two weeks of February and the first two weeks of March 1980. Though various aspects of the criminal justice process were observed, programs classified as crime shows all had at least one instance in which police took into custody

Table 2.2 Patterns of Crime Show Viewing (Percentages)

| | How Often Viewed | | | |
Crime Show*	Never	Sometimes	Often	Almost Always
Quincy	15.7	39.3	18.0	27.0
Chips	24.8	30.4	18.3	26.5
BJ and the Bear	32.6	27.6	19.2	20.6
Charlie's Angels	22.9	48.3	14.9	13.9
Barney Miller	27.7	40.7	20.3	11.3
Vegas	32.1	40.2	16.5	11.2
Rockford File	35.9	38.5	16.7	8.9
Hart to Hart	43.6	33.3	14.2	8.9
B.A.D. Cats	63.8	17.5	8.7	10.0
The Incredible Hulk	49.4	32.5	10.7	7.4
The Misadventures of Sheriff Lobo	56.8	25.4	9.1	8.7
Barnaby Jones	68.7	23.2	5.0	3.1
Eishied	80.0	12.1	4.7	3.2
Stone	82.0	11.7	3.9	2.4
Hawaii Five-O	65.5	28.8	4.4	1.3
Paris	90.5	7.5	.7	1.3

*In order by popularity.

a criminal suspect. There was virtually no intercoder disagreement regarding classification of programs in instances where the same programs were viewed. Sixteen programs were identified as crime shows.

Because some analysts have argued that the public consists of "televisionholics" and that the volume of viewing is most important, while others argue that specific programs are viewed to satisfy specific needs,[3] the index constructed for this study takes into account both the specific content of programs and the volume of viewing.[4] The 16 programs were placed in a list of regularly scheduled network programs. Respondents to the survey were asked to indicate on a scale from 1 (never watch) to 4 (almost always watch) the frequency of viewing each program. The Index of Crime Show Viewing is simply a summation of weights for each of the 16 crime shows. The scale ranges from 16 to 64 and achieves a Cronbach's alpha Reliability Coefficient of .79. The 16 crime shows and their frequency distributions are given in Table 2.2.

MEASUREMENTS

Many of the variables in this study are the result of responses to single survey items. Often times the content of single items is of interest, even though they are part of larger scales. However, the major dependent variables are measured by multi-item scales. What follows is a description of the process of scale construction. At the very least each scale used in this study was subjected to reliability analysis and coefficients of reliability are reported. Scales that are original to this study were subjected to factor analysis to establish that they measure a single attitudinal dimension.

Knowledge of Criminal Legal Processes

One of the relationships of interest in this study is the one between crime show viewing and knowledge of the criminal justice system. Crime shows may be an important source of knowledge concerning arrest rights and the parameters of criminal investigations. Scholars have argued that the maintenance of the legal system depends on at least some citizen knowledge of legal processes. A brief test of knowledge of the criminal justice system was administered to the sample. The items included six true-false questions taken from studies by Sarat and Dominick:[5]

1. When a person is arrested, police have to tell him he has a right to have a lawyer with him before he is questioned. (T)
2. It is the job of the judge to prove that a man accused of a crime is guilty. (F)
3. Criminal trials in the United States are usually secret. (F)
4. If an innocent man is arrested, it is up to him to prove he is not guilty. (F)
5. A man who has committed a crime can be made to answer questions about the crime in court. (F)
6. The amendment to the U.S. Constitution that says a person does not have to testify against himself is the Sixth Amendment. (F)

Each of the items tests knowledge that might reasonably be acquired from the content of television crime shows. The resulting scale, which ranges from 0 to 6, is simply the summation of correct answers for each respondent. The scale achieves a Cronbach's alpha of .53.

Support for the Legal System and Compliance

If crime show programming plays a role in developing support for the system, it will most likely be reflected in attitudes toward the law and the legal system. Two measures using quite different approaches are used in this study to measure support for the legal system and compliance. The first is an Index of Support for the Legal System that consists of six five-point Likert scale items:

1. The individual who refuses to obey the law is a menace to society.
2. I must always obey the law.
3. Personal circumstances should never be considered an excuse for law breaking.
4. A person should obey the law even if it goes against what he thinks is right.
5. Disobedience of the law can never be tolerated.
6. It would be difficult for me to break the law and keep my self-respect.

The items included in the Index of Support for the Legal System were taken directly from a study by Sarat.[6] The scale scores, the result of adding item responses for each respondent, range from 6 to 30. The scale achieves a Cronbach's alpha of .78. Sarat found the items to load significantly on a single factor, and the resulting scale scores correlated significantly with reported compliance behavior.

The Index of Support for the Legal System measures generalized support for the legal system, but does not show *how* adolescents think about the law. To measure the sophistication of attitudes toward compliance, a measurement developed by Rodgers and Taylor, an adaptation of Kohlberg's well-known typology of moral development, was employed.[7] Following Rodgers and Taylor, respondents were asked, "Do you think people should always obey laws?" Those who answered yes were asked, "Why would you obey a law you disagreed with?" Those who answered no were asked, "Why not?" Respondents were urged to elaborate in giving their answers. In this analysis attention was not given to whether respondents answered yes or no to the first question, but to the justifications for the answers.*

Kohlberg's typology of moral development consists of three levels and six stages which are related to cognitive development. The typology is especially useful for classifying ways in which people think about moral dilemmas. The focus in this study is on the three levels of moral development and their relationship to thinking about legal compliance. The lowest level of moral development, the preconventional level, is characterized by an egoistic concern with the avoidance of punishment. The middle level, the conventional level, is characterized by a concern with the maintenance of authority and order—conformity to the expectations of authority or significant others. The highest level, the postconventional level, is characterized by thinking that takes into account principles of conscience or self-accepted moral principles.[8]

Answers to the second question, concerning the reasons for compliance or noncompliance, were used to classify respondents in terms of one of the three levels of moral development. Since the preconventional level is characterized by a concern with reward and punishment, answers that focused on obedience to the law to avoid going to jail were placed in the lowest category. Answers that were placed in the conventional category were ones that mentioned the duty as a citizen to obey the law. Respondents who gave conventional-level answers felt that there was little choice but to obey laws. Few people achieved postconventional styles of reasoning. However, in this study the requirements for classification of answers as postconventional was not rigorous; if a respondent mentioned any circumstances that mitigate

---

*Rodgers and Taylor used the questions to classify respondents in terms of a five-point compliance scale ranging from the lowest, compliance is required to avoid punishment to the highest, compliance is not required because of "self-developed moral principles." In this study attention is given to *how* respondents think about the problem of compliance and not whether they said laws should be obeyed. The coding scheme used here differs from the one used by Rodgers and Taylor in that respect.

compliance, or suggested that compliance might be tempered by personal judgment based on conscience, the answer was classified as post-conventional. To summarize, respondents' answers were classified into preconventional, conventional, or postconventional categories on the basis of justifications for obeying or not obeying laws. One hundred-eight respondents could not be classified because they failed to answer the question or they provided answers that did not clearly fall into one of the categories.

The Index of Support for the Legal System is intended to measure the disposition to comply with the law and generalized support for the legal system, while the second measure taps the cognitive sophistication of respondents who think about the problem of compliance. While both measures are concerned with compliance, they should help answer different questions about the influence of television crime show viewing.

Support for Civil Liberties

Some observers have argued that television police are insensitive to the procedural rights of suspected criminals.[9] Ironically, oftentimes "the law" is portrayed as a hindrance to effective law enforcement. From a systemic point of view procedural guarantees are part of the "rules of the game"; support for civil liberties is a regime orientation fostered in democracies. For the purposes of this study an attempt was made to develop an attitudinal scale to measure support for civil liberties, as they are portrayed in crime shows.

The Civil Liberties Support Scale includes six five-point Likert items, some of which are original to this study and some of which were taken from earlier studies.[10] The scale is the result of an item analysis including a factor analysis of an original pool of twelve items. The final scale achieves a Cronbach's alpha of .62. The six items, which load significantly on a single factor, are:

1. Judges should punish criminals more severely.
2. There are too many restrictions on what police can do.
3. In order to protect the community from further crime, an arrested person should be kept in jail until his case comes to trial.
4. In some cases police should be allowed to search a person or his home, even if they do not have a warrant.
5. Any man who insults a policeman has no complaint if he gets roughed up in return.
6. Evidence which shows that a defendant did commit a crime should be used at his trial regardless of how the police got the evidence.

The scale is simply the sum of scores for each item. The scale scores range from 6 (low support) to 30 (high support).

Images of Police: Effectiveness and Credibility

Representatives of law enforcement agencies have complained that TV crime shows project unrealistic and often unfair images of police officers and their work.[11] It seems likely that the images projected of police by TV crime shows are multidimensional, so it is important to develop measures that tap a variety of perceptions. Fortunately, police image has been the subject of quite a large number of studies. A pool of five-point Likert items was chosen from several studies and subjected to factor analysis.[12] The items and their factor loadings are shown in Table 2.3.

Table 2.3 Factor Matrix: Images of Police

	Factor One	Factor Two
1. Police enjoy pushing people around.	.66	-.38
2. The police don't show proper respect for citizens.	.59	-.38
3. The police in this community are guilty of discrimination against people like the poor and minority groups.	.54	.05
4. The police are often too stupid to solve complicated crimes.	.53	-.27
5. The police spend most of their time going after people who do little things and ignore most of the bad things going on.	.50	-.30
6. The police are too willing to use violence.	.46	.19
7. Policemen are generally more honest than most people.	-.15	.55
8. The police in our city are doing an effective job and deserve our thanks.	-.36	.49
9. Criminals usually get caught.	-.09	.43
10. If I need help, I can rely on the police to come to my aid.	-.26	.41
Percentage of total variance (cumulative)	34.5	44.5
Percentage of explained variance (cumulative)	89.2	100.0

The factor analysis of ten items reveals two dimensions of perceived police image.* The favorable statements and unfavorable statements concerning police loaded on separate factors. The six unfavorable items that loaded on the first factor reflect the opinion that police are brutish and misguided. Four of the items relate to perceived problems with interpersonal relations; police are believed to have a propensity to use violence, to discriminate, or generally fail to treat people with respect. Two of the items hint that police lack the necessary intelligence or drive to deal with major crime. All of the items suggest that police have adversive personality traits.

The items that load significantly on the second factor relate to honesty and effectiveness. The items reflect a feeling that police are effective in controlling crime, are dependable, and are effective in dealing with people.

Two scales were constructed based on the results of the factor analysis. The Police-Community Relations Scale was constructed using the items that loaded significantly on the first factor. The scale is the result of the addition of item scores for the first six items in Table 2.3. The scale achieves a Cronbach's alpha of .78.

The Police Effectiveness Scale was constructed from the items that loaded significantly on the second factor in Table 2.3. The four item scale, the result of adding the scores for each item, achieves a Cronbach's alpha of .60.

Fear of Crime and Trust in People

Perhaps the most consistent finding of previous research concerned with the cultivation of television points of view is that heavy television viewing is associated with perceptions of a "scary and mean" world. It is this finding, reported in numerous instances by Gerbner and his associates that has been the most controversial.[13] Two approaches to measuring perceptions of a hostile world are taken in this study. The first focuses on perceptions regarding the rate of crime and the likelihood of victimization. The second focuses on a more general orientation that has been characterized as trust in people or interpersonal trust.

---

*A principal components analysis using SPSS was conducted. Only two factors with eigenvalues greater than one were extracted. A varimax rotation was used.

The Fear of Crime Scale used in this study is constructed from five five-point Likert items, selected from several previous studies.[14] All five items load significantly on a single factor when subjected to factor analysis.

1. Crime is such a problem that this city is not a safe place to raise children.
2. It just is not safe to go downtown in Providence at night anymore.
3. The extent of crime is one of my major concerns.
4. Crime is such a problem that I am afraid to go out alone at night.
5. The threat of crime is so great that nobody can feel safe in his own home anymore.

Scale scores range from 5 to 25. The scale achieves a Cronbach's alpha of .72.

The measure of interpersonal trust used in this study is taken directly from Gerbner et al. and is called the Mean World Index.[15] The index, based on Rosenberg's "faith in people scale," includes three items:[16]

1. Generally speaking would you say most people can be trusted or that you can't be too careful in dealing with people?
   _____ Most people can be trusted
   _____ Can't be too careful
2. Would you say that most of the time, people try to be helpful or that they are mostly just looking out for themselves?
   _____ Try to be helpful
   _____ Look out for themselves
3. Do you think that most people would try to take advantage of you if they get a chance or would they try to be fair?
   _____ Try to take advantage of me
   _____ Try to be fair

The resulting scale ranges from 3 to 6 and achieves a Cronbach's alpha of .54.

Political Cynicism

One of the hypotheses to be examined in this book is that orientations toward authorities and particular aspects of the regime spill-over and affect more general orientations toward the political system. In other words it is possible that children transfer their feelings toward political authorities such as police to the larger political system.[17] To test this hypothesis this study employs a standard measure of political cynicism. It is a five item scale that has been used in numerous studies:[18]

1. Do you think that people in the government waste a lot of the money paid in taxes, waste some of it, or don't waste much of it?

   _____ Waste a lot

   _____ Waste some

   _____ Don't waste very much

2. Do you think that quite a few of the people running the government are a little crooked, not very many are, or do you think hardly any of them are?

   _____ Quite a few are crooked

   _____ Not very many are crooked

   _____ Hardly any are crooked

3. How much of the time do you think you can trust the government in Washington to do what is right—just about always, most of the time, or only some of the time?

   _____ Just about always

   _____ Most of the time

   _____ Some of the time

4. Do you feel that almost all of the people running the government are smart people who usually know what they are doing, or do you think that quite a few of them don't seem to know what they are doing?

   _____ Almost all know what they are doing

   _____ Quite a few don't seem to know what they are doing

5. Would you say that the government is pretty much run by a few big interests looking out for themselves or that it is run for the benefit of all the people?

   _____ Run by a few big interests looking out for themselves

   _____ Run for the benefit of all

The scores on the items are added to derive a total Political Cynism score. The scale ranges from 5 to 13 and achieves a Cronbach's alpha of .59.

Conditions Affecting Mainstreaming

A major goal of this study is to identify conditions under which television crime show viewing influences the process of development of perceptions of reality and system-relevant attitudes. The measurement of most of the conditional variables such as sex, grade in school, and head of household occupation are straightforward, employing just one or two survey questions. However, several measurements of conditional variables involved the construction of multiple item scales and require explanation.

One variable that deserves attention as a possible condition for mainstreaming is the perceived reality of television programming. The perception that the content of television crime shows reflects reality may make it more relevant and enhance the cultivation effect. A number of studies support this contention.[19] A scale designed to measure the perceived reality of television content was developed using items from a number of previous studies:[20]

1. People in TV shows are just like people in the real world.
2. The criminals on TV are just like the criminals in real life.
3. TV shows tell about life the way it really is.
4. The programs on TV show policemen just the way they are in real life.

The four five-point Likert items load significantly on a single factor when subjected to factor analysis.* The Television Reality Scale ranges from 4 to 20 and achieves a Cronbach's alpha of .71.

It has become almost a basic truism in communication research that communication effects are greatest in the absence of competing information. For that reason it is important to determine the extent to which respondents attend media other than television. This was accomplished by asking three simple yes-no questions: Do you read any newspapers regularly? Do you read any magazines? Have you read any books not required in school lately? The answers to each question were coded as 0 for no and 1 for yes and added to create a scale ranging from 0 to 3 to measure reading habits.

Two additional conditional variables reflect the structural characteristics of respondents' families. The two measures employed are designed to assess the nature of communication patterns in the family and were developed by Chaffee.[21] The measures have been found to be associated with the receptivity to and acquisition of new information. The measure of socio-oriented family communication assesses the extent to which families stress harmonious personal relationships and the avoidance of controversy. It is closely related to measures of

---

*Hawkins (See Robert Hawkins, "The Dimensional Structure of Children's Perceptions of Television Reality," *Communication Research* 4 [1977]: 299-320) has found that perceived reality of television is multidimensional. A "magic window" dimension reflects the extent to which viewers believe they are watching ongoing life or drama, while a "social expectations" dimension is related to whether viewers believe the content of TV matches their expectations about the world. The items in this study fail to separate into clear factors.

family authoritarianism. The highly socio-oriented family stresses deference to adults and the repression of anger. The Socio-Orientation Scale is a five item scale. Respondents were asked if their parents do the following never, rarely, sometimes, or often:

1. Say you shouldn't show anger in a group.
2. Say that parents' ideas are correct and shouldn't be challenged by children.
3. Make it clear that you should not argue with adults.
4. Say the best way to keep out of trouble is to stay away from it.
5. Encourage you to give in on arguments rather than risk making people mad.

A scale score with a possible range from 5 to 20 is the sum of the item scores.

The second measure of family communication patterns assesses a concept-orientation. In a concept-orientation family children are urged to develop their own beliefs, challenge the views of others, and develop their own sources of information. The measure of concept-orientation used in this study uses the same response categories and has the same range of scale scores as the Socio-Orientation Scale:

1. Say that getting your ideas across is important, even if others don't like it.
2. Say that you should look at both sides of issues.
3. Hold family talks about politics or religion, where some people take different sides from others.
4. Visit people who take the other side in arguments about politics or religion.
5. Take a side they don't believe in, just for the sake of argument.

METHODS OF ANALYSIS

The methods used for presentation of the data in this book are eclectic. They range from simple comparison of percentages to regression analysis. However, one of the methods of statistical analysis used in this book requires some explanation. It is the general practice in media analyses to compare zero-order and partial correlation coefficients between media use and the dependent variable for various subgroups.[22] This practice is statistically inadvisable and will be avoided in this study. In a very useful article on conditional relationships Gerald Wright points out that standardized measures such as correlation coefficients are not comparable across subgroups because they are sensitive to differences in standard deviations.[23] In other words, subgroup differences in correlation coefficients may be at least partially attributable to differences in variability. Wright argues persuasively that unstandardized regression coefficients provide a more reliable basis for subgroup comparison. He provides a method for assessing the significance of subgroup differences between regression coefficients that is used in this study.*

NOTES

1. George Gerbner, Larry Gross, Michael Morgan, and Nancy Signorielli, "Charting the Mainstream: Television's Contributions to Political Orientations," *Journal of Communication* 32 (Summer 1982): 100-27.

2. Linda S. Lichter and S. Robert Lichter, *Prime Time Crime* (Washington, D.C.: The Media Institute, 1983); Stephen Arons and Ethan Katsh, "How TV Cops Flout the Law," *Saturday Review*, March 19, 1977, pp. 11-19; Joseph Dominick, "Crime and Law Enforcement on Prime Time Television," *Public Opinion Quarterly* 37 (Spring 1973): 241-50; George Gerbner and Larry Gross, "Living with Television: The Violence Profile," *Journal of Communication* 26 (Spring 1976): 172-99.

3. See Thomas J. Volgy and John E. Schwarz, "TV Entertainment Programming and Sociopolitical Attitudes," *Journalism Quarterly* 57 (January 1980): 150-55.

4. See Jack M. McLeod and Byron Reeves, "On the Nature of Mass Media Effects," in *Television and Social Behavior: Beyond Violence and Children*, ed. S. B. Withey and R. P. Abeles (Hillsdale, N.J.: Erlbaum, 1980) for a good discussion of content-specific versus general effects.

5. Austin Sarat, "Support for the Legal System," *American Politics Quarterly* 3 (February 1975): 3-24; Joseph R. Dominick, "Children's Viewing of Crime

---

*The method for evaluating conditional relationships suggested by Wright involves constructing two regression models. A "restricted model" includes estimates of slopes for the independent variable and group membership. A "full model" includes estimates of slopes for group membership and the independent variable for each category or group. An F-test is then calculated to determine whether group membership significantly affects the original relationship between independent and dependent variable:

$$F = \frac{(R^2 full - R^2 restricted)/df_1}{(1 - R^2 full)/df_2}$$

Where

$R^2 full$ is proportion of variance explained by the full model.

$R^2 restricted$ is the proportion of variance explained by the restricted model.

df_1 is the difference between the number of parameters estimated in the full model and the restricted model.

df_2 is the number of cases minus the number of parameters estimated in the full model.

For further details see Wright.

Shows and Attitudes on Law Enforcement," *Journalism Quarterly* 51 (Spring 1974): 5-12.

6. Sarat, "Support for the Legal System," p. 8.

7. See Harrell Rodgers and George Taylor, "Pre-adult Attitudes Toward Legal Compliance: Notes Toward a Theory," *Social Science Quarterly* 51(December 1970): 539-51; June Tapp and Lawrence Kohlberg, "Developing Senses of Law and Justice," *Journal of Social Issues* 27 (1971): 65-91.

8. Tapp and Kohlberg, "Developing Senses of Law and Justice."

9. Arons and Katsh, "How TV Cops Flout the Law."

10. See Meredith W. Watts, "Anti-Heterodoxy and the Punishment of Deviance: An Explanation of Student Attitudes Toward Law and Order," *Western Political Quarterly* 30 (March 1977): 93-103; Michael Corbett, "Public Support for 'Law and Order': Interrelationships with System Affirmation and Attitudes Toward Minorities," *Criminology* 19 (November 1981): 328-43.

11. See Robert J. Daley, "Police Report on the TV Cop Shows," *New York Times Magazine*, November 19, 1972, pp. 39-40; Alan F. Acuri, "You Can't Take Fingerprints Off Water: Police Officers' Views Toward 'Cop' Television Shows," *Human Relations* 30 (Summer 1977): 237-47.

12. See especially Charles W. Thomas and Jeffrey M. Hyman, "Perceptions of Crime, Fear of Victimization, and Public Perceptions of Police Performance," *Journal of Police Science and Administration* 5 (Fall 1977): 305-17.

13. See George Gerbner et al., "TV Violence Profile No. 8: The Highlights," *Journal of Communication* 27 (Spring 1977): 171-80; Michael Hughes, "The Fruits of Cultivation Analysis: A Reexamination of Some Effects of Television Watching," *Public Opinion Quarterly* 44 (Spring 1980): 287-302; Anthony N. Doob and Glenn E. McDonald, "Television and Fear of Victimization: Is the Relationship Causal?" *Journal of Personality and Social Psychology* 37 (1979): 170-79.

14. Thomas and Hyman, "Perceptions of Crime."

15. George Gerbner, Larry Gross, Michael Morgan, and Nancy Signorielli, "The 'Mainstreaming' of America: Violence Profile 11," *Journal of Communication* 30 (Summer 1980): 10-29.

16. See Morris Rosenberg, *Occupations and Values* (Glencoe, Ill.: Free Press, 1957).

17. David Easton and Jack Dennis, *Children in the Political System* (New York: McGraw-Hill, 1969).

18. Harrell Rodgers, Jr. and Edward B. Lewis, "Political Support and Compliance Attitudes: A Study of Adolescents," *American Politics Quarterly* 2 (January 1974): 61-77.

19. See Bradley S. Greenberg and Byron Reeves, "Children and the Perceived Reality of Television," *Journal of Social Issues* 32 (1976): 86-97.

20. See ibid; Dominick, "Children's Viewing of Crime Shows."

21. See Steven Chaffee, Jack McLeod, and Daniel Wackman, "Family Communication Patterns and Adolescent Political Participation," in *Socialization to Politics*, ed. Jack Dennis (New York: Wiley, 1973): pp. 349-64.

22. Robert P. Hawkins and Suzanne Pingee, "Some Processes in the Cultivation Effect," *Communication Research* 7 (April 1980): 193-226.

23. Gerald C. Wright, "Linear Models for Evaluating Conditional Relationships," *American Journal of Political Science* 20 (May 1976): 349-73.

3

PRIME TIME
CRIMINAL JUSTICE:
THE TELEVISION MAINSTREAM

THE DISTORTED WORLD OF TV CRIMINAL JUSTICE

Prime time television has been experiencing a crime wave for the past 25 years. In 1979 70 percent of prime time programs contained violence. The rate of violent episodes was 5.7 per hour and nearly 54 percent of all leading characters were involved in some violence.[1] Crime on television is at least ten times as rampant as it is in the real world. Those who view an average week's prime time television obtain some notion of the work of 30 police officers, 7 lawyers, 3 judges, but only 1 scientist or engineer and only a small number of blue-collar workers.[2] As early as 1954 as many as 17 percent of the jobs shown on television were connected with police work and 17 percent of the characters shown were criminals.[3] As late as 1976 12 percent of all male television characters had jobs in law enforcement or crime detection.

Television entertainment programming has not always included a large number of shows featuring crime and law enforcement. Joseph Dominick, who has traced the growth of shows featuring crime and law enforcement, found that in the early fifties there were relatively few crime shows, but by the 1959-61 period they accounted for about one-third of prime time programming. There was some decrease in crime show programming in the middle sixties, but the late sixties witnessed a rapid increase in the percentage of prime time given to the subject. The trend reached a peak of 40 percent of prime time schedules given to crime shows in 1975 with a slight drop-off in more recent years.[4]

The trends concerning violence parallel those of crime shows. Gerbner et al. have found, that while there were small fluctuations in their Violence Index, the percent of characters involved in violence remained fairly constant between 1969 and 1979. A notable trend in recent years is an increase in violence in the "family hour" between eight and nine p.m.[5]

The factors that influence the types of programs and the specific content of programs that are scheduled in prime time are numerous and complex.[6] Himmelweit outlined a comprehensive model of how television affects viewers and how viewers and society affect television. Among the factors that she cited that affect the output of the television industry are societal norms, values, and laws; institutions such as the Federal Communications Commission, Congress, and various advocacy groups; the structure and motives of the broadcasting industry itself; and attitudes and values of the viewing audience.[7] A comprehensive review of all the factors that affect crime show programming is not necessary for the purposes of this study, but some attention to how the television mainstream is determined should prove useful.

First and foremost the television industry in the United States is profit seeking. This consideration ultimately affects all other variables that may lead to a particular type of programming. Crime shows have generally been very popular, so despite mounting criticism television network executives have permitted the level of violence in programming to remain high. Crime and violence is not necessarily a subject that is of great interest to the average network executive, but in an industry where rating points translate into higher advertising income, programming that is perceived to attract large audiences is heavily promoted and encouraged. Neither the quality of programming nor the level of violence have much to do with network decisions to return or cancel shows. Network decisionmakers are rewarded for ratings success and have little incentive to concern themselves with the effects of the programming they put on the air.

Network executives need to be responsive to a number of constituencies and still produce programming that will be highly rated. Three of the constituencies include advertisers, advocacy groups, and viewers. Advertisers are, of course, primarily motivated by profits. Until the late 1950s sponsors had a great deal of control over the content of prime time programming.[8] Due to a number of scandals and congressional investigations, the networks have maintained control over content since that time, but it is almost always the case that programming that is offensive to potential advertisers or inconsistent with basic upper-middle class values never gets on the air. Advertisers, television executives, and creators of television program content all are representatives of upper-middle class America, and it would be unreasonable to expect that their values are not expressed in prime time programming.

Network executives have had to deal with the criticism directed at their programming from such groups as the Parent-Teacher Association, Action for Children's Television, and the National Organization of Women. On a number of occasions congressional committees have taken an active interest in the effects of television viewing. For the most part the television industry has managed to avoid "outside" regulation of television content by arguing that the First Amendment to the Constitution protects their right to determine programming. The National Association of Broadcasters, the major lobbyist for the industry, has managed to keep at a minimum the number of regulations concerning broadcasting that do not meet with the approval of the industry. The NAB, which is controlled by the three networks and their affiliates, has attempted to demonstrate that the industry is capable of self-regulation. They have done this through the adoption of the widely quoted National Association of Broadcasters Television Code. Some of the sections of the code particularly relevant to crime show content are:

> Violence, physical or psychological, may only be projected in responsibly handled contexts, not used exploitively. Programs involving violence should present the consequences of it to its victims and perpetrators.
>
> Special sensitivity is necessary in use of material relating to sex, race, color, age, creed, religious functionaries or rites, or national or ethnic derivation.
>
> [T]he treatment of criminal activities should always convey their social and human effects.[9]

Massive amounts of time and energy have been given to finding a formula that will produce high ratings. Over the years police-crime dramas have proven to be popular and have been rewarded with high ratings. Good versus evil seems to be a classic theme that is easily understood and has always had mass appeal. The visual medium of television is especially conducive to programming filled with action: car chase scenes, fistfights, and shootouts. However, producing programs that the public likes and will watch while adhering to standards set by sponsors and the National Association of Broadcasters presents some problems for programmers. Taking into account the tastes and desires of the television audience and the other factors affecting the content of programming, the television industry seems to have arrived at a formula for crime shows that contains at least the following elements:

- The story line must focus on the conflict of good versus evil—the classic theme.
- The distinction between "good" characters and "evil" characters must be clear.
- The evil characters must lose in the end in a way that is vivid, convincing, and consistent with mainstream views of the social order.
- Care must be taken in how bad characters are portrayed, so as not to offend a significant segment of the audience.
- Controversial issues must be avoided.
- The program must be action-packed and exciting, but the story line must be kept simple.

The parameters of the "formula" present some problems for television writers. Each program must include a crime, someone who commits it, someone who is victimized by it, and someone to bring the criminal to justice. How can criminals be portrayed without offending important segments of the viewing audience? How can crimes be portrayed without presenting an image of a threatened society? How can criminals be brought to justice without portraying the "boring" activities usually required in such processes such as arraignments, plea bargaining, etc.? Most importantly, how can crime be portrayed without raising controversial issues? The extent of content control television writers must accept is illustrated by some testimony given by David Rintels, president of the Writers' Guild of America West, before a U.S. Senate subcommittee:

> I was asked to write another episode of "The FBI" on a subject of my choice, at about the time five or six years ago, when four little black girls were killed by the bomb in the Birmingham Church. It had been announced that the FBI was involving itself in the case and I told the producer I wanted to write a fictional account of it. He checked with the sponsor, the Ford Motor Company, and with the FBI—every proposed show is cleared sequentially through the producing company, Quinn Martin; the Federal Bureau of Investigation; the network, ABC; and the sponsor, Ford; and any of the four can veto any show for any reason, which it need not disclose—and reported back that they would be delighted to have me write about a Church bombing subject only to these

stipulations: The Church must be in the North, there can be no Negroes involved, and the bombing could have nothing to do with civil rights. After I said I couldn't write that program, I asked if I could do a show on police brutality, also in the news at that time; certainly the answer came back as long as the charge was trumped up, the policeman vindicated, and the man who brought the specious charge prosecuted.[10]

If Mr. Rintels had written the scripts described above, they would have been very similar to the sanitized view of crime and law enforcement presented on most police-crime shows. For example, Dominick points out that scriptwriters in order to avoid charges of stereotyping have made television criminals as nondescript as possible; he notes that this results in criminals as functions, not people.[11] Characters are usually one-dimensional and inoffensive. Since they are the one group that has the least to complain about with regard to status in American society, white, adult, middle class males are given criminal roles.

Lichter and Lichter point out that the major motive for television crime is greed.[12] The viewing audience is thus assured that crime is understandable and the motivations underlying it are simple. Inexplicable or random violence is rarely shown and the causes of crime are rarely murky. Often violence is removed from reality; it occurs in the past or future, behind closed doors, or in an unidentifiable location. In any event the viewing public is reassured that crime is not a great threat to society as a whole because television crime is almost always unsuccessful; crime, at least on TV, "does not pay."

Violence plays a key role in crime show television programming because it is a dramatic, vivid way of showing who wins and loses. The violent episode at the end of a program often makes it unnecessary for us to view the "boring" postarrest legal process. The solution is quick and clearcut—few TV criminals must face trial and few television law enforcement officers must "prove" their cases in court on television. TV police kill or apprehend criminals; their lives are seldom dull.

Adherence to the "formula" outlined in this section means that television crime shows portray a world that is at great variance with reality. The purpose of the rest of this chapter is to distinguish in some detail the aspects of the television world of crime and law enforcement that reflect accurately the "real" world from those aspects that do not. Fortunately, there has been a great deal of research that has analyzed the content of crime shows.

CRIME SHOWS AS A SOURCE OF INFORMATION

The stability of the sociopolitical order requires that citizens have a basic understanding of the "rules of the game." However, Sarat notes that an increasing number of social scientists argue that legal institutions may function best when citizens are not too well-informed about or interested in their operation.[13] Too much information may lead to "unrealistic" expectations and ultimately cynicism and mistrust. There is considerable controversy concerning whether television crime shows play a role in insuring that "ignorance of the law is no excuse."

Max Gunther, an NBC vice-president, argued in an article written for *TV Guide* a number of years ago that television crime shows play an important role in teaching citizens civil liberties. He attempted to show that creators of crime shows are very much aware of the legal parameters of criminal investigations. The result, according to one executive in charge of programming is that:

> It turns out that TV is a powerful educational medium even when it isn't trying to be, even when it's trying to entertain. There must be millions of people who have learned simply by watching crime dramas in the past few years, that they have the right to remain silent when arrested.[14]

Even the American Civil Liberties Union was quoted as saying that " . . . TV cops behave scrupulously," and that crime shows provide an " . . . excellent legal education for the public." Writers are quoted as complaining that it was much easier to write crime dramas when they did not have to worry about legal accuracy. Besides, they argue, legal accuracy slows the pace of otherwise exciting drama: "Our whole show has to come to a dead stop every week while the cop politely reads the crook his rights."[15]

Despite Gunther's glowing report on the legal accuracy of crime shows, most analysts believe they are, because of omission and distortion, poor sources of knowledge regarding the criminal justice system. Arons and Katsh, for example, conducted a content analysis that revealed 43 scenes where questions could be raised about the legality of police action.[16] The executive producer of "The Mod Squad" (quoted in Gunther) admits that legal accuracy is not necessarily a high priority:

> On our show we feel we can break the rules to some extent when it's dramatically necessary. For instance in a plot situation where the Mod Squaders are in desperate need of some piece of information—where there is some life-and-death reason for acting fast, you know—we don't mind having them search somebody's home without going through all the required legal procedures.[17]

The producer goes on to say that any concern about "breaking the rules" is reduced by the fact that there have been "no complaints from civil rights groups." It is clear that writers are sensitive to complaints about illegal behavior on the part of television police, but systematic content analyses show that dramatic necessity is a higher priority than legal accuracy.

Perhaps the best way to determine the potential of television crime shows for teaching the essentials of law enforcement to viewers is to consider what is shown or not shown. Most shows portray the process of criminal investigation and end with the apprehension, arrest, or violent death of the suspect. Perhaps the story line includes searches and seizures that may be legal or illegal. Often times arrested suspects are "read their rights." The point, however, is that most shows end with an arrest. Arraignments, pretrial hearings, jury selection, bonding, plea bargaining, trials, sentencing, and other postarrest processes are rarely shown. Dominick reported that only 5 percent of the criminals shown in crime shows he analyzed were shown during legal processes that take place after arrest.[18]

In instances where trials are shown, information may still be scarce. Winick and Winick analyzed 28 courtroom drama series to determine the extent to which legal information was provided. They concluded that viewers are highly unlikely to view such processes as jury selection, plea bargaining, arraignments, or instances where cases are resolved before they get to trial.[19] Robert Daley, a former deputy police commissioner, describes the types of distortions that are often present in courtroom dramas:

> I attended a recent murder trial in which the prosecutor subjected the defendant to one of the most scathing personal attacks that any man has ever had to endure. The jury watched the defendant and I watched the jury. It seemed to me that I had seen this scene before, and I had seen the scene before, on TV. On TV the murderer always cracks. At length he can take no more. He suddenly breaks down blubbering and admits his guilt. But this defendant did not break down. He did not admit his guilt. He did not blubber.[20]

Despite the fact that "Perry Mason" for weeks on end was able to elicit courtroom confessions, Daley argues that murderers do not crack. He believes that hardened criminals know how to perform under pressure and informs us that he had never seen a defendant in a murder trial break down on the stand. Lewis, a district attorney, concurs saying that no defendant in his experience admitted guilt during a criminal trial.[21] The reality that most trials do not end in courtroom confessions obviously takes a backseat to dramatic effect on television.

A more subtle set of messages concerning the legal system were discussed in an interesting paper by Ethan Katsh. The argument put forth by Katsh will be discussed in more detail later in this chapter, but at this point it is appropriate to point out that he argues that television communicates a message that may not facilitate learning about the legal system. He argues that television crime shows single out the more visible, tangible aspects of the legal process and ignore abstract qualities. Due to the nature of the medium itself, television personifies the law—television characters, not the rules themselves provide the solutions to conflict. The abstract elements of the law are ignored and the rules are portrayed as concrete and inflexible. Katsh suggests that by portraying the law in this way television makes the legal system and the very foundation of the law less understandable. In the world of crime shows, society is governed by people, not laws, a basic misunderstanding of our constitutional system.[22]

The television mainstream with regard to crime shows and information about the criminal justice system is characterized by distortion and omission. In recent years television writers have begun to include scenes where suspects are read their Miranda rights and search warrants are often served. However, citizens are unlikely to obtain accurate information concerning other aspects of the legal system.

THE IMPORTANCE OF COMPLIANCE

Television executives often argue that crime shows are not pointlessly violent. Some commentators have concurred arguing that they are morality plays in which the "moral is that the bad, evil people who lead criminal, anti-social lives are punished. Thus it pays to be a good, moral person."[23] It seems clear that shows like "Hawaii Five-O" and "CHIPS" portray the lawful life as superior to an unlawful one and may contribute to the forces of social control.

If any message dominates prime time crime shows it is that "crime does not pay" and that criminals are not worthy of imitation. It seems to me that there are three characteristics of crime shows that contribute to the acquisition of the norm of compliance. The first is the sharp distinction drawn between the criminal and the law enforcer. The second is the often violent consequence of criminal activity. The third is the effectiveness of television law enforcement. All three convey the message that compliance is the most appropriate behavior.

Crime shows seldom portray criminals as simple lawbreakers. Aside from their propensity to break the law, television criminals are often given a wide variety of undesirable characteristics. Every attempt is made to guarantee that the audience will find it difficult to sympathize with them. The motives for crime are seldom presented in a way that might induce sympathy; few television bad guys steal to feed their families or kill to avenge the murder of a loved one. Those who break the law most often choose the criminal life because they are greedy or simply mean.

Law enforcers, on the other hand, are imbued with an image of morality. They may not always engage in activities that are admirable and they may make mistakes, but it is perfectly clear that they know right from wrong. Law enforcers may be independent in that they conflict with the "establishment" (often the bureaucracy), but they are always clearly on the side of the law and conventional morality. "Kojak" was the type of law enforcement officer most people can admire. In an interview in *Saturday Review* accompanying an article by Arons and Katsh, Telly Savalas described his character:

> Kojak operates on instinct and decency. It's the same drunk he turns in at night who is back the next morning to borrow a buck. If he kicks a kid who has knocked down an old lady while stealing her purse—and then kicked her while she's down—it's because Kojak doesn't understand that dimension of violence. I'm not talking about police brutality. It's a cautionary kick. A kick is better for the kid than being shut up in a juvenile hall somewhere.[24]

An episode of "Hawaii Five-O" demonstrates the contrast between "good guys" and "bad guys." The bad guy is the son of a gangster, who is romancing a police officer's daughter. The daughter knows nothing about the gangster-son's role as enforcer in his dad's illegal pinball business. The gangster-son, in the process of bombing a bowling alley whose owner would not "knuckle under," kills the best friend of the daughter. In the meantime the police officer has his daughter "picked up" by a squad car and brought to headquarters where she is cautioned about her association with a "known criminal." The father-police officer confronts his daughter in a cool professional manner; he obviously is able to maintain his professionalism, even in an instance where his daughter is making a fatal mistake. Later the gangster-son convinces the young woman that he "is not like the rest of his family," and they are married. In the end, of course, the "bad guy," who not only is a gangster-murderer, but lies to innocent young girls, is shot to death. The point is that the bad-guy role includes a number of negative character traits other than criminality. The police officer is admirable because he is able to separate his professional role from his role as father, and the bad guy, well he certainly got what he deserved.

The second characteristic of crime shows that relates to the norm of compliance is the often violent consequences of criminal activity. A great deal has been written about the symbolic function of violence on television. A violent ending makes it unnecessary to portray the boring legal process that comes after arrest while providing an effective lesson for those who might have sympathized with the lawbreaker. Violence defines social power and status; it makes it clear who is morally superior and inferior at the end of a program. In a detailed analysis of the context of violence on television Gerbner found that 42 percent of all leading characters were injured or killed after they had been violent. Only 8 percent of the characters analyzed who initiated violence escaped without injury or death.[25]

Violent resolutions to criminal investigations are obviously over-represented in television crime shows. Dominick found in his content analysis that 30 percent of the law enforcers on television committed a violent act in the line of duty. This statistic may not be impressive because it included both major and minor characters; looking at the figures from a different perspective, Dominick found that of 24 TV law enforcers who committed violent acts, 94 percent had major roles.[26] Perhaps secondary law enforcers did not often commit violence, but those in leading roles engaged in it. Of course in the real world of criminal investigation police violence is unusual; Robert Daley points out that in his experience most New York police never in their careers fire their guns in the line of duty.[27]

The third characteristic of crime shows that encourages compliance with the law is the effectiveness of police. In a survey that asked a sample of police to evaluate the reality of crime shows, it was the portrayal of police effectiveness that was judged to be the most unrealistic. The following are some comments on the reality of crime shows made by law enforcement officers in the sample:

> The public gets the impression that you can take fingerprints off water. They are under the impression that every criminal leaves a clue. . . .
>
> The public thinks all goddamn crimes should be solved within a half an hour, even with commercials.
>
> All crimes are solved in quick order. All crimes are continually worked on until they are solved. All departments have sophisticated equipment and methods with which to catch criminals. All fingerprints taken lead to arrest. All injuries to a police officer are glorious happenings.

Police work is made to look simple. Police always get their way. They never show crimes that go unsolved, murderers that are not caught, or actions in courts where a jury lets a crook go free.[28]

Sophisticated and systematic content analyses of TV police effectiveness support the impressions of the police in Acuri's sample. Dominick's study of prime time programs in 1972 revealed that 88 percent of television crimes were solved compared to a real-life rate of 23 percent reported by the FBI.[29] An analysis of more recent prime time programs produced similar results. Lichter and Lichter analyzed a six-week sample of prime time series from the 1980-81 television season. They grouped crimes into two major categories. Violent crimes included: murder, kidnapping, robbery, aggravated assault, and rape; serious crimes included burglary, larceny, and auto-theft, as well as all the violent crimes.[30] I have summarized their data with regard to a comparison of television crime and FBI reports in Table 3.1.

A comparison of plot resolution with FBI reports is made difficult by the fact that the FBI reports arrest rates, while the results of crime on television are not always unambiguous. However, the figures in Table 3.1 indicate the tremendous effectiveness of television law enforcers. On television well over 80 percent of violent and serious crimes lead to arrest or defeat of lawbreakers. In less than 20 percent of the shows the criminal was successful or the plot resolution was unclear. With regard to serious crimes the FBI's effectiveness rate is almost the reverse of effectiveness of television law enforcers. In reality police do somewhat better in resolving violent crimes (44 percent), but they are not as nearly as effective as television law enforcers.

Of all of the aspects of television unreality the portrayal of police effectiveness is the most obvious. Aside from real-life police who believe that crime shows create unrealistic expectations, there are few

Table 3.1 Plot Resolution of Crime Shows Compared to FBI Reports

	Serious Crimes		Violent Crimes	
	TV	FBI	TV	FBI
Criminal success/No arrest or unresolved	17%	81%	16%	56%
Criminal defeat/Arrest	83%	19%	84%	44%

Source: Linda S. Lichter and S. Robert Lichter (1983) *Prime Time Crime*. Washington, D.C.: The Media Institute. Compiled from Tables 12 and 13. Reprinted by permission.

who complain about the fact that crime almost never pays on television. In fact the creation of that particular aspect of unreality seems entirely consistent with the section of the Broadcasters Code that says that " . . . the treatment of criminal activities should always convey their social and human effects." The code has been interpreted to mean that all crimes must be solved and all criminals punished.

It seems obvious that compliance with the law is a norm that is clearly and solidly in the center of the television mainstream.

It was noted earlier that legal scholar Ethan Katsh has given considerable thought to the way in which television influences the way people "think" about the law. He points out that the law should be viewed broadly as a process by which abstract and intangible rules, based on certain values and philosophical attributes, determines the resolution of disputes. A great deal of rhetoric has been given to the idea that citizens should support the idea that disputes should be settled by legal institutions applying abstract rules—we are a government of "laws, not men." Television's crime shows give a great deal of lip service to the idea of compliance with the law, but often the message transmitted is that people, not the law, insure compliance. Some dialogue from the detective series, "Bert D'Angelo" quoted by Katsh illustrates the problem:

> *D'Angelo*: "What do I know about the law? I'm not a lawyer, I'm a cop."
> *Inspector Keller*: "It's your job to enforce it."
> *D'Angelo*: "It's my job to protect people from the mugger, the rapist, the armed robber, and the killer. People like Joey, like my partner Mickey, did the law help them? Did the law stop that killer? All the laws in the world won't stop one man with a gun. It's going to take me or somebody like me and you know what? I'll do it any way I can."
> *Inspector Keller*: "You're a dangerous man, Bert."
> *D'Angelo*: "That's right. You'd better be damn glad I'm on your side."

Katsh believes that dialogue such as the above is anti-law in that it fails to encourage the public's belief in the viability of rule of law. The personification of resolution of conflicts reduces the public's awareness of the laws abstract qualities. Katsh argues that the very nature of electronic media like television contributes to the failure to encourage abstract conceptions of law. Historically, the print media contributed to the development of our conceptions of law because it was able to communicate abstract information easily. Instead of verbal thought television emphasizes concrete representations of the law such as police, criminals, courts, and police stations. By focusing on a "legal system" where personalities instead of the law are responsible for the resolution of disputes, the very basis and justification of the legal order become less understandable, and Katsh believes less desirable.[31]

In summary, television crime shows appear to encourage the norm of compliance. That crime does not pay on television is evident when one examines the level of effectiveness of police in terms of killing or arresting suspected criminals. Often the message is reinforced by the fact that suspected criminals are not merely subjected to legal process, but meet a very violent end. While crime shows lack subtlety in the way they enforce the norm of compliance, they fail to promote sophisticated thinking about the "rules of the game." Crime shows fail to convey the abstractness of the law and the idea that it is the law that promotes compliance, not law enforcers. The television mainstream with regard to both the norm of compliance and the nature of law appears to be a gross distortion of reality.

SUPPORT FOR CIVIL LIBERTIES

A noted criminologist, Herbert Packer identified two value systems that compete for priority in the operation of the criminal justice system. The two value systems or models are useful for analyzing the content and point of view of crime shows. The "Crime Control Model" sees repression of criminal conduct as the most important function of the criminal justice process. The view put forth is that criminal conduct must be kept under tight control so as to prevent a breakdown of the public order. Public order and high regard for crime control are seen as an important precondition for social freedom. It is not surprising that the Crime Control Model stresses a high rate of apprehension and conviction of criminals, with a minimum of emphasis placed on ceremonious rituals and technicalities. Packer notes that built into the Crime Control Model is a "presumption of guilt," which is a reflection of confidence in the efficiency of the criminal justice system.

The alternative approach suggested by Packer is a "Due Process Model" that emphasizes the rules by which suspects are treated. The Due Process Model is based on a presumption of innocence, which is conceived as a direction to officials about how they should proceed. It tends to emphasize the formal structure of the law to a greater extent than the Crime Control Model. The Due Process Model emphasizes the elimination of mistakes that might adversely affect individuals, while the Crime Control Model accepts the probability of some mistakes in the interest of controlling crime.[32]

The prevailing evidence indicates that television places a great deal of emphasis on a Crime Control Model of the criminal justice system.

Despite the protestations that police dramas are increasingly giving an accurate picture of police procedures,[33] an analysis by Arons and Katsh indicates otherwise. Take for example the following scene from a "Dragnet" rerun, a series that Gunther cites as particularly accurate: Sergeant Friday has just taken a suspect's photograph from her roommate, Sara, and is continuing his search for information about the absent girl:

Friday: "Do you have any samples of her handwriting?"
Sara: "Yes, the book by the phone. That's her address book."
Friday: "We'll have to take this along with us. It'll be returned."
Sara: "But what do I tell Mary if she notices her picture and address book are gone?"
Friday: "What time do you expect her today?"
Sara: "Right after work, about five."
Friday: "All right. These'll be back by four p.m. Now we'd appreciate it if you wouldn't say anything about it until we have completed our investigation."
Sara: "Oh, don't worry. I don't want to make things any worse than they are. I just know Mary isn't guilty. She's too nice."
Friday: "Well, if she's that nice, she isn't guilty, and if she's guilty, she's not nice."[34]

The problem is, of course, that the audience knows whether or not Mary is guilty. In most crime shows the audience sees the crime committed, so they *know* who committed the crime, a position the television police do not enjoy. So when the police violate the Fourth Amendment and conduct an illegal search, it seems acceptable because guilt has already been established as far as the audience is concerned.*

Most crime shows tend to portray criminals as especially heinous and unregenerate types who deserve whatever treatment they receive from basically strong armed law enforcers. What is emphasized is support for the social order under all circumstances and the idea that the machinery of justice sometimes gets in the way of efficient law enforcement. Robert Alley describes a scene from "Kojak" that illustrates this point:

This particular show opened with Kojak entering an apartment with a warrant to search for jewels. Unable to discover them, the detective re-

---

*The Fourth Amendment of the U.S. Constitution: The right of the people to be secure in their persons, houses, papers, and effects, against unreasonable searches and seizures, shall not be violated, and no warrants shall issue, but upon probable cause, supported by oath or affirmation, and particularly describing the place to be searched, and the persons or things to be seized.

sorted to an arrest based on the possession of a concealed weapon, a kitchen instrument resembling an ice pick. The D.A. angered by the "quick cover-up collar," chastised Kojak for dreaming up a case. He said Kojak had no "right to toy with the law." Kojak's response was bitter. He asked the D.A. whose side he was on and suggested he "get back to reality." "Pick a side," Kojak cried, as he admitted stretching the law. He noted that perhaps it should be stretched "in reverse" once in a while. He concluded with an emotional appeal for the D.A. to "come into my courthouse one night—the streets." Later in the episode the D.A. was painted as the heavy and the script's depiction of murder and other felonious acts exonerated Kojak's actions and indignation.[35]

The message is clear: procedural guarantees like the exclusionary rule simply get in the way of effective law enforcement. The D.A. "went too far" in protecting the rights of a suspected criminal and in the end innocent people suffered.*

A content analysis of crime shows by Arons and Katsh showed that in 15 crime shows there were 43 scenes where questions could be raised about the legality of police action. Included were 21 clear constitutional violations and 15 instances of police brutality. Another study, cited by Arons and Katsh, indicated the number of instances where TV police fail to secure a search warrant and fail to advise suspects of their rights is on the increase.[36]

Haney and Manzolati in a content analysis of crime shows found an average of between two and three constitutional violations by police per hour-long program. They found that in most programs illegal searches were portrayed as essential, always turning up a vital missing piece of evidence. Witnesses brutalized by police often provided the crucial lead that resulted in the capture of vicious criminals. Haney and Manzolati point out that violations of suspects' constitutional rights are almost never identified as such, but when they are they are portrayed as necessary for effective police work. They noted that in over 70 percent of the cases where the police mention the Constitution, the courts, or judges the reference was negative or critical. Haney and Manzolati conclude that on television crime shows the message is: "The law and the Constitution stand in the way of effective solutions to our crime problem."[37]

Taken together, an overwhelming amount of evidence supports the conclusion that television presents a crime control point of view.

---

*The "exclusionary rule", based on a Supreme Court decision (*Mapp v Ohio*), states that evidence that is seized, but was not included in a search warrant cannot be used against the accused in a court of law.

The procedural guarantees due to suspected criminals are either ignored or portrayed as impediments to effective law enforcement. Because the viewer, but not necessarily the television police, often witnesses crimes, a presumption of guilt prevails on crime shows. With regard to civil liberties the television world of crime and police work bears little resemblance to reality.

IMAGES OF POLICE

The images of police are distorted by the scriptwriters for television crime shows. The relative overrepresentation of characters engaged in law enforcement was noted earlier in this chapter. Dominick found that most law enforcers on television were directly connected with the police or some governmental agency. The law enforcers were overwhelmingly male, white, and middle-aged (36 to 50 years of age). The work of television's police is primarily investigative; routine police work is rarely shown.[38] All in all the work of law enforcers is portrayed as much more glamorous than it is in reality.

Police Work and Effectiveness

It has been noted earlier in this chapter that television police are extremely effective and real-life police find this aspect of crime shows especially disturbing because it creates unrealistic expectations of police performance. The police in the survey conducted by Acuri were also critical of the way the work of police has been portrayed in crime shows. The focuses of the criticism seem to be on two characteristics of crime show portrayals of police: The idea that police work is glamorous and undertaken independently, and that police have tremendous resources at their disposal to solve crimes.[39]

Acuri's respondents complained that crime shows portrayed the police as "supermen," while real police work is "humdrum," not filled with "glory and excitement." Two police officers remarked:

> The public gets the picture that cops are gods . . . and that every cop is on his own without any department supervision. Many crime incidents are blown out of proportion. . . . The average patrolman on the street may become involved in one homocide investigation in his career but cover 5,000 accidents. . . . He will probably never fire his weapon in anger in his entire career.
>
> The public must think, what fun it is to be a cop . . . work undercover and solve big crimes. They never have been punched in the mouth and they're told you didn't act properly when you made an arrest. . . .

The "big crimes" are more often a complaint about a neighbor's dog pissing on a favorite bush.[40]

Haney and Manzolati correctly point out that in reality the major portion of police time is given to dealing with victimless crimes like public drunkenness, but television crime shows rarely show police dealing with domestic disputes, heart attack victims, or stuck elevators.[41]

Acuri's police respondents were also critical of the way in which television crime shows portray the resources available to police for investigations. On television police have sophisticated equipment at their disposal. In contrast police officers said that

Police shows badly mislead the public and create the impression that the solution to a crime is a wild adventure. Cannon can hop on a plane to check out a routine lead, when most police require eight pages of justification to make a toll call.

The uninformed public gets false impressions of the way police departments operate. They, the public, feel that all experts are at our fingertips . . . as well as all up-to-date crime labs. In most cases that is crap.[42]

Robert Daley finds it particularly irritating when police stations and offices are portrayed as neat and efficient with lots of books lining the walls and sophisticated equipment in view. He describes most police offices he has seen:

On the whole, police offices are among the shabbiest that exist in our world. They are manned 24 hours a day. They are the personal office of nobody. In most cases, the only permanent decorations are wanted posters and maps of sectors or precincts or divisions. Police offices are manned almost exclusively by men; they are not used to impress anybody; no outsider sees what they look like except suspects, who are usually too scared to notice. If such offices are often badly cleaned, this is partly because the men who man them don't complain and partly because they're in use much of each day. There are no rugs on the floor and there are no books on the walls.[43]

Daley also pointed out that television police always seem to have the most up-to-date sophisticated equipment at their disposal. Police radios always work and patrol cars are never run down or dented.

Aside from the unrealistically high rate of success of television police in solving crimes, it appears that the nature of everyday police work is not accurately portrayed. Television police, as opposed to real-life police, spend their time dealing with major crime. They have experts and sophisticated equipment at their disposal, as well as unlimited budgets. Their surroundings are often pleasant and some police offices could even be described as scholarly. All of these distortions may lead the viewing audience to have unrealistic expectations of police performance.

Honesty and Integrity

It is clear that in general, images of police can be described in terms of a number of dimensions. Still, most television police are characters without a great deal of depth; they are in fact one-dimensional in that we seldom see them in roles other than law enforcer. Lichter and Lichter found that two out of three law enforcers are never shown engaging in activities other than purely occupational tasks. Only 6 percent were featured in a personal role. Private eyes, as opposed to police officers, were more likely to have well-rounded roles.[44]

The two characteristics of television's police that have received the most attention are integrity and competence. Two of Acuri's respondents provide comments on how they feel law enforcers are portrayed:

> Cops are either lazy and dumb or smart and sarcastic. Cops are either hardnosed, honest, or corrupt. Wives are neurotic and feel sorry for themselves.
>
> And as far as detective fiction is concerned the "dumb" cop is a fixture because the public demands him! In fact, it is as necessary to have a "dumb" cop in a detective story as it is to have a clever detective.[45]

In many shows in which a private eye is the major character police are often portrayed as incompetent or corrupt. The ineffectiveness or dishonesty of police makes it necessary for a "Barnaby Jones" or "Jim Rockford" to step in and solve the crime. In reality private investigators are usually involved in missing-person cases or are busy gathering evidence for divorce proceedings.

Actually the image of law enforcers projected by crime shows is generally a positive one. Dominick found that television police were basically honest and law-abiding. Only 2 percent were shown as villians and only 11 percent used illegal means to gather evidence.[46] Haney and Manzolati found that television police almost never made a mistake. They did not find a single instance where the wrong man was in custody at the end of the show.[47] Lichter and Lichter found that only 8 percent of the law enforcers in their content sample "bent the rules" in criminal investigations. They did find a tendency, however, for the "man in the trenchcoat" to solve crimes when police were unequal to the task.

Table 3.2 Plot Functions of Law Enforcers

Positive (Total)	54%
Friendly	14%
Competent	36%
Heroic	4%
Negative (Total)	28%
Illegal	8%
Malevolent	2%
Greedy	5%
Foolish	5%
Incompetent	8%
Neutral (Total)	18%

Source: Linda S. Lichter and Robert Lichter (1983) *Prime Time Crime*. Washington, D.C.: The Media Institute. Reprinted by permission.

The results of a systematic analysis of the plot functions of law enforcers conducted by Lichter and Lichter are shown in Table 3.2. The figures in the table show that almost twice as many law enforcers are positively portrayed as negatively portrayed (54 percent vs. 28 percent). Positive portrayals were most likely to emphasize the competence of law enforcers, while heroic portrayals were least likely to be shown.*

Very few law enforcers were portrayed as malevolent (2 percent). Most of the negative portrayals focused on incompetence and illegal behavior. Perhaps, given the complaints of some police, it is surprising that only 5 percent of the law enforcers were portrayed as foolish.[48]

When Lichter and Lichter cross tabulated the plot functions of law enforcers with law enforcer characteristics some interesting patterns were revealed. Law enforcers who were the stars were much more likely to be portrayed in a positive manner than those who had minor roles. Nonwhite and younger law enforcers were more likely to be portrayed in a positive way than white or older law enforcers. When police are compared with private investigators, the data showed that the former were less likely to be portrayed positively than the latter.[49]

In summary, it appears that television law enforcers are much more likely to be portrayed positively than negatively. They are also likely

---

*Lichter and Lichter describe "heroic" police as those who engage in activity "beyond the call of duty" to solve crimes.

to be portrayed as competent, but not necessarily heroic. The one situation where police are most likely to be shown in a negative way is when the star of the program is a private investigator. It would appear to be necessary in such shows to demonstrate police incompetence or corruptibility in order to elevate the status of the star as law enforcer.

THE SCARY WORLD

Imagine living in a place where almost six violent crimes are seen by the average citizen every hour. Most of the crimes are vicious attacks by truly frightening calculating criminals on innocent victims. They are committed out of greed or to avoid detection and take place in the victim's home or place of business. The police are almost as likely to commit violent acts as the criminals. Most crimes involve attacks against people, not property. Attackers are likely to be unknown to victims. Furthermore, violence seems to permeate all human activity and acts of murder, rape, kidnapping, and especially terrorism are on the increase.

This is a place created by television scriptwriters who believe that in order to entertain an audience that has become increasingly sophisticated, it is necessary to focus on the darkest and most violent aspects of human behavior. The television world is a dangerous place where every citizen must use extreme caution to avoid becoming a victim of some terrible crime.

Systematic analyses of the content of prime time crime shows reveal the extent to which the television world is a scary world, one considerably removed from reality. Table 3.3 shows that television crime is likely to be violent and directed against people, while in the "real world" crime is most likely to be directed against property. Lichter and Lichter found that 36 percent of television crimes involved murder, while FBI reports reveal that in reality murders contribute less than 1 percent to the total proportion of crimes. Crimes against property are almost invisible on television, but FBI reports reveal that burglary and larceny make up 90 percent of all reported crime. In all, 88 percent of television crimes are classified as violent compared to 10 percent of real-life crime according to the FBI.[50] These findings are consistent with the results of an earlier study conducted by Dominick that showed that murder is the most frequent TV crime followed by aggravated assault, simple assault, and armed robbery.[51] One must come to the conclusion that the television world of crime is a gross distortion of the real one. Evidently scriptwriters are convinced that

Table 3.3 Rankings of Serious Crimes on Television Entertainment Programs Compared to FBI Reports (Frequency of Occurrence)

	Television	FBI
Murder	36%	*
Robbery	23%	4%
Kidnapping	13%	*
Aggravated Assault	13%	5%
Burglary	6%	28%
Larceny-Theft	6%	62%
Rape	3%	*
Total	100%	100%

*Indicates less than 1 percent.

Source: Linda S. Lichter and Robert Lichter (1983) *Prime Time Crime*. Washington, D.C.: The Media Institute, p. 16. Eighty-eight percent of TV crime is classified as violent compared to 10 percent of crimes according to FBI Reports. Reprinted by permission.

crimes such as public drunkenness, vandalism, prostitution, and fraud are humdrum and not titillating enough to attract an audience.

George Gerbner and his associates believe that it is possible to infer power relationships in television's "scary world" by examining the characteristics of victims of crimes. Analyses by Gerbner et al. and Dominick have given a clear picture of the characteristics of victims. Women (regardless of age), young boys, nonwhites, and members of the lower or upper class are most likely to be victims.[52] Female victimization seems to be on the increase.[53] Crime shows, according to Gerbner et al. may provide "lessons of victimization." It is possible for viewers in a rough sort of way to calculate the risks and opportunities of violent behavior. In several studies Gerbner and his associates have undertaken the calculation of "risk ratios" for characters of crime shows with different characteristics. The risk ratio is obtained by dividing the more numerous of two roles (Violent vs. Victim or Killer vs. Killed) by the less numerous for each group. A positive sign indicates there are more violents or killers in a category than victims of violence or killed. A negative sign indicates that there are more victims or killed than violents or killers within a group. Table 3.4 shows the risk ratios for major characters on programs from 1968 to 1978. The figures were taken from a large table constructed by Gerbner et al.[54]

Table 3.4 Risk Ratios for Major Characters, 1969-78 (Top Five and Bottom Five)

Violent-Victim Ratio		Killer-Killed Ratio	
Top Five			
"Bad" females	+1.05	"Good" males	+3.85
Elderly males	+1.07	Child/Adolescent male	+3.00
"Bad" males	-1.01	Middle class male	+2.20
Settled adult males	-1.12	Young adult male	+2.17
Settled adult females	-1.12	Settled adult male	+2.13
Bottom Five			
Child/Adolescent male	-1.69	Elderly male	+1.00
Lower class female	-1.71	Child/adolescent female	0.00
Young adult female	-1.82	Elderly female	-0.00
Upper class female	-2.00	Lower class male	-1.13
Elderly female	-3.33	"Good" female	-1.60

Source: George Gerbner, Larry Gross, Nancy Signorielli, Michael Morgan, and Marilyn Jackson-Beeck, (1979) "The Demonstration of Power: Violence Profile No. 10." *Journal of Communication* 29: 187. The rankings and the figures were obtained from Table 4. Reprinted by permission.

Table 3.4 reveals some interesting patterns. The characters at the top of the table are most likely to be aggressors, while the ones at the bottom are likely to be victims. The most distinctive differences in the ratios relate to sex roles. Four out of the bottom five who are most likely to be victims of violence are women. Elderly women followed by upper class females are most likely to be victims of violence. "Good" female characters have the most negative killer-killed ratio. The males who have the most "unfavorable" risk ratios are lower class, elderly, or young.

An examination of the characteristics of those with positive risk ratios reveals some interesting differences between those who are violent and those who kill. "Bad" men and women seem to give more violence than they receive; the evil characters seem to be the most provocative with regard to committing general violence. On the other hand the fact that "good" middle class-type males have the "most favorable" killer-killed ratios indicates that the heroes on television may be the most violent of all. The status distinctions on crime shows seem clear: it is the weak (women, elderly, lower class) who are the victims, the "bad" who create general mayhem, and the "good" middle class male hero who does the killing in the name of retribution.

So, what lessons concerning victimization are there in crime shows for those who "live" in the world of television? First and foremost all those in the television world must be cautious; the likelihood of being involved in violent activity is great. Second, one must remember that crime can occur most anywhere; victimization is especially likely in places of business or in the home. Third, the criminal aggressor is likely to be a stranger, not someone the victim knows, so it is important to be careful around strangers. Finally, if you are young or elderly, female, or a member of the lower class the likelihood you will be a victim of crime is greater.

CONCLUSIONS

The television mainstream with regard to criminal justice is for the most part an inaccurate reflection of the real world. The reasons for distortion are many, but the primary motivation of the television industry is to attract an audience for advertisers. Television writers and executives simply do not believe that "reality sells." Audiences are perceived to be uninterested in petty crimes, mundane everyday police work, or complicated plots.

The following generalizations can be derived from the studies reviewed in this chapter:

- Crime shows are a poor source of information about the criminal justice system. Most of the legal process is not shown. Aspects that are shown are distortions of reality.
- Crime shows are unable to convey the abstract nature of law. Emphasis is given to the concrete.
- Television police are much more effective than real-life police.
- Unlike in the real world, there is little ambiguity or confusion on television regarding the differences between legal and illegal behavior.
- On television criminals meet a violent end much more frequently than in real life.
- Television crime shows do not promote a sophisticated understanding of the reasons why compliance with the law might be desirable.
- The rights of accused are portrayed on crime shows as unfortunate hindrances to law enforcement.
- Police are portrayed positively in most instances, but the occupation of law enforcer is glamorized. There is a vast difference between how TV police spend their time and real police spend their time.
- The television world is an extremely violent world where the probability of victimization is much higher than in reality.

Television crime shows seem to put forth a "crime control" point of view that is highly supportive of the status quo and conventional views of proper behavior, ethics, and morality.

NOTES

1. George Gerbner, Larry Gross, Michael Morgan, and Nancy Signorielli, "The Mainstreaming of America: Violence Profile 11," *Journal of Communication* 30 (Summer 1980): 10-29.

2. George Gerbner et al., "Charting the Mainstream: Television's Contributions to Political Orientations," *Journal of Communication* 32 (Summer 1982): 100-27.

3. Sydney Head, "Content Analysis of Television Drama Programs," *Quarterly Journal of Film, Radio, and Television* 9 (1954): 175-91.

4. Joseph R. Dominick, "Crime and Law Enforcement in the Mass Media," in *Deviance and Mass Media*, ed. Charles Winick (Beverly Hills: Sage, 1978).

5. Gerbner et al., "The Mainstreaming of America," p. 13.

6. Muriel G. Cantor, *Prime-Time Television: Content and Control* (Beverly Hills: Sage, 1980).

7. Hilde T. Himmelweit, "Social Influence and Television," in *Television and Social Behavior: Beyond Violence and Children*, ed. S. B. Withey and R. P. Abeles (Hillsdale, N.J.: Erlbaum, 1980).

8. Cantor, *Prime-Time Television*, p. 69.

9. National Association of Broadcasters, *The Television Code* (1976) Sec. 4:2.

10. Hearings on Freedom of the Press, Subcommittee on Constitutional Rights of the Senate Committee on the Judiciary, 92nd Cong., 1st and 2nd sessions, 1972, 522.

11. Joseph R. Dominick, "Crime and Law Enforcement on Prime Time Television," *Public Opinion Quarterly* 37 (Spring 1973): 241-50.

12. Linda S. Lichter and S. Robert Lichter, *Prime Time Crime* (Washington, D.C.: The Media Institute, 1983).

13. Austin Sarat, "Support for the Legal System," *American Political Quarterly* 3 (February 1975): 3-24.

14. Max Gunther, "You Have the Right to Remain Silent," *TV Guide*, December 18, 1971, pp. 7-9.

15. Ibid.

16. Stephen Arons and Ethan Katsh, "How TV Cops Flout the Law," *Saturday Review*, March 19, 1977, pp. 11-19.

17. Gunther, "You Have the Right to Remain Silent," p. 8.

18. Dominick, "Crime and Law Enforcement."

19. Charles Winick and Mariane Winick, "Courtroom Drama on Television," *Journal of Communication* 24 (1974): 67-73.

20. Robert J. Daley, "Police Report on the TV Cop Shows," *New York Times Magazine*, November 19, 1972, pp. 39-40.

21. W. H. Lewis, "Witness for the Prosecution," *TV Guide*, November 30, 1974, pp. 5-7.

22. Ethan Katsh, "Is Television Anti-Law?: An Inquiry into the Relationship Between Law and Media," *ALSA Forum* 7 (1983): 26-40.

23. Benjamin Stein, "The Social Value of TV Thrillers," *Wall Street Journal*, May 28, 1975, p. 8.

24. Arons and Katsh, "How TV Cops Flout the Law," p. 12.

25. George Gerbner, "Violence and Television Drama: Trends and Symbolic Functions" in *Content and Control*, vol. 1 of *Television and Social Behavior*, ed. G. A. Comstock and E. A. Rubinstein (Washington, D.C.: U.S. Government Printing Office, 1972).

26. Dominick, "Crime and Law Enforcement on Prime Time Television," p. 245.

27. Daley, "Police Report on TV Cop Shows," p. 40.

28. All quotations are from Alan F. Acuri, "You Can't Take Fingerprints Off Water: Police Officers' Views Toward 'Cop' Television Shows," *Human Relations* 30 (Summer 1977): 237-47.

29. Dominick, "Crime and Law Enforcement on Prime Time Television," p. 245.

30. Lichter and Lichter, *Prime Time Crime*.

31. Katsh, "Is Television Anti-Law?"

32. Herbert Packer, *The Limits of Criminal Sanction* (Stanford, Calif.: Stanford University Press, 1968).

33. Gunther, "You Have the Right to Remain Silent."

34. Arons and Katsh, "How TV Cops Flout the Law," p. 12.

35. Robert S. Alley, *Television: Ethics for Hire?* (Nashville: Abingdon Press, 1977): p. 110.

36. Arons and Katsh, "How TV Cops Flout the Law," p. 14.

37. Craig Haney and John Manzolati, "Television Criminology: Network Illusions of Criminal Justice Realities," in *Readings About the Social Animal*, ed. E. Aronson (San Francisco: Freeman, 1980): p. 128.

38. Dominick, "Crime and Law Enforcement on Prime Time Television."

39. Acuri, "You Can't Take Fingerprints Off Water."

40. Ibid., p. 243.

41. Haney and Manzolati, "Television Criminology."

42. Acuri, "You Can't Take Fingerprints Off Water," p. 243.

43. Daley, "Police Report on the TV Cop Shows," p. 40.

44. Lichter and Lichter, *Prime Time Crime*, p. 37.

45. Acuri, "You Can't Take Fingerprints Off Water," pp. 245-46.

46. Dominick, "Crime and Law Enforcement on Prime Time Television," p. 244.

47. Haney and Manzolati, "Television Criminology."

48. Lichter and Lichter, *Prime Time Crime*.

49. Ibid., pp. 40-41.

50. Ibid., p. 16.

51. Dominick, "Crime and Law Enforcement on Prime Time Television," p. 243.

52. George Gerbner et al., "Cultural Indicators: Violence Profile No. 9," *Journal of Communication* 28 (Summer 1978): 176-207; Dominick, "Crime and Law Enforcement on Prime Time Television," p. 244.

53. George Gerbner et al., "The Demonstration of Power: Violence Profile No. 10," *Journal of Communication* 29 (Spring 1979): 177-96.

54. Ibid., p. 187.

4

MAINSTREAM VIEWS OF CRIME AND LAW ENFORCEMENT

REQUIREMENTS OF THE SYSTEM

In the first chapter it was argued that the historical role of the mass media has always been to promote support for the prevailing social and political order. In this chapter the focus is on the concept of support and the orientations necessary for the persistence of the system. There is general agreement that political systems require a process of socialization for persistence, but there has been considerable disagreement regarding the conceptualization of goals of social and political systems.

For the most part research in the social sciences has been dominated by a system-maintenance theory of socialization; socialization has been viewed as a process by which current social patterns are replicated and the status quo maintained. The system-maintenance perspective consciously links stability to system constancy or lack of change; emphasis is placed on socialization's conserving function.

More recently the system-maintenance perspective has been criticized:

> The major drawback of a theoretical perspective that emphasizes system maintenance is that research inspired by a concern for stability, vertical or horizontal, must overlook a whole range of consequences that socialization has for political diversity, conflict, and change.[1]

Easton and Dennis go on to argue that socialization may be destabilizing as well as system maintaining. Furthermore, most analysts would

55

agree that systems that cannot or do not change are among the least likely to survive. It is more useful from the perspective of theory development to view socialization as a process that may produce constancy *or* change and to focus on the "persistence" of systems as opposed to their maintenance. Easton and Dennis argue that all successful systems change because change is necessary in response to changing environments. They focus on the sources of "stress" on political systems, arguing that socialization is a process that may serve to reduce stress by insuring that the system receives minimal levels of support. At the same time recognition is given to the idea that socialization processes can contribute to disorder and increases in system stress. It is important to note that the system-maintenance perspective emphasizes homogeneity as a condition of stability. System constancy is usually viewed as a situation where peace, cohesion, consensus, and harmony prevail. In contrast, the system-persistence perspective allows that stability may not be inconsistent with diversity and some conflict.

In an analysis of the role of mass media in the process of socialization it seems reasonable to focus on the "persistence" of systems rather than more narrowly on their stability. Indeed it is quite easy to understand how, compared to such agents as the family, mass media may contribute to instability and conflict. However, having left open the possibility of socialization processes contributing to stress on the political system, this research like that conducted by Easton and Dennis gives attention to ways in which socialization plays a vital role in enabling political systems to persist. In fact the focus is narrowed to how socialization is relevant to how political systems deal with one kind of stress: insufficient support for authorities, regime, and political community.

The question of interest here is: What citizen orientations are necessary to guarantee the persistence of the current system? It has been noted that certain levels of diffuse support for the community, regime, and authorities are necessary in order to keep systemic stress at a manageable level. There have been numerous attempts to operationalize support for the three objects of the political system. For the purposes of this study each of the measures described in the second chapter serve as an operationalization of support for one of the three systemic objects. Orientations toward the regime or rules of the game are measured by the Index of Knowledge of Criminal Legal Process, the Index of Support for the Legal System, the measurement of moral development, and the Civil Liberties Support Scale. Orientations toward political authorities are measured in terms of the Police-Community Relations Scale and the Police Effectiveness Scale. The Fear of Crime Scale and the Mean World Index tap basic orientations toward the "community." Finally, the Political Cynicism Scale measures more general orientations toward the political system.

In this chapter the task is to identify the systemic mainstream. There are really three "mainstreams" that are of concern to this book. In the previous chapter an attempt was made to identify the television mainstream. The systemic mainstream can be described as the set of citizen orientations toward systemic objects that produce the least amount of stress. The third mainstream can be described as the most common orientations toward the system held by citizens. System persistence is maximized to the extent there is isomorphism among the three mainstreams. Obviously, the three mainstreams may differ, but the discussion in Chapter 3 supported the idea that the television mainstream is system supportive. This chapter is concerned with the correspondence between system requirements and citizen orientations. An analysis of the distributions of scale items serves as a baseline for later examination of the influence of the television mainstream on orientations.

KNOWLEDGE OF CRIMINAL LEGAL PROCESSES

Is the political system's goal of persistence consistent with the ideal of an "informed citizenry"? It would seem that citizen familiarity with and understanding of the "rules of the game" would be essential to the persistence of any regime. To be sure, regime persistence depends on citizen knowledge of the norms of behavior—a basic understanding of the difference between legal and illegal behavior—but there is some evidence that knowledge concerning legal systems is negatively related to support. Some social scientists argue that democratic legal systems function best when the public is relatively uninformed about their operation.[2] The greater the knowledge, according to this argument, the more likely citizens will be aware of a gap between how they expect institutions to function and how they actually perform.

A number of studies have found that the public generally gives a great deal of diffuse support to the courts, but that those who are most informed about court operations and especially decisions are the least supportive.[3] The inverse relationship between knowledge and support has also been found in studies of attitudes toward police.[4] Perhaps a finding reported by Sarat is more relevant to this study; he found that knowledge of the law was unrelated to willingness to comply with the law, but negatively related to satisfaction with the legal system. His conclusion was that the norm of compliance is so strong that knowledge of how the legal system operates has little effect on law-abidingness.[5]

It is clear that citizen knowledge of laws designed to maintain social order contributes to system persistence, but what about laws that protect the individual from the system? It is obvious that in some instances in a democracy the goals of citizens conflict with the goal of system persistence. As Sarat points out:

> Legal knowledge is a fundamental requisite for citizens in a competitive economic and political system. Only people who know what their rights are and how the legal system works can defend themselves against intrusions on their freedom and use that system to achieve their goals and ameliorate undesired conditions.[6]

Ultimately in situations where the goals of citizens conflict with the goal of system persistence, agents of socialization will stress system goals. Most observers would agree that "civic training" that takes place in schools and within such groups as Boy/Girl Scouts emphasizes knowledge of rules related to social control rather than rules protecting citizen rights. The public mainstream probably involves some, but not extensive, knowledge of criminal legal processes.

The frequency distributions for items included in the Index of Knowledge of Criminal Legal Processes are shown in Table 4.1. Not surprisingly, the adolescents in the sample indicated an awareness of the fact that police have to inform suspects of their rights at the time of arrest. They also knew that trials are public (60.4 percent) and that judges are not prosecutors (64.3 percent). Less than half of the sample (44.2 percent) knew that in the United States there is a presumption of innocence and less than one-fourth understood the Fifth Amendment guarantee against self-incrimination.

Direct comparisons with the distributions in Sarat's adult sample are possible for five of the items included in the index. As might be expected, adults in Sarat's Wisconsin sample were more knowledgeable than the adolescents in the Rhode Island sample. However, aside from the differences in the percentage of correct answers, the pattern of results are very similar; both samples were most likely to know about arrest rights, the nonprosecutorial role of the judge, and the fact that trials are public. They were least likely to be aware of the Fifth Amendment. The only major difference occurred on the item concerning the

Table 4.1 Knowledge of the Law

	Percentage providing each answer		
	True	False	Don't Know
1. When a person is arrested, police have to tell him he has a right to have a lawyer with him before he is questioned. (T)	87.1*	6.0	7.0
2. It is the job of a judge to prove that a man accused of a crime is guilty. (F)	26.2	64.3	9.6
3. Criminal trials in the United States are usually secret. (F)	19.7	60.4	19.9
4. If an innocent man is arrested, it is up to him to prove that he is not guilty. (F)	43.7	44.2	12.1
5. A man who has committed a crime can be made to answer questions about the crime in court. (F)	64.1	21.9	13.9
6. The amendment to the U.S. Constitution that says a person does not have to testify against himself is the Sixth Amendment. (F)	19.0	19.4	61.6

*Missing data were excluded. The number of respondents range from 602 to 619.

presumption of innocence; the adult sample (73.2 percent) was much more likely to be aware of this right than the adolescent sample (44.2 percent).[7]

These findings are consistent with those reported by others who have assessed legal knowledge.[8] Citizens seem to be aware of their rights when they are confronted by agents of law enforcement, but their knowledge of postarrest legal processes and civil law is scanty.

The mainstream of public opinion with regard to knowledge of criminal legal processes can be described as conducive to system persistence. Citizens seem to have limited information regarding their rights after an arrest has taken place. In other words the postarrest legal process if viewed as vague and ambiguous by most citizens.

SUPPORT FOR THE LEGAL SYSTEM AND COMPLIANCE

A great deal of research indicates that the disposition to obey the law is firmly established at an early age.[9] The system requires a great deal of diffuse support for the legal system so that political authorities can " . . . make decisions, get them accepted as binding, and put them into effect."[10] Political systems have alternative means to guarantee compliance such as coercion or promises of special benefits, but the most efficient way to maintain social control is to have a legal system in which

> people apply rules to their own conduct, not one in which people are manipulated by officials . . . [I]t is one in which people have made a commitment to follow uniformly applicable societal rules when their conduct affects the interests of others, not one in which they make such decisions on the basis of their own unfettered discretion.[11]

Easton and Dennis argue that socialization is a very important way to reduce system stress by insuring that members accept most of the outputs as binding most of the time.[12]

The general acceptance of the norm of compliance, established very early in childhood, persists throughout the adolescent years and into adulthood. Even very deprived black adolescents are positively oriented toward compliant behavior.[13] Hess and Torney found that cynicism regarding the legal system increases with age, but while maturation moderates attitudes toward compliance most researchers have found as Sarat that, "In almost overwhelming numbers the people interviewed . . . agreed that the law must always be obeyed."[14]

The collapsed frequency distributions for the items included in the Index of Support for the Legal System are shown in Table 4.2. The distributions in the table show that there is not as much consensus regarding support for the legal system as might be expected. However, on each item the sample takes the supportive position by a wide margin. There are no instances where more than 30 percent of the sample take a nonsupportive position. The item (Number 3) that provoked the most disagreement suggested the possibility of conflict between compliance and personal circumstances. The response pattern on this item may be a reflection of maturation. The most personal statements (Numbers 2 and 6) affirming compliance receive high support.

Again it is possible to make some comparisons with the results of the study of adults conducted by Sarat. A comparison of the distributions in Table 4.2 with the distributions for Sarat's adult sample reveals no surprises; Sarat's sample appears to be generally more supportive

Table 4.2 Collapsed Frequency Distributions for Items Included in the Index of Support for the Legal System

	Percentage who:		
	Disagree	Neutral	Agree
1. The individual who refuses to obey the law is a menace to society.	13.9*	23.8	62.3
2. I must always obey the law.	15.6	15.0	69.4
3. Personal circumstances should never be considered an excuse for lawbreaking.	29.1	31.3	39.6
4. A person should obey the law even if it goes against what he thinks is right.	22.6	25.9	51.6
5. Disobedience of the law can never be tolerated.	21.7	39.3	39.0
6. It would be difficult for me to break the law and keep my self respect.	19.8	19.5	60.7

*Number of respondents ranges from 601 to 617.

of the legal system, but this can be attributed to the fact that a seven-point scale was used, while a five-point scale was used in the present study. Consequently fewer responses appear in the middle (neutral) category in Sarat's study. In terms of the patterns of responses the results of the two studies are nearly identical; both studies show strong support for the norm of compliance.[15]

From the perspective of system persistence what should be the basis of legal compliance? In terms of social control it is inefficient for the system to rely on reward and punishment to guarantee obedience; a system with legal compliance based entirely on coercion would require a police officer on every corner. On the other hand it would create a great deal of stress on the system if people applied their own rules of conduct. In terms of Kohlberg's typology of levels of moral development it would probably be the least stressful for the system if citizens maintained a Level 2 orientation, where emphasis is on rule conformity in order to maintain authority.

Most studies have found that the Conventional Level characterizes the ways in which most people think about compliance. Rodgers and

Table 4.3 Levels of Moral Development Regarding Compliance with the Law[a]

	Percentage
Preconventional	18.8[b]
Conventional	44.8
Postconventional	36.4

[a]Coded on the basis of responses to the question, Do you think people should always obey laws? Why or why not.
[b]Only 511 respondents provided enough information so their answers could be coded.

Taylor, however, classified almost half of their sample of adolescents into the highest level of moral development. Fewer than 20 percent were at the lowest level where rule conformity to avoid punishment is emphasized, almost one-third were classified as "conventional."[16]

The classification used in this study was very liberal with regard to placing responses in the postconventional category, but as shown in Table 4.3 the largest proportion of respondents gave conventional answers when asked about the basis for compliance or noncompliance. Despite the fact that the respondents in this study were younger than those in the Rodgers and Taylor study about the same proportion (18.8 percent) gave preconventional answers. Still a surprising proportion of the sample (36.4 percent) was able to identify circumstances that might mitigate compliance. The mainstream view, however, is that there is little choice but to obey the law. The persistence of the system requires obedience and that is justification enough for the largest proportion of the sample.

SUPPORT FOR CIVIL LIBERTIES

It seems clear that systemic stress will be minimized when citizens hold a crime control point of view. A crime control viewpoint assumes that the criminal justice system is efficient; in contrast to the Due Process Model it involves orientations that are supportive of the system in a specific situation when systemic and citizen goals are in conflict.

Most research on political socialization has shown that children and adolescents have a great deal of admiration for the government, so it is not surprising that few worry about the government's violation of the rights of those accused of crimes.[17] Support of freedom from capricious government power seems to increase with age.[18]

Adult public opinion has been largely supportive of crime control.[19] In an analysis of several national samples Stinchcombe and his associates found not only a relatively high level of support for punitiveness in criminal justice, but that in contrast to other elements of "liberalism" the public is increasingly taking a conservative crime control point of view. In fact the crime control issue has in recent years become less closely associated with issue positions that usually define liberalism and conservatism.[20] In general most surveys on the topic have shown that the American public has little sympathy for the rights of accused; the mainstream view is a crime control point of view.

The collapsed frequency distributions for each item in the Civil Liberties Support Scale are shown in Table 4.4. In general the adolescents included in the sample have a crime control point of view. The greatest sensitivity to civil liberties is displayed on the questions dealing with the requirement of a search warrant and police brutality. Fully one-fourth of the sample, however, is willing to tolerate brutality in some circumstances. Less than one-fourth disagree that "judges should punish criminals more severely." There seems to be some ambivalence about restrictions on police. The sample definitely does not support the exclusionary rule and does not believe that suspects should be released on bail.

On first examination the figures in Table 4.4 do not appear to indicate consensus on crime control. However, on closer examination the lack of sensitivity to constitutionally protected rights seems remarkable; less than half of the sample (46.8 percent) rejected the idea of police brutality, while almost one-third (27.2 percent) thought that search warrants should be unnecessary. The large percentage of respondents who were "undecided" also indicates a lack of sensitivity to issues regarding procedural rights.

The data from previous studies considered along with the distributions in the sample analyzed in this study indicate that mainstream public opinion is not supportive of civil liberties.[21] Assuming the perspective of system-persistence, the large proportion of responses in the undecided category of Table 4.4 indicates that moderately repressive measures aimed at social control will receive little opposition.

Table 4.4 Collapsed Frequency Distributions for Items Included in Civil Liberties Support Scale

	Percentage who:		
	Disagree	Neutral	Agree
1. Judges should punish criminals more severely.	24.1*	31.0	44.9
2. There are too many restrictions on what police can do.	33.2	36.5	30.3
3. In order to protect the community from further crime, an arrested person should be kept in jail until his case comes to trial.	17.7	23.9	58.4
4. In some cases police should be allowed to search a person or his home even if they do not have a warrant.	57.4	15.4	27.2
5. Any man who insults a policeman has no complaint if he gets roughed up in return.	46.8	28.0	25.2
6. Evidence which shows that a defendant did commit a crime should be used at his trial regardless of how the police got the evidence.	27.6	29.5	42.9

*The number of respondents ranged from 610 to 618.
Source: James M. Carlson (1983) "Crime Show Viewing by Preadults: The Impact on Attitudes Toward Civil Liberties," *Communication Research* 10: 540. Reprinted by permission.

IMAGES OF POLICE

The earliest studies of political socialization demonstrated that the police officer is among the first representatives of the political system to be recognized by young children. Easton and Dennis believe that the police officer plays a key role in the process of socializing a sense of legitimacy of external authority:

> If as children mature they come to despise, distrust, scorn, or reject police, the probabilities would be considerable (assuming no compensatory mechanisms come into operation in the later years) the acceptance of the whole structure of authority at all levels would suffer.[22]

Easton and Dennis go on to argue that while positive orientations toward police may initially be critical in the development of the norm of compliance, the police officer remains an important symbol of external authority throughout the adult years.

The police officer receives a great deal of respect from young children. The very youngest children surveyed by Easton and Dennis understood that the "policeman is a compelling force, one whom there is a special obligation to obey. . . . "[2][3] Furthermore children see police officers as essentially benevolent, trustworthy, and helpful. This viewpoint is relatively stable, though as children mature they come to see police as less infallible and dependable. Perhaps most important is a finding by Hess and Torney that noncompliance in face to face encounters with police officers is unthinkable to young children; only 6 percent said they would disobey a police officer if they knew the officer was wrong.[2][4]

Numerous surveys show that adults hold police in high regard and feel they are doing an effective job. These findings are ironic in light of the fact that many police believe that the public has negative images of them. Among the most impressive results are those reported by Smith and Hawkins who found that 71.8 percent of their sample had "very favorable" images of police.[2][5] Peek and Alston used an eleven-point scale to compare public orientations toward various institutions. They found that the FBI and local police were held in higher regard than Congress, the Supreme Court, the press, and the American Medical Association among others.[2][6] Almost all of the survey evidence available points to the fact that the vast majority of adults retain the positive orientation toward police they acquired during childhood.

Police-Community Relations

It is clear that the mainstream point of view regarding police is highly positive. It is possible to examine in some detail the various aspects of these orientations by focusing on the frequency distributions of the survey items used in this study. The distributions for the items that loaded significantly on the factor labeled Police-Community Relations are given in Table 4.5.

The sample of adolescents examined in this study have surprisingly negative images of how police deal with citizens; they are more likely to agree than disagree that police are too willing to use violence and that they spend too much time on unimportant crimes. On four of the six items a much larger proportion of the sample gave positive responses than negative ones, but the magnitude of support and the degree of consensus is not as great as one might expect.

Table 4.5 Collapsed Frequency Distributions for Items Included in the Police-Community Relations Scale

	Percentage who:		
	Disagree	Neutral	Agree
1. Police enjoy pushing people around.	43.6*	23.9	32.5
2. The police don't show proper respect for citizens.	47.5	29.8	22.7
3. The police in this community are guilty of discrimination against people like the poor and minority groups.	42.2	37.1	21.7
4. The police are often too stupid to solve complicated crimes.	55.0	23.5	21.5
5. The police spend most of their time going after people who do little things and ignore most of the bad things going on.	28.5	25.6	35.9
6. The police are too willing to use violence.	32.7	30.9	36.4

*The number of respondents range from 611 to 618.

It is possible to compare the distributions on three of the items with the distributions of an adult sample analyzed by Thomas and Hyman. Nearly 72 percent of the adult sample disagreed that, "The police don't show proper respect for citizens," while only 47.5 percent of the adolescent sample disagreed with the statement. Seventy-two percent of the Thomas and Hyman sample disagreed that, "The police in this community are guilty of discrimination against people like the poor and minority groups," while only 42.2 percent of the adolescent sample disagreed with the statement.[27]

Care must be taken not to make too much of the lack of consensus regarding perceptions of police-community relations; on only two of the six statements do as many as one-third of the sample indicate that they have negative images of police. The general trend in the table is toward positive orientations or ambivalence. The mainstream viewpoint is certainly not nonsupportive.

Police Effectiveness

In an interesting article Jensen points out that general images of police and the disposition to comply with the law depend to some extent on the perception that "crime does not pay" or that police are effective. He, like many other analysts, found that young children see police as very effective; 70 percent of the seventh graders in his sample agreed that, "People who break the law are almost always caught and punished."[28] Hess and Torney found that 57 percent of second graders believed that people who break laws are always caught.[29] As children mature they learn that the police are not infallible, but 50 percent of the twelfth graders in Jensen's sample believed that most criminals are caught.[30]

Hess and Torney's study showed that children develop images of police as helpful and benevolent. The judgments of helpfulness are more stable across age groups than the judgments of effectiveness. Perhaps most impressive is the finding that children feel that it is more important to comply with the wishes of police officers than those of their parents or teachers.[31]

The collapsed frequency distributions for the items that loaded significantly on the factor labeled "Police Effectiveness" are shown in Table 4.6. The figures in the table show that the adolescents in the sample generally view police as effective, but once again positive orientations are not as numerous as one might expect. Nearly 60 percent viewed police as reliable and helpful. Only one-third do not think police are more honest than other people, and 44 percent agree that in general police are doing an effective job. The surprising figures in the table show that nearly equal proportions of the sample agree and disagree that, "Criminals usually get caught." There appears to be consid-

Table 4.6 Collapsed Frequency Distributions for Items Included in the Police Effectiveness Scale

	Percentage who:		
	Disagree	Neutral	Agree
1. Policemen are generally more honest than most people.	34.3*	25.4	40.3
2. The police in our city are doing an effective job and deserve our thanks.	20.0	36.0	44.0
3. Criminals usually get caught.	41.9	16.6	41.5
4. If I need help, I can rely on the police to come to my aid.	21.1	19.3	59.6

*The number of respondents range from 610 to 618.

erable polarization on this particular item; only 16.6 percent demonstrated any uncertainty.

In summary, the mainstream view of police seems to be supportive, but there is some skepticism about effectiveness. Only 41.5 percent of the adolescent sample analyzed in this book agreed that "criminals usually get caught" and 35.9 percent thought that "police spend too much of their time going after people who do little things and ignore most of the bad things." Still, few disagreed that police are honest, respectful, and helpful.

FEAR OF CRIME AND TRUST IN PEOPLE

Fear of victimization and a general trust in people are orientations that are related to a sense of community. Systems that are unable to insure a degree of personal safety among the citizenry are likely to experience a great deal of stress. Indeed, from a Hobbesian point of view the primary function of the polity is to protect citizens from each other. A system's persistence would seem to rest on its ability to maintain social order, but the threat of victimization allows it to prosper. The mainstream point of view probably reflects a moderate amount of fear of crime. If citizens live in terror, then the system's inability to maintain social control is revealed, but if fear of crime is nonexistent one justification for the polity's existence is absent.

The existence of a political community assumes that in general citizens trust each other enough so that they agree implicitly to be governed together. The American political system, some have argued, requires a relatively high degree of mutual trust on the part of citizens because legitimacy rests on popular participation in leadership selection and to some extent in policymaking. However, to some extent the system depends on mutual mistrust on the part of the citizenry; the American system is based largely on individualism and its legitimacy rests on the idea that people are predisposed to oppress each other.[32] Mainstream viewpoints probably reflect a moderate amount of interpersonal distrust.

Fear of Crime

The collapsed frequency distributions for the items included in the Fear of Crime Scale are shown in Table 4.7. The percentages in the table indicate that the sample is aware of the threat of victimization, but is not preoccupied with the problem of crime. Only 45 percent of the sample indicated that crime was one of their major concerns.

Table 4.7 Collapsed Frequency Distributions for Items Included in the Fear of Crime Scale

	Percentage who:		
	Disagree	Neutral	Agree
1. Crime is such a problem that this city is not a safe place to raise children.	61.1*	18.0	20.9
2. It just is not safe to go downtown in Providence at night anymore.	21.2	17.9	60.9
3. The extent of crime is one of my major concerns.	27.3	27.5	45.2
4. Crime is such a problem that I am afraid to go out alone at night.	50.5	14.2	35.3
5. The threat of crime is so great that nobody can feel safe in his own home anymore.	43.1	20.5	36.4

*The number of respondents range from 609 to 618.

This figure is low in comparison with the results of an analysis of an adult sample drawn from Virginia that indicated that nearly 80 percent were very concerned with crime.[33] The sample is prudent in that about 61 percent felt that it is not safe to be downtown at night, but it largely rejected the more extreme statement concerning whether the city is a safe place to raise children. Over one-third of the sample (36.4 percent) felt that "the threat of crime is so great that nobody can feel safe in his home anymore." These figures correspond closely to the response patterns to the same items by the Thomas and Hyman sample.

The figures in Table 4.7 indicate that the adolescents in the Rhode Island sample, like adults in many nationwide samples, are concerned about crime and its consequences for them, but they are not preoccupied by the problem. In fact responses to the item, "The extent of crime is one of my major concerns," are striking in that over half of the sample indicated disagreement or ambivalence. Still, the mainstream view seems to be that victimization is a real threat and that caution is necessary.

Table 4.8 Frequency Distributions for Items Included in the Mean World Index

	Percentage who say:	
1. Generally speaking, would you say most people can be trusted or that you can't be too careful in dealing with people?	Most people can be trusted	Can't be too careful
	42.5*	57.5
2. Would you say that most of the time, people try to be helpful or that they are mostly just looking out for themselves?	Try to be helpful	Look out for themselves
	40.7	59.3
3. Do you think that most people try to take advantage of you if they get a chance or would they try to be fair?	Try to take advantage	Try to be fair
	52.6	47.4

*The number of respondents range from 612 to 619.

The Mean World

National surveys indicate that the American public is not characterized by a great deal of interpersonal trust. Children are generally less trustful than adults.[34] The distribution of responses to the items in the Mean World Index given in Table 4.8 show that the sample of Rhode Island adolescents is generally mistrustful; on the items a majority of respondents felt that people cannot be trusted, are not helpful, and will try to take advantage.

A comparison of the response patterns in Table 4.8 with responses given by adults and children in other samples to the same items indicates a general pattern of mistrust. Gerbner et al. showed that only about one-third of the adults in the National Opinion Research Corporation (NORC) General Social Survey gave mistrustful responses to each of the three items, but over half of a sample of children agreed that "people will take advantage" and that "you can't be too careful in dealing with people."[35] Well over two-thirds of the sample of children analyzed by Gerbner et al. agreed that "people . . . are mostly just looking out for themselves."[36] The responses of adolescents in the present study seem to fall between those of adult and children samples analyzed by Gerbner and his colleagues. Once again the mainstream view seems to be one of moderate amounts of interpersonal mistrust. There is cynicism regarding fellow citizens, but mistrust is not extreme.

POLITICAL CYNICISM

One of the most dramatic trends in public opinion in recent years has been the decline in political trust. Although there is no absolute standard by which one can determine whether a population is generally trustful of the political system, some generalizations are possible. It is clear that responses to all of the items included in the standard Political Cynicism Scale indicate a dramatic decline in trust in government since 1958. For example, in 1958 74 percent of white adults nationwide agreed that the "government in Washington can be trusted to do what is right just about always or most of the time." By 1980 only 25 percent of white adults agreed with the statement.[37]

Socialization studies have shown that children are generally more trustful than adults; political trust seems to decline rapidly between eighth and twelfth grades, though adults are less trustful than twelfth graders.[38] There is also some evidence that political trust has decreased among children and adolescents as well as adults in the past 25 years.

While there is general agreement that political trust has declined, the significance of the decline has been hotly debated. Arthur Miller has argued that feelings of basic discontent "are very likely to be accompanied by hostility toward political and social leaders, the institutions of government, and the regime as a whole."[39] Jack Citrin on the other hand argues that "the meaning of recent increases in the level of political cynicism remains ambiguous, and to decisively conclude that there exists widespread support for radical political change or pervasive alienation from the political system is premature, if not misleading." Citrin goes on to argue that the decline in trust is a reflection of "ritualistic responses" to current events and personalities.[40] Whether Miller or Citrin are correct about the gravity of the situation, it seems clear that a high degree of mistrust is stressful for the system; trust not cynicism is more conducive to system persistence.

The response patterns of the adolescent sample examined in this study to the items included in the Political Cynicism Scale are shown in Table 4.9. In general the same patterns of cynicism that have been found in other studies are shown in Table 4.9. As might be expected the adolescents included in this study are not as cynical as the adults included in other studies. Cynicism on items dealing with waste of tax money, whether government officials are crooked, and whether people running the government know what they are doing are highly comparable to the sample reported by Abramson.[41] In comparison to other samples the adolescents in this study were more likely to say

Table 4.9 Frequency Distributions for Items Included in the Political Cynicism Scale

	Percentage who say:		
1. Do you think that people in the government waste a lot of the money paid in taxes, waste some of it, or don't waste much of it?	Waste lot	Waste some	Don't waste very much
	54.7*	41.4	3.9
2. Do you think that quite a few of the people running the government are a little crooked, not very many are, or do you think hardly any of them are?	Quite a few	Not very many	Hardly any
	49.3	42.3	8.5
3. How much of the time do you think you can trust the government in Washington to do what is right—just about always, most of the time, or only some of the time?	Just about always	Most of the time	Some of the time
	48.9	7.7	43.5
4. Do you feel that almost all of the people running the government are smart people who usually know what they are doing, or do you think that quite a few of them don't seem to know what they are doing?	Almost all know what they are doing		Quite a few don't seem to know what they are doing
	39.8		60.2
5. Would you say that the government is pretty much run by a few big interests looking out for themselves or that it is run for the benefit of all the people?	Run by a few big interests		Run for the benefit of all
	53.0		47.0

*The number of respondents range from 614 to 619.

that government officials could be trusted and that the government is run for the benefit of all.

It appears that mainstream public opinion includes a dose of political cynicism. It is unclear whether this reflects a healthy skepticism about government or a threat to the stability of the political system. Mainstream public opinion appears to be somewhat out of line with the needs of the system to maintain low levels of stress. Public opinion regarding government or the system may also be inconsistent with the television mainstream, though television may in fact contribute to low levels of trust.

CONCLUSIONS

Mainstream views on issues concerning crime and law enforcement can be described as "moderate." The means and standard deviations for scale scores on each of the linear scales included in this study are shown in Table 4.10. When the means are examined in light of the possible ranges of each of the scales, what is remarkable is the absence of extreme viewpoints. There does not seem to be an extremely high degree of knowledge of the law, support for the legal system, or support for civil liberties, but scores are also not at a remarkably low level. There is neither a high nor low degree of fear of crime or distrust of people. Police are viewed realistically, not idealistically or overly cynically. Perhaps the most remarkable figure in the table is the mean on the Political Cynicism Scale. The sample of adolescents appears to be more trustful of representatives of the political system than one might reasonably expect.

It was necessary in this chapter to get a "feel" for the mainstream of public opinion regarding crime and law enforcement because in the following chapters it will be argued that crime show viewing has its greatest effects on those individuals whose views are outside of the systemic, television, and public opinion mainstream. What was found in this chapter was surprising homogeneity with regard to views on

Table 4.10 Mean Scores for Scales*

Scale	Possible Range	Mean	Standard Deviation
Knowledge of the law	0-6	3.1	1.4
Support for the legal system	6-30	20.9	4.1
Support for civil liberties	6-30	17.7	3.9
Police-Community relations	6-30	19.0	4.6
Police effectiveness	4-20	12.7	2.9
Fear of crime	5-25	14.9	3.8
Mean world	3-6	4.7	1.0
Political cynicism	5-13	7.8	1.8

*Number of respondents range from 600 to 619.

crime and law enforcement. In the next chapter those people who hold views that are "outside of the mainstream" will be identified, so that specific hypotheses can be developed about media effects.

NOTES

1. David Easton and Jack Dennis, *Children in the Political System* (New York: McGraw-Hill, 1969), p. 36.

2. See Austin Sarat, "Support for the Legal System," *American Politics Quarterly* 3 (February 1975): 5.

3. Walter Murphy and Joseph Tanenhaus, "Public Opinion and the United States Supreme Court," *Law and Society Review* 2 (1968): 365-84; William Skogan, "Judicial Myth and Judicial Reality," *Washington University Law Quarterly* (1971): 309-34.

4. David H. Bayley and Harold Mendelsohn, *Minorities and Police* (New York: Free Press, 1969).

5. Sarat, "Support for the Legal System."

6. Ibid., p. 13.

7. Ibid.

8. M. Williams and J. Hall, "Knowledge of the Law in Texas," *Law and Society Review* 7 (1972): 99-118.

9. Robert Hess and Judith Torney, *The Development of Political Attitudes in Children* (Garden City, N.Y.: Doubleday, 1967).

10. David Easton, *A System Analysis of Political Life* (New York: Wiley, 1965), p. 158.

11. Robert Gerstein, "The Practice of Fidelity to Law," *Law and Society Review* 4 (1970): 479-90.

12. Easton and Dennis, *Children in the Political System.*

13. Harrell Rodgers and George Taylor, "Pre-Adult Attitudes Toward Legal Compliance: Notes Toward A Theory," *Social Science Quarterly* 51 (December 1970): 539-51.

14. Sarat, "Support for the Legal System," p. 5.

15. Ibid., p. 6.

16. Rodgers and Taylor, "Pre-adult Attitudes Toward Legal Compliance," p. 543.

17. H. H. Remmers and Richard D. Franklin, "Sweet Land of Liberty," in *Anti-Democratic Attitudes in American Schools*, ed. H. H. Remmers (Evanston, Ill.: Northwestern University Press, 1963).

18. Judith Gallatin and Joseph Adelson, "Legal Guarantees of Individual Freedom: A Cross-National Study of Development of Political Thought," *Journal of Social Issues* 27 (1971): 80-101.

19. Michael Corbett, "Public Support for 'Law and Order': Interrelationships with System Affirmation and Attitudes Toward Minorities," *Criminology* 19 (November 1981): 328-43.

20. Arthur L. Stinchcombe, et al., *Crime and Punishment—Changing Attitudes in America* (San Francisco: Jossey-Bass, 1980).

21. Corbett, "Public Support for Law and Order."

22. Easton and Dennis, *Children in the Political System*, p. 240.

23. Ibid., p. 221.

24. Hess and Torney, *The Development of Political Attitudes in Children*, p. 64.

25. Paul Smith and Richard O. Hawkins, "Victimization, Types of Citizen-Police Contacts, and Attitudes Toward Police," *Law and Society* 7 (Fall 1973): 135-52.

26. Charles W. Peek, Jon P. Alston, and George D. Lowe, "Comparative Evaluation of Local Police," *Public Opinion Quarterly* 42 (Fall 1978): 370-79.

27. Charles W. Thomas and Jeffrey M. Hyman, "Perceptions of Crime, Fear of Victimization, and Public Perceptions of Police Performance," *Journal of Police Science and Administration* 5 (Fall 1977): 305-17.

28. Gary F. Jensen, "'Crime Doesn't Pay': Correlates of a Shared Misunderstanding," *Social Problems* (1971): 189-201.

29. Hess and Torney, *The Development of Political Attitudes in Children*, p. 64.

30. Jenson, "Crime Doesn't Pay," p. 195.

31. Easton and Dennis, *Children in the Political System*, p. 226.

32. David Schuman, *A Preface to Politics* (Lexington, Mass.: D. C. Heath, 1973).

33. Thomas and Hyman, "Perceptions of Crime," p. 312.

34. George Gerbner et al., "TV Violence Profile No. 8: The Highlights," *Journal of Communication* 27 (Spring 1977): 178.

35. Ibid.

36. Ibid.

37. Paul R. Abramson, *Political Attitudes in America: Formation and Change* (San Francisco: W. H. Freeman, 1983), p. 230.

38. M. Kent Jennings and Richard G. Niemi, *The Political Character of Adolescence: The Influence of Families and Schools* (Princeton: Princeton University Press, 1974), p. 142.

39. Arthur H. Miller, "Political Issues and Trust in Government: 1964-1970," *American Political Science Review* 68 (December 1974): 951-72.

40. Jack Citrin, "Comment: The Political Relevance of Trust in Government," *American Political Science Review* 68 (December 1974): 973-88.

41. Abramson, *Political Attitudes in America*, p. 230.

5

CONDITIONS AFFECTING MAINSTREAM VIEWS

INTRODUCTION

Public attitudes related to crime and law enforcement likely evolve as a result of interactions of influences emanating from family, school, peers, actual contact with the criminal justice system, and the mass media. Though there is general agreement that a media-effects model, which simplistically attributes powerful, direct effects to the mass media, has been discredited,[1] theoretical justification for considering television entertainment as an important influence on the socialization of adolescents is not difficult.

As noted in the first chapter, the theoretical approach taken in this research comes from George Gerbner and his associates who argue that television viewing may not have easily discernible strong direct causal effects on beliefs and opinions, but can "cultivate" a symbolic structure that is used by viewers to interpret reality.[2] A major premise of what has come to be called "cultivation analysis" is that the very persistence and pervasiveness of television's images cultivate the dominant beliefs and values of American society; cultivation contributes to a common, system-supportive perspective. Media-cultivated facts increasingly become standards by which Americans judge their own beliefs and behavior, as well as others.[3]

The evidence that television viewing cultivates certain views of social reality has generally been consistent and persuasive, though the body of research in this area has not been produced without criticism. Critics have charged that correlations between television viewing and conceptions of social reality are often very small, and in some instances fall below statistical significance when multiple controls are placed on bivariate relationships.[4] Gerbner's research has been criticized for ignoring key variables, using poor or unrepresentative samples, and improperly measuring television viewing.[5] However, despite the criticism the cumulative results of over a decade's research on the topic seem to indicate that while relationships are often statistically small, television's independent effects usually survive controls for third variables.[6] Gerbner et al. are unconcerned about the small correlations found in most of their studies because, they argue " . . . just as an average temperature shift of a few degrees can lead to an ice age or the outcomes of elections can be determined by slight margins, so can a relatively small but pervasive influence make a crucial difference. The 'size' of the effect is far less critical than the direction of its steady contribution."[7]

The concern of this chapter is with "how cultivation works." As Hawkins and Pingee point out, cultivation theory has been approached primarily from a sociological perspective, and little attention has been given to the psychological processes and the conditions that determine how cultivation occurs.[8] In recent years a few scholars have given attention to *how* learning from television occurs; the most interesting development in this area—the idea of passive learning—will be briefly discussed. The idea that the influence of television is equally probable for every viewer is no longer accepted. Instead more attention is being given to the conditions that increase or decrease the probability of effects. Later in the chapter some types of conditions that influence cultivation will be discussed, with special attention given to the idea of mainstreaming. Finally, groups that hold views that are deviant from the mainstream, and thus more likely to be influenced by viewing crime shows, will be identified for further analysis.

Before beginning a discussion of conditions and processes of cultivation it is important to point out that the present research diverges from the research of Gerbner and his colleagues in one important respect. Gerbner et al. make two assumptions:

> One is that commercial television, unlike other media, presents an organically composed total world of interrelated stories (both drama and news) produced to the same set of market specifications. Second, television audiences (unlike those for other media) view largely non-selectively and by the clock rather than by the program. Television is a ritual, almost like religion, except that it is attended more regularly.[9]

This study is based on the assumption that the content of television programming is relevant to the probability of effects. This assumption is supported by a number of data-based studies. Hawkins and Pingee related the Mean World Index and a measure of perceptions of violence in society to viewing programs of ten different content types. They found that viewing crime-adventure shows was associated with high scores on the Mean World Index. Viewing of crime-adventure shows, situation comedies, game shows, cartoons, and children's shows was associated with perceptions of violence in society. News and documentaries, as well as several other content types including sports shows, were not associated with either measure.[10] Other data analyzed by Berman and Stookey support the argument that the effects of viewing programs of all content types is not uniform with respect to perceptions of social reality.[11] It seems clear that the particular type of program habitually viewed is a condition that is relevant to cultivation effects. Hawkins and Pingee conclude correctly that it is unnecessary to assume uniform content and habitual, indiscriminate viewing to explain the cultivation of relevant attitudes and perceptions.[12]

PASSIVE LEARNING AND CULTIVATION

The process of learning is usually associated with conscious motivation and activity; it is a form of behavior that has been conceptualized as goal-directed and purposive, where the learner understands the salience of what is being learned and gives it his or her attention. Given these assumptions about the process of learning, it is not surprising that television has not been viewed as an effective teacher; television viewing is usually seen as a passive experience that involves little motivation or attention. It has already been noted that some believe that programs are viewed indiscriminately and that the content of the programs viewed is largely unrelated to viewer interests or a goal of knowledge acquisition.

In recent years researchers have been giving increasing attention to the idea that it is possible to learn through passive experiences such as television viewing. Krugman and Hartley, who provide the theoretical justification for passive learning, argue that neither interest nor motivation are necessary for the acquisition of knowledge or attitudes. In their view the mere absence of resistance may be all that is necessary for learning to occur; the substance of television entertainment, they argue, may be "caught rather than taught."[13]

To understand how television might be a source of knowledge and attitudes it is important to make some important distinctions between the more active type of classroom learning and passive learning. One of the distinctions has to do with the physiological qualities of attention. Relying on an argument made by William James, Krugman and Hartley point out that voluntary attention, as opposed to involuntary attention, requires a great deal of effort and cannot be sustained for long periods of time. Since voluntary attention requires effort and cannot be continuous most of what is experienced is involuntarily attended. In other words much of what is learned is learned when there is an absence of an effort to attend. Krugman and Hartley provide a complex physiological argument in support of their position, but for the purposes of the present research it is most important simply to recognize that learning can be involuntary and effortless.

Perhaps the most important distinction between active and passive learning as they relate to television viewing is the one between excitement and relaxation. Krugman and Hartley point out that television viewing may be a relaxing experience, one in which defenses are "down" and the viewers are receptive to information and viewpoints that do not challenge their basic values. In contrast to active learning that requires arousal, passive learning is facilitated by television viewing that relaxes; the flickering light of the television, according to Krugman and Hartley, affects the brain's alpha rhythms, and hence relaxes.

The idea of passive learning compliments cultivation theory in that they both emphasize the subtlety of the process of learning; cultivation analysis emphasizes the pervasiveness of messages and the idea that the very persistence with which they are transmitted ultimately influences perceptions of reality and attitudes. The idea that the repetition of essentially the same message is necessary to "cultivate" a perception of reality seems inconsistent with a model of learning that involves a high degree of attention to a single message. The theoretical advancements made by Krugman and Hartley, as well as Gerbner and his associates provide ample justification for a search for "effects" of television entertainment.

SOME CONDITIONS AND PROCESSES
AFFECTING CULTIVATION

Most recent research has shown that television does not have an across-the-board impact. Even Gerbner and his associates have begun to focus on the conditions under which effects are present and the probability of their occurrence. There is some confusion concerning the classification of the many conditional variables affecting relationships between television viewing and perceptions of social reality.[14] Although it is beyond the scope of this book to discuss all of the issues regarding the classification of conditional variables, several types of conditions relate directly to this study. These conditions were outlined in some detail by Hawkins and Pingee.[15]

The Ability to Process Television's Messages

Cultivation effects may depend on individual abilities concerning the reception and processing of messages. As Hawkins and Pingee point out the number of variables related to individual differences in message processing is quite large.[16] Several variables included in the present study may be related to cognitive functioning and deserve to be examined.

Intelligence is probably related to the ability to critically evaluate the messages transmitted by television crime shows. Critical abilities reflected by a measure of intelligence may enhance or inhibit cultivation effects. Those with high intelligence may be most susceptible to cultivation because they understand the messages being transmitted and are able to discriminate between conflicting messages. On the other hand highly intelligent viewers may have a wider range of experience with diverse forms of information and may view the message of crime shows more critically.

Measures of achievement are probably relatively poor surrogates for measures of intelligence, but IQ scores are often unavailable. In the present study an approximation of grade average is used to examine the influence of processing abilities on cultivation of mainstream points of view. A major problem with using grades is that they may reflect conformity to teacher or school norms as much as they reflect academic achievement. However, there is also considerable controversy concerning the validity of IQ scores.

Age or grade in school may also be indicative of the ability to process television's messages. Hawkins and Pingee point out that cognitive development theories predict that children's receptivity to messages varies depending upon the stage of development. At some stages children may be much more dogmatic and inflexible than at other stages.[17] In this study cultivation effects will be examined among the varying grades in school.

Antecedent variables that may ultimately condition cultivation of mainstream views are the structural characteristics of families. Two measures of family communication patterns used in this study, socio-orientation and concept-orientation, may have a great deal to do with how respondents process information. Respondents from highly socio-oriented families may be extremely receptive and deferential; they may be highly likely to "learn" from television. Adolescents from highly concept-oriented families may view the content of television entertainment more critically and be less receptive or they may have a greater ability to understand messages and therefore more susceptible to cultivation.

Perceptions of the Reality of Television Programming

Those who perceive that the content of television is "real" are more likely to see television's messages as relevant and are more susceptible to cultivation. This basic hypothesis has received a great deal of attention in recent years. Generally the hypothesis has not found a great deal of support. Reeves found that perceived reality made little difference in the effects of television viewing on a variety of behaviors.[18] Hawkins and Pingee found that cultivation was most likely to occur at *lower* levels of perceived reality.[19]

The perception of reality may in fact be related to the idea of passive learning discussed earlier. When television is perceived as "unreal" individuals may be more relaxed and more susceptible to cultivation. "Real" television may arouse viewers and make them defensive and less open to the messages being transmitted. A measure of perceived reality is included in the present study so that its conditioning effects can be examined.

Previous Experience and Cultivation Effects

Hawkins and Pingee outline a number of ways in which previous experience may condition the cultivation effects of television. The first situation is one in which television messages simply confirm perceptions of reality and values that were developed from previous experience. If the messages of television confirm real-world experiences of the individual there would likely be very little cultivation effect aside from reinforcement.

A second situation may involve the case where the messages transmitted by television are disconfirmed by previous experience. Television content may be seen as lacking credibility because other sources of information are presenting or have presented conflicting messages.

The third condition outlined by Hawkins and Pingee is the most interesting and relevant to this study. That is the situation where the messages being transmitted by television are congruent with dominant, mainstream social beliefs. If one's previous experiences have led one to hold mainstream views, television will contribute little more than reinforcement. If previous experience has produced a viewpoint that is outside of the mainstream, then heavy television viewing is likely to cultivate mainstream values; cultivation is a process, as has been noted previously, that tends to promote homogeneity of viewpoints.[20]

The characteristics that may influence previous acceptance of mainstream viewpoints are numerous, but an example using socioeconomic status should serve to illustrate the process. As Gerbner et al. point out, people from high-status backgrounds tend to be lighter viewers of television and exhibit greater diversity of attitudes.[21] However, high-status persons who are heavy viewers of television tend to hold mainstream viewpoints that could not be predicted given their demographic characteristics; heavy viewers regardless of social background characteristics tend to share a homogeneous, mainstream viewpoint. A large number of variables that may be reflections of personal experiences and that may affect views on crime and law enforcement will be reviewed later in this chapter.

Related to the question of previous experience is the volume of information individuals hold regarding aspects of social reality. It is generally held that the effects of communication are greatest when there is an absence of competing information, experience, or pre-existing knowledge regarding the subject matter. If that is the case, younger, less experienced individuals should be more susceptible to cultivation effects. Those who do not consume other media such as books, magazines, and newspapers would also be more likely to accept the messages of television. Several variables, including a measure of reading habits, will be used in this study to assess the possible effects of competing information.

The Context of Mass Media Effects

The social groups surrounding the individual may condition the cultivation process. There are numerous ways to characterize an individual's social context. For example, Hawkins and Pingee cite a study where children's peer groups were categorized as cohesive or noncohesive and the effects of cohesiveness on the cultivation process were examined.[22] Many have noted that televison viewing does not take place in a vacuum; people view television in a context. In this study such factors as urban/suburban residence, public/private school attendance, and family structure will be examined to see if they affect the process of cultivation.

ISOLATING CHARACTERISTICS THAT CONTRIBUTE TO MAINSTREAMING

A thorough cultivation analysis requires that groups that hold views outside of the mainstream be identified because it is precisely those groups that are hypothesized to be affected most by television viewing. In addition to characteristics associated with previous experience a number of other conditions that may influence the cultivation process have been identified. The problem of identifying variables that characterize the conditions of cultivation is that single variables may stand for more than one condition. Hawkins and Pingee note that "I(t) is easy to forget that demographic characteristics are reifications of very meaningful processes. They are locators that are simpler to use than the processes themselves, but as demographics they mean nothing."[23]

An example of the problem can be provided by thinking about the possible implications of controlling for one of the variables that will be considered later--grade in school. Suppose that it is found that the respondents in the lower grades are more likely to be influenced by crime show viewing than those in the higher grades. How can this finding be interpreted? Grade in school may be a reflection of cognitive development or processing abilities. It may also reflect personal experiences or simply the amount of information held about a particular subject. In other words, grade in school may be a surrogate for a number of conditions and processes; there may be a number of explanations for the effects of grade in school or other variables on the media-effects relationship.

A major concern of this chapter is to identify groups that are most likely to be mainstreamed. This is accomplished by examining the relationships between characteristics of respondents and support for mainstream views concerning criminal legal processes. For purposes of organization conditional variables are grouped into three categories: individual characteristics, family characteristics, and contextual characteristics.

Individual Characteristics

Measures of quite a large number of individual characteristics were included in the survey of Rhode Island adolescents. In this and following chapters attention will be given to the conditioning effects of six of them. Sex, grade in school, and head of household occupation can be described as demographic characteristics. Grade in school is the analytical equivalent of age. Head of household occupation serves as an indicator of social economic status.* Several background characteristics including religion, race, and ethnicity are not included in the analysis because they were found to have little or no influence on television crime show viewing–criminal justice attitude relationships.†

Three additional individual characteristics may be related to how respondents "process" the messages that are being transmitted by crime shows. They include a very rough measure of achievement in school, the extent to which respondents read newspapers, books, and magazines, and perceptions of the reality of television content.†† These variables may be more of a reflection of processing abilities than the socialization of mainstream viewpoints. However, as noted earlier, in some instances when conditional relationships are found, more than one explanation for the conditioning effect of the third variable are possible. With that possibility taken into account each of the "processing" variables are examined to determine whether or not they are related to mainstream criminal justice attitudes.

A great deal of attention has been given to sex differences in recent years. Studies of socialization lead us to believe that males and

---

*Grade in school and age produced almost identical results when related to the dependent measures examined in this study. Head of household occupation was the only SES measure that it was possible to obtain. White-collar occupations included those classified as professionals, owners, managers, clerical, and sales. Blue-collar occupations included: craftsmen, operators, laborers, service workers, and all others.

†These variables were included in preliminary statistical analyses, but were excluded because they added nothing to explanations of media effects. These variables may have theoretical significance, but in Rhode Island the population is not representative with respect to ethnicity, religion, and race; there are relatively few blacks in Rhode Island and Irish and Italian Catholics are overrepresented.

††School officials in some districts would not allow access to student records or questions about grade-point average. The question about grades that produced only two response categories was a result of a compromise. The measures of reading habits and perceptions of TV reality described in Chapter 2 are dichotomized at the median for purposes of analysis of conditional relationships.

females differ with regard to system-relevant attitudes. Boys have been found to have greater interest in public affairs and consequently display greater knowledge of politics.[24] Most research regarding sex and political interest, involvement, and knowledge would seem to lead to the expectation that females will be less likely to have a high degree of knowledge about criminal legal processes.

Socialization research also indicates that females are more likely than males to be positively oriented toward authority and obedience. For example, Hess and Torney found that girls were more likely than boys to say that it is the duty of the "good citizen" to obey laws.[25] Weissberg in a review of socialization literature concluded that girls are more oriented toward conformity to rules than are boys.[26] With regard to mainstream attitudes the research would seem to indicate that males are more likely to be less supportive of the legal system and less oriented toward compliance; female attitudes are more likely to fall in the mainstream.

Given the differences in orientations toward conformity with the law, it is reasonable to expect that females as opposed to males are likely to take a crime control point of view. The evidence regarding sex and crime control orientations is not extensive, but Stinchcombe and his associates found that among adults females are more likely than males to endorse harsh treatment of criminals.[27] Hess and Torney report that young girls are more likely to emphasize the protective quality of the political system. With regard to support for civil liberties females are likely to hold mainstream views, while males may hold views relatively outside of the mainstream.[28]

Males and females differ considerably with regard to perceptions of police. Females show a greater attachment to police officers at a young age.[29] They are more likely than boys to rate police officers as powerful, responsive, and helpful.[30] This evidence is consistent with that reported by Bouma who found that males had less favorable attitudes toward police regardless of the controls imposed. Males are consistently outside of the mainstream, compared to females, with regard to positive orientations toward police.[31]

The evidence regarding fear of crime and perceptions of a "mean world" consistently indicates that females are less trustful of people and fear victimization. Stinchcombe et al. found that in a nationwide sample of adults females demonstrate a greater fear of crime.[32] The Thomas and Hyman study of adults in Virginia confirms this finding. Females, it appears, feel more vulnerable than males and are more likely to feel threatened by strangers.[33]

Almost every study of socialization has examined the effects of age differences on system-relevant orientations. Generally most studies have found that as respondents age they become more knowledgeable and less idealistic regarding the system. These basic trends hold with respect to attitudes concerning the criminal justice system.

There is ample evidence that young children acquire knowledge about the political system rapidly as they move through the grades. Schools spend a great deal of time on "civics education," and with regard to the "basics" there is a great deal of evidence of successful socialization.[34] There is also substantial evidence that children develop the ability to think analytically about politics as they mature, but there is no real development until after the age of eleven.[35] It is highly likely that adolescents in the higher grades will demonstrate greater knowledge of criminal legal processes than those in the lower grades.

Orientations toward the legal system and compliance also change with age. In general, maturity brings the view that rules and laws are more flexible and less absolute.[36] For example Hess and Torney show that there is a tremendous decline from grade two to grade eight in agreement that "all laws are fair."[37] Given the evidence that shows that respondents in higher grades see law as more flexible, results reported by Rodgers and Taylor that show that age has little influence on levels of moral development are surprising.[38] Perhaps age is related to movement to the conventional level, but not the postconventional level. The evidence from previous research points to the expectation that respondents in the higher grades are more likely to be outside of the mainstream with respect to support for the legal system and compliance.

Since younger respondents are more positively oriented toward authority, it should come as no surprise that they are not particularly supportive of civil liberties. Weissberg reports that younger children have no problem with the extensive use of government power. However, by the time students reach the teenage years they are more sensitive to democratic values and in particular due process guarantees. Older respondents are more likely to hold views regarding civil liberties that are outside of the mainstream.[39]

It was noted in the previous chapter that the police officer is one of the first authorities recognized by young children. Early views of the police officer are extremely positive. The positive images of police decline dramatically with age.[40] Not only are police seen as less helpful and powerful, but they are also seen as less effective; Jensen reports that the belief that "criminals are usually caught" declines dramatically between the seventh and twelfth grade.[41] The image of the police officer among young children is so highly idealized that declines in positive orientations are to be expected. Generally, younger respondents are more likely to hold mainstream views regarding police than older respondents.

There is little consistent evidence regarding the effects of age on fear of crime and perceptions of a mean world. Stinchcombe presents some evidence that among adults older men have a greater fear of victimization than younger men. Generally, younger people are more optimistic in their dealings with other people.[42] Jennings and Neimi, however, reported that their parent sample displayed greater trust in people than their student sample.[43] Age probably interacts with a number of other variables such as parental overprotection, place of residence, and self-confidence in affecting fear of crime and trust in people. Perhaps older students with more experience outside of the home will be less fearful of victimization, but more careful in interpersonal relations.

Social status, a variable included in most studies of socialization, is often confounded with a wide variety of other variables. It can serve as a surrogate for such factors as parental characteristics, cognitive abilities, and self-confidence. Weissberg reports that students of higher social status demonstrate greater involvement, interest, and knowledge of public affairs.[44] Students from higher status families obviously have some educational advantages not enjoyed by those with a lower status background; they tend to develop cognitive abilities more easily than their lower status cohorts. It would be consistent with earlier studies if students from higher status homes demonstrated greater knowledge of criminal legal processes than students from lower status homes.

Higher status students are among the first to see laws as less than absolute, rigid guides for behavior.[45] Lower status students place more emphasis on compliance and support for the legal system; they generally are less cynical about authority.[46] Previous research would support the proposition that students from families where the head of the household has a low-status occupation are more likely to demonstrate support for the legal system and the norm of compliance.

Adult studies have consistently shown that working-class citizens are the least supportive of democratic principles.[47] Evidently orientations toward democracy are developed early because Litt found that among students in the Boston area those with middle class backgrounds were more democratic.[48] Studies reviewed by Weissberg would lead to the expectation that students whose parents have high-status occupations will be supportive of civil liberties, while those from low-status homes will be more likely to have a mainstream crime control point of view.[49]

Consistent with their orientation toward legal compliance, lower status students have more positive attitudes toward police than high-status students. Hess and Torney reported that low-status students were more likely to agree that "people who break the laws always get caught."[50] They also see police as more helpful, powerful, and friendly.[51] These findings are confirmed by studies of adults.[52] In this study students from higher status families should exhibit attitudes that are outside of the mainstream with respect to orientations toward police.

There is strong evidence that lower status individuals have a greater fear of crime than those with greater status.[53] This has been found to be the case regardless of whether education, income, or occupation is used as an indicator of status. There is also some evidence that status is associated with perceptions of a mean world; Jennings and Neimi report that in both their student and parent samples high-social status individuals display a high degree of interpersonal trust.[54] With regard to television crime shows, high-status respondents are outside of the mainstream with respect to perceptions of a mean world and fear of victimization.

It is desirable to include some measures of cognitive capabilities for a number of reasons. Cognitive skills may be associated with some of the attitudinal variables under study, such as support for civil liberties or moral development. It is also likely that the influence of viewing crime shows varies depending on how well individuals are able to discriminate and process the information being transmitted. Previous studies have included measures of intelligence, as well as achievement. Care must be taken in interpreting results based on standard IQ tests or grade average. Many professionals question the validity of IQ tests. As noted earlier, grade average may measure achievement, but it might also measure conformity to teacher and school norms. Intelligence and achievement are independent concepts, but their measurements probably reflect, at least in a general way, cognitive abilities.

It should come as no surprise that both IQ scores and grade-point averages are associated with high levels of knowledge about public affairs.[55] Children with high IQ scores are among the first to be able to discriminate the functions and institutions of government.[56] When the data collected from Rhode Island adolescents is analyzed a positive relationship between grades and knowledge of criminal legal processes should be revealed.

Students with well-developed cognitive skills are among the first to depersonify political institutions and view them abstractly. Hess and Torney reported that regardless of age children with low IQ scores were more likely to personify government institutions.[57] Those with high IQ's are less likely to hold the legal system in high regard or support the norm of compliance; Hess and Torney report that high IQ students see the laws as less rigid, while Rodgers and Taylor found a very strong negative relationship between grade average and compliance disposition.[58] Based on earlier studies students with higher grades can be expected to exhibit lower support for the legal system and to be found among those at the postconventional level of moral development. In general, students with well-developed cognitive capabilities should hold attitudes that are outside of the mainstream.

Support for democratic values is associated with cognitive sophistication.[59] Given previous findings that indicate that students with high IQ scores and grade averages are less supportive of the legal system, it is reasonable to expect that they will not hold a crime control point of view. Students who display cognitive sophistication are likely to see inconsistency between government coercion and democracy; with regard to support for civil liberties they likely hold views outside of the mainstream.

Hess and Torney report that students with low IQ scores are more likely to see police as benevolent and knowledgeable than those with high scores. Those with lower intelligence persist in idealization of political authorities for some time after their high intelligence cohorts become cynical. Furthermore, low-IQ students tend to retain the belief that "most criminals are caught" long after their cohorts develop a more realistic view of police performance.[60] Most research seems to indicate that people with high cognitive abilities have a realistic view of police image and performance; this view puts them outside of the mainstream.

There is little or no research that relates cognitive abilities and fear of crime or perception of a mean world. However, it is possible to infer the possibility of a relationship. Individuals with high IQ scores or grade-point averages often have a great deal of self-confidence. It is likely that persons with high self-confidence would be less concerned about the threat of crime or would display a high degree of interpersonal mistrust; high grades should be associated with low scores on the measures of fear of crime and perceptions of a mean world.

Two other individual characteristics included in this study, reading habits and perceptions of the reality of television entertainment, are

Table 5.1 Mean Scores and T-Tests of Significance on Measures of Criminal Justice Attitudes, by Demographic Characteristics*

Measure	Sex			Grade			Parents' Occupation		
	Male	Female	$p <$	6th-8th	9th-12th	$p <$	Blue-collar	White-collar	$p <$
Knowledge of the law	3.34	2.88	.001	2.70	3.63	.001	2.97	3.21	.05
Support for the legal system	20.65	20.86	ns	21.45	19.82	.001	20.70	20.93	ns
Support for civil liberties	17.48	18.00	ns	17.19	18.46	.001	17.95	17.58	ns
Police-community relations	18.81	19.10	ns	19.40	18.37	.01	18.97	19.01	ns
Police effectiveness	12.78	12.58	ns	13.03	12.18	.001	12.51	12.90	ns
Fear of crime	13.93	16.18	.001	15.42	14.67	.05	15.08	15.08	ns
Mean world	4.74	4.66	ns	4.68	4.73	ns	4.77	4.59	.05

*The number of respondents range from 598 to 619.
ns = not significant

90

probably more related to processing abilities than to mainstream viewpoints. It is reasonable to expect that students who regularly read newspapers, magazines, and nonschool books will display higher scores on the scale designed to measure legal knowledge. They should be outside of the mainstream—generally more cynical—on measures of support for the legal system and police image. Those who read a great deal should be more supportive of civil liberties and perhaps less negative about crime and the trustworthiness of people.

Students who believe television entertainment reflects reality probably are not exposed to other sources of information. If that is the case then those who perceive television content as real will probably have low scores on the measure of legal knowledge. On all of the attitudinal measures used in this study they will likely hold mainstream viewpoints; if respondents accept the television viewpoint as accurate then they will probably share that viewpoint.

The mean scores on each of the scales by sex, grade in school, and head of household occupation are shown in Table 5.1. The sexes differ significantly on only two of the measures; males have higher scores on the measure of legal knowledge, while females exhibit a greater fear of crime than males. Differences on the other measures are not statistically significant. Males are outside of the mainstream on the two measures where differences are significant; they may be susceptible to cultivation by television crime shows.

Grade in school is highly related to all but one of the measures in Table 5.1. Students in the higher grades demonstrated more extensive knowledge of criminal justice processes, were less positively oriented toward the legal system, were more supportive of civil liberties, had less positive images of police, and feared crime less than students in the lower grades. All of the relationships are in the predicted direction; with age comes increased knowledge and increased cynicism concerning the criminal justice system. Maturity also brings confidence concerning the threat of crime and sensitivity regarding the criminal procedural rights of the individual. Older students hold views that are outside of the mainstream and are most likely to be influenced by heavy crime show viewing.

The measure of socioeconomic status used in this study, head of household occupation, is only significantly related to two of the scales. As might be expected, students from middle class families exhibit higher scores on the legal knowledge scale than those from blue-collar families. Students from blue-collar families also perceive the world as "mean," compared with those whose parents has a white-collar occupation. It is the middle class students who hold views outside of the mainstream on these two scales, and it is they who are most likely to be influenced by heavy viewing of crime shows.

Relationships between conditional variables and moral development are shown in Table 5.2. The relationship between sex and moral development is not statistically significant, though there appears to be a tendency for males as opposed to females to give postconventional responses. Since moral development is partially based on cognitive development it is not surprising that students in the higher grades were more likely to provide postconventional answers; the relationship is highly significant. Students from blue-collar families were more likely to respond to the question regarding compliance in a preconventional or conventional manner than students from white-collar homes. To the extent that heavy crime show viewing affects "thinking" about compliance, its greatest influence is likely on students in the higher grades and those from middle class backgrounds.

It was noted earlier that the measure of achievement in school used in this study should be interpreted with caution because it involved a self-report of grades. The problems with the measure may be reflected in Table 5.3 where all the significant relationships run in a direction that is opposite to that predicted; high grades are associated with support for the legal system, a crime control point of view, and positive images of police. There is no significant relationship between grades and knowledge of criminal legal processes.

The most likely explanation for these findings is that the subjective measure of academic achievement used in this study reflects a need for respondents to give socially acceptable answers. If that is the case, the results in Table 5.3 are not surprising; social desirability is probably associated with mainstream views of compliance and police image. It may also be the case that the grades reported are accurate, but they reflect conformity to teacher and school values more than achievement. If that is true, then it is not surprising that there is a relationship between grades and support for the system. Though the measure of grades may have problems with validity, it will be included in later tables because it is the only measure of cognitive capabilities available.

Students who read extensively have higher scores on the measure of legal knowledge, as expected. The only other significant difference

Table 5.2 Moral Development and Conditional Variables (Percentages)[a]

	Pre-conventional	Conventional	Post-conventional	
Sex				
Male	17.0	42.3	40.7	p = ns[b]
Female	20.7	47.0	32.3	
Grade				
6th-8th	24.2	47.3	28.5	$p < .001$
9th-12th	12.2	42.2	45.6	
Head of Household *Occupation*				
Blue-collar	21.0	48.6	30.5	$p < .05$
White-collar	16.4	42.8	40.8	
Grades				
Mostly A's and B's	18.3	47.1	34.6	p = ns
Mostly C's or lower	21.3	36.9	41.8	
Reading Habits				
Light reader	20.6	44.5	34.8	p = ns
Heavy reader	16.7	44.9	38.3	
Perception of TV *Reality*				
Low	14.1	42.8	43.1	$p < .001$
High	24.7	48.5	26.9	
Socio-Orientation				
Low	20.7	35.7	43.1	$p < .01$
High	17.9	50.6	31.4	
Concept-Orientation				
Low	19.8	38.9	41.2	$p < .05$
High	17.8	49.4	32.7	
Residence				
Urban	19.8	46.9	33.3	p = ns
Suburban	18.0	42.4	39.6	
School				
Private	18.8	47.3	33.9	p = ns
Public	19.2	41.1	39.7	

[a]The number of respondents range from 502 to 511.
[b]Chi Square tests of significance.
ns = not significant

Table 5.3 Mean Scores and T-Tests of Significance on Measures of Criminal Justice Attitudes, by Individual Characteristics Relevant to Information Processing Abilities*

Measure	Grades			Reading Habits			Reality		
	A's and B's	C's or lower	$p <$	Light	Heavy	$p <$	Low	High	$p <$
Knowledge of the law	3.11	3.06	ns	2.91	3.38	.001	3.33	2.87	.001
Support for the legal system	21.09	19.72	.001	20.62	20.95	ns	20.51	21.07	ns
Support for civil liberties	17.44	18.66	.01	17.76	17.74	ns	18.03	17.37	.05
Police-community relations	19.42	17.54	.001	18.60	19.48	.05	18.93	19.00	ns
Police effectiveness	12.85	12.14	.01	12.62	12.74	ns	12.38	13.07	.01
Fear of crime	14.75	15.20	ns	15.28	14.83	ns	14.58	15.72	.001
Mean world	4.68	4.67	ns	4.73	4.64	ns	4.76	4.64	ns

*The number of respondents range from 592 to 618.
 ns = not significant

between light and heavy readers is on the measure of police-community relations; heavy readers have a more positive image of police. This finding was unexpected.

Students who believe that television entertainment presents content that reflects reality have scores on the measure of legal knowledge that are significantly below those students who do not see television entertainment as real. The perception of high reality is also associated with a crime control point of view, a feeling that police are effective, and fear of crime; all of these relationships are in the expected direction. While the measure of the perception of reality may have a lot to do with how the content of television is processed, it may also be related to mainstream viewpoints. Exposure to limited amounts of information may lead respondents to exaggerate the credibility of television. Those with limited information may be precisely the individuals who are predisposed toward the mainstream.

The figures in Table 5.2 show that there are no significant relationships between grades, reading habits, and level of moral development. Again the effect of grade average is in the opposite direction predicted; respondents with lower grades exhibited postconventional styles of reasoning, while those with high grades are found to be conventional. These figures give some support to the argument that grade average may reflect conformity to conventional norms.

There is a significant relationship between the perception that television reflects reality and characteristic reasoning about compliance; respondents who believe television reflects reality were at the preconventional or conventional levels, while "low reality" respondents were more likely to give postconventional responses. It follows that respondents who are sophisticated enough to understand the fictional character of television are the most likely to understand the complications of compliance.

Family Characteristics

Of all of the agents of socialization the family has received the most attention from researchers. In this study attention is given to two structural characteristics of families that are likely related to both attitudes in the mainstream and information-processing abilities. Socio-oriented family communication patterns are related to the idea of authoritarianism; highly socio-oriented families stress conformity to adult viewpoints and avoidance of controversy. Concept-oriented family communication patterns are related to the extent that children are urged to acquire multiple sources of information and develop their own viewpoints.

Not surprisingly socio-orientation and concept-orientation family experiences are associated with a wide variety of system-relevant orientations. Chaffee reported that both dimensions are related to political knowledge; students from families with a low socio-orientation and a high concept-orientation demonstrated the greatest amount of knowledge.[61] It is reasonable to expect that levels of knowledge of the law will be higher for students from low socio-oriented and high concept-oriented families. Respondents from highly structured families that stress conformity—socio-oriented—are likely to be oriented positively toward compliance. A great deal of research indicates that authoritarian families produce offspring who are submissive when faced with authority.[62] For similar reasons the products of socio-oriented families would likely support a crime control point of view and be supportive of police.

Socio-oriented families may be described as "protective"; children are urged to conform and avoid controversy for their own good. Some interesting research has shown that protective families tend to produce offspring who are mistrustful and fearful of people outside of their immediate families and peers.[63] If that is the case, then products of socio-oriented families can be expected to be fearful of crime and exhibit low levels of interpersonal trust.

Concept-orientation has more to do with the flow of information in the family than socio-orientation. Consequently, products of concept-oriented families likely exhibit characteristics associated with high levels of information such as a realistic view of laws, compliance, and authorities. They probably also exhibit orientations that are characteristic of those who are sophisticated in their political thinking; these orientations may include support for a more democratic, due process point of view and postconventional views of compliance. A product of a high concept-oriented family will likely be self-confident and consequently be trustful of people and fear victimization less than those from families where information seeking is discouraged.

In Table 5.4 relationships between characteristics of families and attitudes concerning the criminal justice process are displayed.* As expected, high socio-orientation is associated with lower levels of knowledge of the legal system, support for the legal system, and a crime control view regarding civil liberties. The only other significant

---

*The socio-orientation and concept-orientation scales are dichotomized at the median.

Table 5.4 Mean Scores and T-Tests of Significance on Measures of Criminal Justice Attitudes, by Family Structural Characteristics*

Measure	Socio-orientation			Concept-orientation		
	Low	High	$p <$	Low	High	$p <$
Knowledge of the law	3.37	2.93	.001	3.00	3.23	.05
Support for the legal system	19.80	21.42	.001	20.25	21.24	.01
Support for civil liberties	18.25	17.42	.05	18.28	17.31	.01
Police-community relations	18.86	19.04	ns	18.20	19.70	.001
Police effectiveness	12.39	12.87	.05	12.17	13.19	.001
Fear of crime	14.78	15.35	ns	14.88	15.22	ns
Mean world	4.66	4.75	ns	4.80	4.62	.05

*The number of respondents range from 604 to 619.
ns = not significant

relationship regarding socio-orientation shows that students from highly structured homes tend to see police as more effective than those from homes that are less structured or oriented toward conformity. The percentages in Table 5.2 show that, as expected, students from socio-oriented families are significantly more likely to give conventional responses when justifying compliance attitudes; over half gave conventional answers, while less than one-third gave postconventional answers.

The figures in Table 5.4 regarding the effects of growing up in concept-oriented families show some relationships that were unexpected. As expected, high concept-orientation is significantly and positively related to knowledge of the legal system and interpersonal trust. However, high concept-orientation in the family is related to support for the legal system, a crime control point of view, and positive orientations toward police. It is possible that the free flow of information in families simply results in more strongly reinforced mainstream views. In any case it appears that contrary to expectations, students from low-concept families are in some cases more likely to hold views outside of the mainstream.

Percentages in Table 5.2 regarding concept-orientation and levels of moral development also run in an unexpected direction; students from high concept-oriented families are most likely to be characterized by conventional thinking, while low concept-orientation is related to postconventional responses. These findings regarding concept-orientation are not necessarily inexplicable; there is some evidence that indicates that attitude acquisition and change is most likely when subjects "believe" they have the freedom to choose what to believe.

Contextual Factors

In recent years increasing attention has been given to the effects of contextual characteristics on attitudes and behavior. There are two characteristics of respondents' environments that will be given attention in this study: whether they attend a private or public school and whether they live in a central city or suburb. Current research offers ample justification for suspecting that these characteristics might be associated with attitudes concerning law enforcement.

To some extent urban or suburban residence reflects social status; it is likely that some of the attitudes that are related to status are also related to place of residence. This is probably the case with knowledge of the legal system; it is likely that residents of the suburbs will demonstrate higher scores than urban residents. However, there is some evidence that urban residents are more likely to be supportive of the norm of compliance and take a crime control point of view. Stinchcombe et al. found that central city residents have punitive attitudes toward crime and Block found low support for civil liberties in the same group.[64]

There also appears to be a relationship between place of residence and images of police. Thomas and Hyman in their study of Virginia adults found that suburban residents had more positive orientations toward police than urban residents.[65] In an analysis of a nationwide sample of adults Block found a similar pattern.[66]

Central cities generally have higher crime rates than the suburbs, so it is reasonable to expect that city dwellers will have an understandable fear of victimization. Most previous research seems to indicate that this is the case. Thomas and Hyman found that those who reside in central cities are more concerned about crime and Stinchcombe et al. found a greater fear of victimization in the same group.[67]

A surprisingly small amount of attention has been given to the effects of school structure on attitudes and beliefs. Private schools, especially parochial schools, are usually more highly structured in that they require conformity to rules and norms. Generally private school students can be expected to hold a mainstream point of view. There may be little difference between students who attend the two types of schools in terms of knowledge of the law, but private school students likely have a positive orientation toward compliance and are disposed

Table 5.5 Mean Scores and T-Tests of Significance on Measures of Criminal Justice Attitudes, by Contextual Factors*

Measure	Residence			School		
	Urban	Suburban	$p <$	Private	Public	$p <$
Knowledge of the law	2.96	3.29	.01	3.03	3.17	ns
Support for the legal system	21.24	20.11	.001	21.10	20.38	.05
Support for civil liberties	17.58	17.97	ns	17.60	17.90	ns
Police-community relations	19.41	18.75	.01	19.06	18.85	ns
Police effectiveness	12.75	12.55	ns	12.64	12.72	ns
Fear of crime	15.06	15.13	ns	15.14	15.04	ns
Mean world	4.69	4.71	ns	4.67	4.74	ns

*The number of respondents range from 601 to 619.
ns = not significant

toward crime control as opposed to due process.[68] Private school students, according to a study by Bouma, are more likely to believe that "criminals usually get caught" and are more likely to characterize police as "nice guys."[69] Perhaps since private school students are in a more protected environment, they will exhibit greater interpersonal mistrust and fear of victimization than public school students.

The relationships between contextual factors and attitudes concerning criminal justice are shown in Table 5.5. Place of residence is significantly related to only three of the measures. Suburban students have significantly higher scores on the measure of legal knowledge than urban students; this finding may be due largely to social status differences between urban and suburban residents. It is perhaps surprising that urban residents demonstrate significantly higher support for the legal system and positive images of police-community relations than suburban residents.

Public/private school attendance fails to have a significant effect on all but one of the dependent measures in Table 5.5. As expected, private school students are more likely to support the legal system and the norm of compliance than public school students. All of the other means in the table are in the predicted direction, but differences fail to be greater than one would expect randomly. Table 5.2 shows that public/private school attendance, like urban/suburban residence, has no significant effect on levels of sophistication regarding thinking about compliance.

CONCLUSIONS

The major purpose of this chapter has been to identify conditions and processes that may influence the cultivation of mainstream points of view. Special attention has been given to identifying groups that hold views on law enforcement that are outside of the television and public opinion mainstream. According to the hypothesis put forward by Gerbner et al. it is these groups that are most likely to exhibit cultivation effects.[70]

There was some variation depending on the orientation being examined, but a general description of groups that hold views outside of the mainstream is possible. With regard to individual demographic characteristics males, students in the higher grades, and respondents from homes where the head of the household has a white-collar occupation are most likely to be influenced by viewing crime shows. With regard to individual characteristics related to information-processing abilities students with high (but in some cases low) grade-point averages, those who are heavy readers, and those who believe that television *does not* reflect reality are most susceptible to cultivation.

Respondents whose families are characterized by a low socio-orientation have views outside of the mainstream and are likely candidates for cultivation by crime shows. The conditioning effects of family concept-orientation are less clear; respondents from high concept-oriented families have views outside of the mainstream with regard to legal knowledge and trust in people, but are clearly in the mainstream with regard to several other orientations.

Generally, suburban residents have views outside of the mainstream with respect to legal knowledge, support for the legal system, and perceptions of police-community relations. Public school students have nonmainstream views with respect to compliance and support for the legal system.

In the chapters that follow the effects of viewing television crime shows on each of the orientations toward the legal system will be examined in detail. The results reported in this chapter indicate which conditional variables will receive attention in the chapters that follow.

NOTES

1. Joseph Klapper, *The Effects of Mass Communications* (Glencoe, Ill.: Free Press, 1960).

2. George Gerbner et al., "Cultural Indicators: Violence Profile No. 9," *Journal of Communication* 28 (Summer 1978): 176-207.

3. George Gerbner, Larry Gross, Michael Morgan, and Nancy Signorielli, "The 'Mainstreaming' of America: Violence Profile 11," *Journal of Communication* 30 (Summer 1980): 10-29.

4. Paul M. Hirsh, "The 'Scary World' of the Nonviewer and Other Anomalies," *Communication Research* 7 (October 1980): 403-56.

5. Ibid.; Michael Hughes, "The Fruits of Cultivation Analysis: A Reexamination of Some Effects of Television Watching," *Public Opinion Quarterly* 44 (Spring 1980): 287-302.

6. Robert P. Hawkins and Suzanne Pingee, "Television's Influence on Social Reality," in *Technical Reviews*, vol. 2 of *Television and Behavior: Ten Years of Scientific Progress and Implications for the Eighties*, ed. David Pearl, Lorraine Bouthilet, and Joyce Lazar (Washington, D.C.: National Institute of Mental Health, 1982).

7. Gerbner et al., "The 'Mainstreaming' of America," p. 14.

8. Hawkins and Pingee, "Television's Influence on Social Reality."

9. Gerbner et al., "The Demonstration of Power: Violence Profile No. 10," *Journal of Communication* 29 (Spring 1979): 177-96.

10. Robert P. Hawkins and Suzanne Pingee, "Some Processes in the Cultivation Effect," *Communication Research* 7 (April 1980): 193-226.

11. David R. Berman and John A. Stookey, "Adolescents, Television and Support for Government," *Public Opinion Quarterly* 44 (1980): 330-40.

12. Hawkins and Pingee, "Television's Influence on Social Reality."

13. Herbert E. Krugman and Eugene L. Hartley, "Passive Learning from Television," *Public Opinion Quarterly* 34 (Winter 1970): 184.

14. See Jack M. McLeod and Byron Reeves, "On the Nature of Mass Media Effects," in *Television and Social Behavior*, ed. S. B. Withey and R. P. Abeles (Hillsdale, N.J.: Erlbaum, 1980).

15. Hawkins and Pingee, "Television's Influence on Social Reality."

16. Ibid.

17. Ibid.

18. Byron Reeves, "Perceived TV Reality as a Predictor of Children's Social Behavior," *Journalism Quarterly* 55 (Winter 1978): 682-95.

19. Hawkins and Pingee, "Some Processes in Cultivation Effect," p. 204.

20. Hawkins and Pingee, "Television's Influence on Social Reality."

21. Gerbner et al., "The 'Mainstreaming' of America," p. 15.

22. Hawkins and Pingee, "Television's Influence on Social Reality," p. 243.

23. Ibid., p. 246.

24. See Fred I. Greenstein, *Children and Politics* (New Haven: Yale University Press, 1965); Robert Weissberg, *Political Learning, Political Choice and Democratic Citizenship* (Englewood Cliffs, N.J.: Prentice-Hall, 1974).

25. Robert Hess and Judith Torney, *The Development of Political Attitudes in Children* (Garden City, N.Y.: Doubleday, 1967).

26. Weissberg, *Political Learning*, p. 114.

27. Arthur L. Stinchcombe et al., *Crime and Punishment—Changing Attitudes in America* (San Francisco: Jossey-Bass, 1980).

28. Hess and Torney, *The Development of Political Attitudes in Children*, p. 203.

29. Ibid., p. 209.

30. Ibid., p. 210; David Easton and Jack Dennis, *Children in the Political System* (New York: McGraw-Hill, 1969).

31. Donald Bouma, *Kids and Cops* (Grand Rapids: W. B. Erdman, 1969), p. 55.

32. Stinchcombe et al., *Crime and Punishment*, p. 26.

33. Charles W. Thomas and Jeffrey M. Hyman, "Perceptions of Crime, Fear of Victimization, and Public Perceptions of Police Performance," *Journal of Police Science and Administration* 5 (Fall 1977): 305-17.

34. Weissberg, *Political Learning*, p. 72.

35. Joseph Adelson and Robert O'Neal, "The Growth of Political Ideas in Adolescence: The Sense of Community," *Journal of Personality and Social Psychology* 4 (July 1966): 295-306.

36. Hess and Torney, *The Development of Political Attitudes in Children*, p. 160.

37. Ibid., p. 62.

38. Harrell Rodgers and George Taylor, "Pre-adult Attitudes Toward Legal Compliance: Notes Toward a Theory," *Social Science Quarterly* 51 (December 1970): 539-51.

39. Weissberg, *Political Learning*, p. 135.

40. Easton and Dennis, *Children in the Political System*, p. 375.

41. Gary F. Jensen, "'Crime Doesn't Pay': Correlates of a Shared Misunderstanding," *Social Problems* (1971): 181-201.

42. Stinchcombe et al., *Crime and Punishment*, p. 89.

43. M. Kent Jennings and Richard G. Niemi, *The Political Character of Adolescence: The Influence of Families and Schools* (Princeton: Princeton University Press, 1974), p. 145.

44. Weissberg, *Political Learning*, p. 102.

45. Hess and Torney, *The Development of Political Attitudes in Children*, p. 160.

46. Ibid., p. 160.

47. James W. Prothro and Charles M. Grigg, "Fundamental Principles of Democracy: Bases of Agreement and Disagreement," *Journal of Politics* 23 (May 1960): 276-84.

48. Edgar Litt, "Civic Education, Norms, and Political Indoctrination," *American Sociological Review* 28 (February 1963): 69-75.

49. Michael Corbett, "Public Support for 'Law and Order': Interrelationships with System Affirmation and Attitudes Toward Minorities," *Criminology* 19 (November 1981): 328-43.

50. Hess and Torney, *The Development of Political Attitudes in Children*, p. 307.

51. Easton and Dennis, *Children in the Political System*, p. 243.

52. Thomas and Hyman, "Perceptions of Crime," p. 312.

53. Ibid., p. 314.

54. Jennings and Neimi, *The Political Character of Adolescence*, p. 106.

55. Ibid., p. 99; Hess and Torney, *The Development of Political Attitudes in Children*, p. 149.

56. Easton and Dennis, *Children in the Political System*, p. 367.

57. Hess and Torney, *The Development of Political Attitudes in Children*, p. 153.

58. Ibid., p. 161; Rodgers and Taylor, "Pre-adult Attitudes Toward Legal Compliance," p. 223.

59. Judith Gallatin and Joseph Adelson, "Legal Guarantees of Individual Freedom: A Cross National Study of the Development of Political Thought," *Journal of Social Issues* 27 (1971): 80-101.

60. Hess and Torney, *The Development of Political Attitudes in Children*, p. 304.

61. Stephen Chaffee et al., "Mass Communication in Political Socialization" in *Handbook of Political Socialization*, ed. Stanley Renshon (New York: Free Press, 1977), pp. 223-58.

62. J. P. Kirscht and R. C. Dillehay, *Dimensions of Authoritarianism: A Review of Theory and Research* (Lexington: University of Kentucky, 1967).

63. Frank A. Pinner, "Parental Overprotection and Political Distrust," *The Annals* 361 (September 1965): 58-70.

64. Stinchcombe et al., *Crime and Punishment*, p. 132; Richard Block, "Support for Civil Liberties and Support for the Police," *American Behavioral Scientist* (July 1970): 781-96.

65. Thomas and Hyman, "Perceptions of Crime," p. 314.

66. Block, "Support for Civil Liberties and Support for the Police," p. 784.

67. Thomas and Hyman, "Perceptions of Crime," p. 313; Stinchcombe et al., *Crime and Punishment*, p. 135.

68. Bouma, *Kids and Cops*, p. 78.

69. Ibid., p. 77.

70. Gerbner et al., "The 'Mainstreaming' of America."

6

KNOWLEDGE OF CRIMINAL LEGAL PROCESS AND RIGHTS

INTRODUCTION

"The Paper Chase," a critically acclaimed television series, presented an accurate portrayal of life in law school. To the disappointment of critics and faithful fans the series was cancelled after a short period of time because it had received poor ratings. Recently Showtime, a pay TV network, has revived the series. Lynn Roth, the executive producer of the new segments, in a recent interview offered some insights concerning the failure of "The Paper Chase" to catch on with the commercial network. She gave an example of how "... we did a show on search and seizure, a complicated, interesting legal issue. If we had done that for the network, they might have said the audience wouldn't understand."[1] This view provides support for the conclusion drawn in Chapter 3 that television executives have little interest in using television to "educate" viewers. It is often assumed that the audience cannot or will not attend entertainment that deals with complex issues.

The analysis of the content of crime show programming showed that there is a paucity of information about criminal legal processes. What information is presented is often inaccurate, and much of the activity of television police is technically illegal. Emphasis in crime shows seems to be on people, not rules or abstract elements of the law.

Given the content of crime shows it can hardly be expected that heavy viewers would be more informed about criminal legal processes than light viewers. In fact, earlier findings that crime shows distort the reality of the criminal justice system might lead to the expectation of a negative relationship between crime show viewing and the possession of accurate information about criminal legal processes and rights.

As might be expected, there has been a relatively large amount of research on relationships between television viewing and knowledge. However, most research has centered on the relationship between viewing news and public affairs programming and knowledge of politics and current events. The evidence concerning the news and levels of political information is fairly consistent. Atkin and Gantz found that children who watch the news and pay attention to Saturday morning news briefs have higher levels of political knowledge.[2] This finding has been confirmed for adolescents by Chaffee and Conway et al.[3]

The relationship between overall television viewing and levels of information has been found to run in the opposite direction; those who view a great deal of television have lower levels of political information. Rubin found this contrasting relationship in a study of adolescents. Public affairs viewing was positively associated with high levels of political information, while overall viewing was negatively associated with the measure of political information and a measure of information specificity.[4] Jackson-Beeck specified the relationship somewhat, finding that there was a powerful negative impact of television exposure on political information among those in lower grades and boys.[5] Chaffee found a negative relationship between consumption of electronic media, including radio, and political information scores.[6]

It is ironic that children and adolescents report that television is their primary source of information; they believe that they are learning from television entertainment as well as news.[7] The evidence seems clear as Rubin states that " . . . extensive television viewing *per se* may be dysfunctional for the acquisition of political information and the understanding of the workings of government."[8] Presumably, heavy viewers of television spend less time consuming newspapers, magazines, and books that make a positive contribution to knowledge. It is also possible that those who are heavy television viewers have characteristics that predispose them toward low levels of knowledge. However, in the studies cited above the negative relationship between television viewing and political knowledge survived controls for a variety of background variables often associated with information acquisition.

There have been few attempts to link the viewing of entertainment television with the acquisition of specific information. The only study that dealt specifically with knowledge of the law and crime show viewing was one undertaken by Dominick.[9] Dominick developed two measures of legal knowledge: one emphasized arrest rights and the other dealt with knowledge of legal terms. He related these two measures to an Index of Crime Show Viewing that is very similar to the one used in this research. The results showed that heavy viewing of crime shows was associated with high knowledge of arrest rights, but not with knowledge of legal terms. Dominick attributed this finding to the fact that crime shows often portray law enforcers "reading rights" to suspects, but little else regarding the criminal justice process is shown.

Despite Dominick's finding there is little that would lead one to expect a positive relationship between crime show viewing and knowledge of criminal legal processes and rights. The analysis of crime show content undertaken in Chapter 3 showed that the televison mainstream does not emphasize substantive knowledge. The discussion of requirements of the political system in Chapter 4 pointed to the fact that system stability is likely enhanced by a citizenry that is not aware of its rights when in conflict with the system. The representatives of the system have an interest in keeping citizens informed about laws relating to social control, but not about laws that protect the citizen from the system. Overall, an examination of the distributions for items included in the measure of legal knowledge used in the present study showed that adolescents were aware of their right to an attorney at the time of arrest, but at least one-third of the sample could not provide correct answers to the remaining items in the scale. The mainstream appears not to be characterized by widespread knowledge of criminal justice processes.

The relationship between the Index of Crime Show Viewing and Knowledge of Criminal Legal Processes is shown in Table 6.1. The figures in the table are unstandardized partial regression coefficients accompanied by their standard errors. The figures in the table indicate a strong negative relationship between viewing crime shows and legal knowledge ($r = -.178, p < .001$). All of the coefficients in the table are at least twice their standard errors, so they are statistically significant. The original relationship survives controls for ten variables. The only control that has a major impact on the original relationship is grade in school, but the crime show viewing-legal knowledge relationship remains significant.

Table 6.1 The Effects of Crime Show Viewing on Knowledge of Criminal Legal Processes by Selected Control Variables

Uncontrolled	-.340[a]
	(.008)[b]
Controlling For:	
Sex	-.433
	(.008)
Grade in school	-.149
	(.008)
Head of household occupation	-.329
	(.008)
Grade average	-.342
	(.008)
Reading habits	-.319
	(.008)
Perception of TV reality	-.307
	(.008)
Family socio-orientation	-.306
	(.008)
Family concept-orientation	-.333
	(.008)
School (public/private)	-.327
	(.008)
Residence (urban/suburban)	-.327
	(.008)
All controls	-.167
	(.008)
Final *df*	(554)

[a] Regression coefficients

[b] Standard errors of regression coefficients. If the regression coefficients are at least twice their standard errors, they are significantly different from zero.

When the Index of Crime Show Viewing is broken down into low, medium, and high categories and the distributions for the six items in the Legal Knowledge Scale are examined for each group, some interesting patterns appear. Crime show viewing does not have a positive impact on any of the items. On the item dealing with the right to an attorney before questioning, 96.2 percent of the respondents who were light crime show viewers gave the correct answer compared to 92.3 percent of the heavy viewers; the difference is not statistically significant. Relationships between crime show viewing and the other five items in the scale are all negative; three out of five of the negative relationships are statistically significant.*

With regard to knowledge of criminal legal processes the cultivation hypothesis appears to be supported. What is being cultivated is ignorance of the criminal justice system. Misinformation and the lack of information in crime shows is reflected in the low knowledge scores of heavy viewers. The basic relationship survives an impressive number and variety of controls. With the cultivation hypothesis supported, it will be interesting to examine the mainstreaming hypothesis as it relates to knowledge of the law.

INDIVIDUAL CHARACTERISTICS AND LEGAL KNOWLEDGE

The evidence indicates that in general crime show viewing is associated with low scores on the index of legal knowledge, but is the relationship conditional? Are groups that are outside of the mainstream more likely to be influenced by the negative effects of crime show viewing? In the previous chapter the relationships between a number of individual characteristics and knowledge of legal processes were examined. Since the sample as a whole is characterized by relatively low levels of knowledge regarding the legal system it was suggested that those who have relatively high knowledge scores are outside of the mainstream. Those who do not share the dominant view or characteristic are hypothesized to be most likely influenced by crime show viewing.

Individual characteristics are broken into two categories: demographic characteristics and characteristics related to information-processing abilities. All three of the demographic characteristics examined were related significantly to knowledge of the legal system. The three groups with high scores and thus outside of the mainstream are males, respondents in the higher grades, and those from families where the head of the household has a professional or white-collar occupation. According to the mainstream hypothesis these three groups, since their characteristics are inconsistent with the television and sample mainstream, should be most influenced by heavy crime show viewing. The figures necessary to test the mainstream hypothesis with regard to demographic characteristics and legal knowledge are shown in Table 6.2.

---

*The three categories for crime show viewing are low (16-24), medium (25-32), and high (33-57).

Table 6.2 The Effects of Crime Show Viewing on
Knowledge of Criminal Legal Process in Subgroups
Defined by Demographic Characteristics

Uncontrolled	-.340[a]	
	(.008)[b]	
Sex		
Male	-.261	
	(.010)	$p < .05$[c]
Female	-.511	
	(.012)	
Grade in School		
Lower grades (6th-8th)	-.111	
	(.011)	$p = $ ns
Higher grades (9th-12th)	-.159	
	(.014)	
Head of Household Occupation		
Blue-collar	-.318	
	(.012)	$p < .01$
Professional—white-collar	-.154	
	(.011)	

[a] Regression coefficients

[b] Standard errors of regression coefficients. If the regression coefficients are at least twice their standard errors, they are significantly different from zero.

[c] F-tests for difference between regression coefficients.

ns = not significant

The figures in Table 6.2 are unstandardized regression coefficients. The accompanying standard errors are shown in parentheses. The regression coefficients for each value of each conditional variable were derived from the regression equation outlined in Chapter 2. An F-ratio is calculated to determine the significance of differences between relationships in groups. Wright, who outlined this method for evaluating conditional relationships, explains that the F-ratio essentially indicates whether a model, where slopes are allowed to vary, explains significantly more variance in the dependent variable than a model where slopes are not allowed to vary.[10] In some instances highly divergent slopes may not characterize a model where the variance explained is increased appreciably. It may also be the case that a small divergence of slopes increases the variance explained a great deal. In other words, there may be instances where the divergence of slopes is of interest even if the additional variance explained by the more complex model is not statistically significant. Both the differences in unstandardized regression coefficients *and* tests of significance will be considered in interpretations of figures in this chapter and those that follow.

The figures in Table 6.2 support the cultivation hypothesis, but not the mainstream hypothesis. Regardless of the condition the regression coefficients that describe relationships between crime show viewing and legal knowledge are negative and significantly different from zero. However, the relationship is not significantly stronger in the three groups that were hypothesized to be subject to mainstreaming. An examination of two of the conditional relationships reveals patterns that are the opposite of those expected; females not males were most likely to be mainstreamed while the relationship is stronger for adolescents from a working-class household than a middle class household. Differences between respondents of lower and higher grade levels are not significant, but crime show viewing is more strongly associated with legal knowledge among those in higher grades, as predicted.

The results regarding the conditioning effects of demographic-background characteristics are for the most part not consistent with those reported by Jackson-Beeck.[11] She found that overall television viewing was most negatively associated with levels of political information among boys, those in the lower grades, and those from a relatively lower socioeconomic status background. The results reported in Table 6.2 indicate that heavy crime show viewing interacts with background characteristics in a way that contributes to lower levels of knowledge among those who are generally predisposed to low knowledge in the first place.

The other set of individual characteristics considered as conditional variables includes those that may be related to cognitive abilities or how messages transmitted by crime shows are processed. These characteristics may not be theoretically related to mainstream attitudes, but when grade average, reading habits, and the perception of the reality of television were correlated with legal knowledge in the previous chapter, some interesting patterns were revealed. Surprisingly grade-point average was not significantly related to knowledge of criminal legal processes. Those who consume a great deal of written communications and those who do not believe that television content is real exhibited relatively high knowledge scores. With regard to knowledge of the law adolescents who are heavy readers and who perceive television as unreal are outside of the mainstream and should be most susceptible to the influence of crime show viewing.

Table 6.3 The Effects of Crime Show Viewing on
Knowledge of Criminal Legal Process in Subgroups
Defined by Individual Characteristics Related to
Information Processing

Uncontrolled	-.340[a]	
	(.008)[b]	
Grade Average		
Mostly C's or lower	-.336	
	(.015)	$p = ns$[c]
Mostly A's and B's	-.297	
	(.009)	
Reading Habits		
Light reader	-.116	
	(.012)	$p < .05$
Heavy reader	-.477	
	(.012)	
Perception of TV Reality		
Low	-.374	
	(.011)	$p = ns$
High	-.143	
	(.011)	

[a] Regression coefficients

[b] Standard errors of regression coefficients. If the regression coefficients are at least twice their standard errors, they are significantly different from zero.

[c] F-tests for difference between regression coefficients.

ns = not significant

The statistics necessary to examine the conditioning effects of characteristics relevant to information-processing abilities are found in Table 6.3. The regression coefficients and their standard errors all support the cultivation hypothesis; regardless of the condition high levels of crime show viewing are associated with low levels of knowledge of the criminal justice process. The original relationship differs little with regard to grade averages; adolescents with relatively lower grade averages appear to exhibit greater cultivation effects, but the differences between regression coefficients are not large or statistically significant. However, if those with low levels of achievement in school have lower levels of knowledge of the law, heavy viewing of crime shows seems to compound the negative effect.

The conditioning effects of reading habits are as expected. Heavy readers exhibited knowledge of the law that was outside of the mainstream and the figures in Table 6.3 show that it is this group that is most likely to be mainstreamed by heavy viewing of crime shows. Differences in the magnitude of the crime show viewing-legal knowledge association are significant; while heavy crime show viewing is significantly associated with legal knowledge among light readers, it is among heavy readers that television has the strongest negative influence. Reading contributes to knowledge of criminal law, while viewing crime shows inhibits the process of acquiring accurate information.

The figures related to the conditioning effects of the perceived reality of television portrayals are interesting. Though the regression coefficients for the low and high reality groups are not significantly different, the magnitude of the difference is quite large and in the expected direction. It is those who do not think television reflects reality whose knowledge of criminal law is most influenced by viewing crime shows. These results are consistent with those of a number of studies that have shown that the perception of television reality does not enhance television's influence.[1][2] The opposite seems to be the case with respect to knowledge of the law. These findings are consistent with the concept of passive learning; critical viewing of programs makes little difference whether or not learning, or in this case nonlearning, takes place.

To summarize, the examination of the conditioning effects of individual characteristics revealed some interesting patterns. Regardless of the control for individual factors the negative relationship between crime show viewing and knowledge of criminal law survives. However, the strength of the relationship varies for different values of three of six individual characteristics considered. In only one of the three instances where there were significant differences between regression coefficients was the mainstream hypothesis supported; the group with levels of knowledge higher than the mainstream was most influenced by viewing crime shows. However, when only the magnitude of differences between regression coefficients are considered, in three out of five instances the mainstream hypothesis seemed to be supported.

FAMILY CHARACTERISTICS AND LEGAL KNOWLEDGE

The influence of television viewing is subject to mediation of other agents of socialization such as family and school. It is likely the case that crime show viewing will have the greatest influence on knowledge of the legal system when parents do not intervene in the process of communication. That is to say that individuals from families who are "open" to information from a wide variety of sources would be the most likely to be influenced by entertainment television. In terms of the measures of family structure employed in this study, members of families who are high in concept-orientation and low in socio-orientation should be more open to nonfamily sources of information.

Previous studies have shown that concept- and socio-orientation are highly related to political knowledge and system awareness; high concept-orientation and low socio-orientation are related to high levels of knowledge and system awareness.[13] This is not surprising given the fact that concept-orientation is related to "thinking for one's self" and socio-orientation is related to openness to communication.

Family communication patterns were found to be significantly related to knowledge of the law in Chapter 5. As expected, respondents from low socio-orientation and high concept-orientation families had significantly higher scores on the legal knowledge scale; they are outside of the mainstream and should be most influenced by viewing crime shows.

The figures necessary to examine the effects of family communication patterns on the crime show viewing-legal knowledge relationship can be found in Table 6.4. The regression coefficients in Table 6.4 provide additional support for the cultivation hypothesis; regardless

Table 6.4 The Effects of Crime Show Viewing on Knowledge of Criminal Legal Process by Family Communication Characteristics

Uncontrolled	-.340[a]	
	(.008)[b]	
Family Socio-orientation		
Low	-.228	
	(.013)	$p = \text{ns}^c$
High	-.297	
	(.010)	
Family Concept-orientation		
Low	-.160	
	(.011)	$p < .05$
High	-.463	
	(.013)	

[a] Regression coefficients

[b] Standard errors of regression coefficients. If the regression coefficients are at least twice their standard errors, they are significantly different from zero.

[c] F-tests for difference between regression coefficients.

ns = not significant

of the structure of family communications, crime show viewing is associated with lower levels of legal knowledge.

The mainstreaming hypothesis receives only partial support. Family socio-orientation does not appear to modify the effects of crime show viewing on knowledge of criminal law; while the regression co-efficients for both low and high socio-oriented groups are significantly different from zero, they are not significantly different from each other.

Concept-orientation does seem to influence the strength of the original relationship. As expected, respondents from high concept-oriented families are influenced to a greater extent by crime show viewing than those from low concept-oriented families. These findings are consistent with those reported by Chaffee that indicate that concept-orientation has a greater influence on knowledge acquisition than socio-orientation.[14] It appears that those families who urge their members to think for themselves run the risk of the acquisition of misinformation on the part of family members. It also appears that individuals who are encouraged to attend a variety of media may in fact give their attention to communications that offer little accurate information.

To summarize, it appears that one dimension of family communication structure, concept-orientation, modifies the relationship between crime show viewing and levels of knowledge about the legal system. Regardless of the type of family structure, crime show viewing has a negative influence on levels of accurate knowledge of the law, but the influence is greatest on those who come from families where "open-mindedness" is encouraged; those from concept-oriented families are most likely to be mainstreamed.

CONTEXTUAL FACTORS AND LEGAL KNOWLEDGE

Characteristics of the environment other than the family may also modify the relationship between crime show viewing and knowledge of criminal justice processes. One important agent of socialization of children and adolescents is the school. School as an influence on socialization may be operationalized in terms of a number of dimensions, but in this study a simple distinction between public or private schools is made. Private schools, especially parochial schools, are probably much like socio-oriented families in that they are highly structured and stress conformity to rules. Inasmuch as many private schools emphasize a "back to basics" approach to education they probably could not be described as concept-oriented.

As a communication environment private schools are probably more "closed" than public schools. Students who attend private schools are often homogeneous with respect to background characteristics, consumption of mass media, and attitudes. In all likelihood there is simply more conformity and less diversity with respect to viewpoints in a private school than in a public school. If that is the case private school students should be "less open" to the influences of television crime shows than public school students.

It is also the case that private schools stress rule conformity and adherence to conventional norms; public school students should be more likely to hold levels of knowledge outside of the mainstream and hence be more influenced by messages transmitted by crime shows. In Chapter 5 a comparison of public and private school students in terms of levels of legal knowledge revealed no significant difference, though private school students were slightly closer to the mainstream.

Place of residence may mediate the crime show viewing-legal knowledge relationship, where one lives influences daily interpersonal interactions, experiences, and norms. Suburban residence may indicate access to higher quality education, interaction with higher status neighbors, and less exposure to diverse points of view. Obviously some of the characteristics associated with surburban residence may be associated with higher levels of knowledge (for example, higher quality education, middle class status, highly educated parents), while others may be related to lower levels (for example, lack of diversity, stress on conformity). The comparison of urban and suburban residents undertaken in Chapter 5 showed that residents of the suburbs had high levels of knowledge of criminal legal procedures and were outside of the mainstream. The mainstreaming hypothesis suggests that suburban residents will be most likely to be influenced by television crime show viewing.

The figures necessary to examine the mediating effects of contextual factors can be found in Table 6.5. The figures show that regardless of the condition the cultivation hypothesis is supported; crime show viewing is significantly associated with lower levels of knowledge of the legal system. The regression coefficients for public versus private school students are not significantly different, but the differences in magnitude suggest support for the mainstreaming hypothesis; the legal knowledge of public school students is influenced to a greater extent than that of private school students. It appears that public school students were more open and receptive to the distorted messages concerning the legal system transmitted by crime shows.

Table 6.5 The Effects of Crime Show Viewing on Knowledge of Criminal Legal Process by Contextual Factors

Uncontrolled	-.340[a]	
	(.008)[b]	
School Attended		
Public	-.406	
	(.012)	$p = ns$[c]
Private	-.196	
	(.010)	
Place of Residence		
Urban	-.250	
	(.012)	$p = ns$
Suburban	-.290	
	(.010)	

[a] Regression coefficients

[b] Standard errors of regression coefficients. If the regression coefficients are at least twice their standard errors, they are significantly different from zero.

[c] F-test of significance of difference between regression coefficients.

ns = not significant

Residence does not appear to mediate the crime show viewing-legal knowledge relationship. Despite the fact that suburban residents display higher levels of knowledge and are outside of the mainstream, the evidence does not strongly support the mainstreaming hypothesis.

To summarize, it appears that school structure, but not place of residence, modifies the relationship between crime show viewing and knowledge of criminal legal processes. Schools appear to be an important source of competing information. The structure of schools likely has something to do with the reception of messages transmitted by crime show programming.

CONCLUSION

Television crime shows contribute nothing to levels of knowledge about the criminal justice system. The standardized partial regression coefficients (beta weights) shown in Table 6.6 reveal that only grade in school has a larger influence on scores on the legal knowledge scale. Crime show viewing does not allow the invasion of little TV rays that

Table 6.6 The Relative Influence of 11 Variables on
Knowledge of Criminal Legal Process

Variable	Beta	
Sex	-.181*	
Grade in school	.281	
Head of household occupation	-.048	
Grade average	.093	
Reading habits	-.119	
Perception of TV reality	.078	
Family socio-orientation	-.109	
Family concept-orientation	-.109	
Public/private school	.025	
Residence	.034	
TV crime show viewing	-.187	
Final *df*	(554)	$R = .464$

*All of the beta weights are significantly different from
zero.

drain off knowledge of the criminal justice system. Instead crime shows present a distorted image of how the criminal justice system works. Distorted information about the legal process competes with more accurate information from other sources for attention so that even those students who might be predisposed to attend media that provide accurate information are likely to be confused. The argument made by Gunther that crime shows are highly informative is clearly without support.[15]

The findings in this chapter support the cultivation hypothesis and in doing so run counter to the only other study that has dealt with the subject.[16] The mainstreaming hypothesis with regard to legal knowledge received mixed support. Of the ten conditional variables examined, only four influenced the original relationship significantly and only two in the direction predicted by the mainstream hypothesis. Still, the negative impact of crime show viewing was very strong among two groups that normally would be expected to have high levels of knowledge—those from concept-oriented families and heavy readers.

If television programming serves the status quo and the status quo is best served when most members of the political system are ignorant of their rights when confronted by law enforcement officials, then crime show programmers serve the system well. The mainstream is characterized by low levels of knowledge of the criminal justice system and the television programs that deal with law enforcement reinforce the mainstream.

NOTES

1. Ben Brown, "A New Semester of 'Paper Chase' on Showtime," *USA Today*, May 21, 1984, p. 50.

2. Charles K. Atkin and Walter Gantz, "Television News and Political Socialization," *Public Opinion Quarterly* 42 (1978): 183-98.

3. Stephen Chaffee et al., "Mass Communication in Political Socialization," in *Handbook of Political Socialization*, ed. Stanley Renshon (New York: Free Press, 1977), pp. 223-58; Margaret Conway et al., "The News Media in Children's Political Socialization," *Public Opinion Quarterly* 45 (1981): 164-78.

4. Alan M. Rubin, "Child and Adolescent Television Use and Political Socialization," *Journalism Quarterly* 55 (Winter 1978): 125-29.

5. Marilyn Jackson-Beeck, "Interpersonal and Mass Communication in Children's Political Socialization," *Journalism Quarterly* 56 (1979): 48-53.

6. Chaffee et al., "Mass Communication in Political Socialization," p. 239.

7. Ibid., p. 236.

8. Rubin, "Child and Adolescent Television Use," p. 127.

9. Joseph R. Dominick, "Children's Viewing of Crime Shows and Attitudes on Law Enforcement," *Journalism Quarterly* 51 (Spring 1974): 5-12.

10. Gerald C. Wright, Jr., "Linear Models for Evaluating Conditional Relationships," *American Journal of Political Science* 20 (May 1976): 349-73.

11. Jackson-Beeck, "Interpersonal and Mass Communication in Children's Political Socialization."

12. Byron Reeves, "Perceived TV Reality as a Predictor of Children's Social Behavior," *Journalism Quarterly* 55 (Winter 1978): 682-95.

13. Chaffee et al., "Mass Communication in Political Socialization," p. 246.

14. Ibid.

15. Max Gunther, "You Have the Right to Remain Silent," *TV Guide*, December 18, 1971, pp. 7-9.

16. Dominick, "Children's Viewing of Crime Shows."

7

COMPLIANCE AND SUPPORT
FOR THE LEGAL SYSTEM

INTRODUCTION

While many social and behavioral scientists were busy trying to discern the possible effects of violent television programming on deviant-aggressive behavior, George Gerbner and Larry Gross were pointing out that, "Instead of threatening the social order, television may have become our chief instrument of social control."[1] The idea that television viewing tends to produce passivity and compliance is certainly not new; giant television screens played prominent roles in manipulating the behavior of citizens in works of fiction such as George Orwell's *1984* and Ray Bradbury's *Fahrenheit 451*.[2] More recent years have witnessed the publication of mass market books on television with such dramatic titles as *The Plug-In Drug* and *Remote Control: Television and the Manipulation of American Life*.[3] The image of television viewing as an "activity" that promotes passivity and quiescence in the face of authority is widespread.

In an earlier chapter it was shown that television crime dramas are morality plays that encourage viewers to be good law-abiding, moral people. This is accomplished by portraying law breakers as basically immoral individuals, whose motives for criminal activity are never treated sympathetically. In addition the consequences of unlawful behavior are never ambiguous; criminals often meet a violent end and police are always successful. Support for the legal system is also encouraged by the fact that there is a perpetual crime wave taking place in prime time. Gerbner and his associates point out that enforcing the

119

law takes three times as many characters as the number of all blue-collar and service workers on television.[4]

Given what is known about the interests of those who control the content of television programming, the National Association of Broadcasters Code, and the content of television crime shows, it is reasonable to expect a strong association between crime show viewing and support for the legal system. Regarding the ability to think philosophically or abstractly about legal dilemmas, crime show viewing should encourage preconventional or conventional approaches to compliance.

Taking into account the great deal of attention that has been given to the relationship between violent programming and deviant behavior, it is not surprising that few have attempted to link crime show viewing and support for the criminal justice system. A few studies have dealt indirectly with the question. Gerbner et al. found that heavy television viewers compared to light viewers were likely to believe that the government is spending too little on crime control.[5] The observed relationship was not statistically significant for self-identified conservatives. Berman and Stookey found that viewers of "Police Story," "Kojak," and "Police Woman" were more supportive of local government. However, they also found that viewers of "Starsky and Hutch" and "Hawaii Five-O" had negative images of government.[6] Dominick examined the relationship between two television use measures--a crime show viewing index and an index measuring the importance of television as a source of information about law enforcement—and propensity to report witnessed crimes. He found that the television as an information source measure was negatively associated with willingness to report witnessed crimes. The crime show viewing index had a positive, but insignificant, relationship with willingness to report witnessed crimes in the male subsample. Dominick suggested that television viewing might be encouraging a "don't get involved" syndrome.[7]

The one study that is most relevant to the concern of this chapter is one by Weigel and Jessor that linked television viewing to adolescent conventionality; it deserves detailed attention. Weigel and Jessor used two samples, one of adolescents and one of college students, to examine the relationships between television viewing and a wide variety of measures of adherence to conventional norms. Their independent variable was a summation of estimates of the number of hours per week spent viewing entertainment and news programming. Among their dependent measures were: a 10-item scale designed to measure independence (autonomous decision-making and freedom from culturally prescribed behavior); a 30-item measure of attitudes toward deviance; a 30-item measure of self-reported deviant behavior (lying, stealing, fighting, etc.); and a 4-item measure of reporting involvement in marijuana use. For purposes of analysis television involvement was classified as low, medium, or high.

In the college student sample male subjects who were heavy television viewers were significantly less independent, less likely to report behavioral deviance, and less likely to be involved with marijuana than light viewers. In the adolescent sample heavy television viewing was significantly associated with low attitudinal deviance and marijuana use among boys. Relationships between television viewing and attitudinal deviance among girls and reported deviance among boys were in the predicted direction, though statistically insignificant. The findings of Weigel and Jessor are important because they document a relationship between involvement with television and a syndrome of conventionality.[8]

It seems clear that compliance with the law is a disposition that is solidly in the television mainstream; the review of crime show content undertaken in Chapter 3 showed that virtually every crime drama reinforces the view that obedience to the law is desirable behavior. In Chapter 4 it was emphasized that the norm of compliance must be in the mainstream of the population in order for the political system to maintain a tolerable level of system stress; the mainstream in the United States and in the sample of adolescents examined in the present study is characterized by a great deal of support for the legal system. Since the population and television mainstream consists of support for the norm of compliance and the legal system, it is reasonable to expect that heavy viewers of crime shows will show signs of cultivation of the mainstream view.

The relationship between the Index of Crime Show Viewing and support for the legal system is shown in Table 7.1. The figures in the table are unstandardized partial regression coefficients, accompanied by their standard errors. The figures in the table show a fairly strong positive relationship between crime show viewing and support for the legal system ($r = .138, p < .01$). All of the coefficients in the table are at least twice their standard errors, so they are statistically significant; the original relationship survives controls for ten variables. Controls for grade in school and family socio-orientation reduce the strength of the relationship somewhat, but the partial regression coefficients remain significant.

Table 7.1 The Effects of Crime Show Viewing on Support
for the Legal System by Selected Control Variable

Uncontrolled	.687[a]
	(.024)[b]
Controlling For:	
Sex	.755
	(.025)
Grade in school	.356
	(.025)
Head of household occupation	.678
	(.025)
Grade average	.661
	(.024)
Reading habits	.707
	(.024)
Perception of TV reality	.649
	(.025)
Family socio-orientation	.548
	(.024)
Family concept-orientation	.721
	(.024)
School (public/private)	.640
	(.024)
Residence (urban/suburban)	.625
	(.025)
All controls	.350
	(.026)
Final *df*	(551)

[a] regression coefficients

[b] Standard errors of regression coefficients. If the regression coefficients are at least twice their standard errors, they are significantly different from zero.

When the Index of Crime Show Viewing is broken into three categories ranging from low to high and the distributions for the six items in the Index of Support for the Legal System are examined, some interesting variations are revealed.* The difference between low and high viewers of crime shows is greatest (8.1 percent) on the item that states,

---

*The three categories for crime show viewing are low (16-24), medium (25-32), and high (33-57).

"A person should obey the law even if it goes against what he thinks is right." The smallest difference (1.3 percent) occurs on the item that is stated in the most absolute terms: "Disobedience of the law can never be tolerated." The distributions for all six items are in the expected direction—high viewers are more supportive of the legal system than low viewers.

The cultivation hypothesis seems to be strongly supported by the figures in Table 7.1. Crime shows appear to be cultivating the mainstream view that support for the legal system is desirable. The relationship survives controls for a number of key variables that might be associated with crime show viewing or support for the law. Attention will be given to the influence of crime show viewing on *thinking* about the law later in the chapter. First, consideration will be given to the mainstreaming hypothesis as it relates to support for the legal system.

INDIVIDUAL CHARACTERISTICS AND MAINSTREAMING SUPPORT FOR THE LEGAL SYSTEM

The evidence presented above indicates that crime show viewing cultivates support for the legal system and the norm of compliance, but does the strength of the relationship vary across groups defined in terms of individual characteristics? In Chapter 5 individual characteristics were related to support for the legal system so that those who held views outside of the mainstream could be identified. Few respondents were extremely nonsupportive of the norm of compliance, but it was possible to isolate some groups that were less supportive of the legal system than others.

Three demographic characteristics were related to support for the legal system in Chapter 5. Two of the characteristics, sex and parents' occupation, were not significantly related to support for the norm of compliance. These findings were contrary to what was predicted; it was expected that, based on previous research, males and respondents from middle class homes would be outside of the mainstream with respect to support for the legal system. It was found that, as expected, older students were more cynical regarding the legal system and held views outside of the mainstream. According to the mainstreaming hypothesis students in the higher grades should be more influenced by crime show viewing than those in the lower grades when support for the legal system is considered. The figures necessary to test the hypothesis that crime shows mainstream certain demographic groups' views of the legal system can be found in Table 7.2.

Table 7.2 The Effects of Crime Show Viewing on Support for the Legal System in Subgroups Defined by Demographic Characteristics

Uncontrolled	.687[a]	
	(.024)[b]	
Sex		
Male	.632	
	(.033)	$p = ns$[c]
Female	.659	
	(.039)	
Grade in School		
Lower grades (6th-8th)	.310	
	(.032)	$p < .05$
Higher grades (9th-12th)	.824	
	(.042)	
Head of Household Occupation		
Blue-collar	-.219	
	(.040)	$p < .01$
Professional—white-collar	.124	
	(.033)	

[a] regression coefficients
[b] Standard errors of regression coefficients. If the regression coefficients are at least twice their standard errors, they are significantly different from zero.
[c] F-tests for difference between regression coefficients.
ns = not significant

The unstandardized regression coefficients in Table 7.2 show that crime show viewing influences support for the legal system regardless of the control placed on the relationship, but in one instance the relationship is not in the direction predicted by the cultivation hypothesis. As expected, crime show viewing influences the support given to the legal system by boys and girls in about the same way. The mainstream hypothesis receives strong support with regard to grade in school; crime show viewing has a significantly greater impact on older students, who are predisposed not to give unqualified support to the legal system, than on younger students. It appears that crime shows tend to counteract the cynicism regarding the legal system that grows with age. The findings regarding head of household occupation are intriguing; viewing crime shows cultivates support for the legal system among respondents whose parents have professional or white-collar occupations, but the effects run in the opposite direction for those from working-class households. Why would heavy viewing of crime shows cultivate lower levels of support for the legal system among respondents from blue-collar homes? Perhaps working-class students identify less strongly with the goals of television police than middle class students. It might be the case that working-class students know from experience that police are not as effective as portrayed on television.

Another set of individual characteristics considered as conditional variables included those related to how students process the messages transmitted by television crime dramas. In Chapter 5 it was suggested that students with low grades in school, who read very little, and who perceive that the messages of television reflect reality might be more supportive of the legal system. None of these suppositions received support from the data; reading habits and the perception of television reality are unrelated to support for the criminal justice system, while it is students who achieve high grades, not those with low grades, who are in the mainstream with respect to compliance attitudes. It was suggested that achievement in school, as measured by grades, may be partially related to compliance to school norms. It is entirely possible that the three variables related to information-processing abilities have less to do with determining mainstream viewpoints than they do with facilitating the process of mass media cultivation of support for the legal system. The statistics necessary to examine the conditioning effects of information-processing variables are found in Table 7.3.

The regression coefficients in Table 7.3 provide some strong, but not perfectly consistent, support for the cultivation hypothesis; in five out of six conditions related to information-processing abilities the heavy viewing of crime dramas encourages support for the law. However, the conditional variables included in the table are not without influence. Students who achieve relatively high grades in school appear to become more supportive of the legal system as a result of viewing crime shows, while low achievers become *less* supportive. Why would low achievers become less supportive of the law as a result of heavy crime show viewing? There is no obvious explanation, but perhaps low achievers are subjected to peer influence that conditions the crime show viewing-law support relationship.

Consistent with earlier reports, Table 7.3 shows that the perception of television reality does not condition the cultivation process.[9] The coefficients for light and heavy readers are not significantly different, but the difference is large enough to deserve comment. Heavy readers appear to exhibit the stronger relationship between crime show viewing and support for the criminal justice system. One might expect

Table 7.3 The Effects of Crime Show Viewing on Support for the Legal System in Subgroups Defined by Individual Characteristics Related to Information Processing

Uncontrolled	.687[a]	
	(.024)[b]	
Grade Average		
Mostly C's or lower	-.121	
	(.047)	$p < .05$[c]
Mostly A's or B's	.937	
	(.028)	
Reading Habits		
Light reader	.271	
	(.034)	$p =$ ns
Heavy reader	.925	
	(.037)	
Perception of TV Reality		
Low	.663	
	(.036)	$p =$ ns
High	.572	
	(.036)	

[a] regression coefficient

[b] Standard errors of regression coefficients. If the regression coefficients are at least twice their standard errors, they are significantly different from zero.

[c] F-test of significance of difference between regression coefficients.

ns = not significant

heavy readers to be more cynical about the legal system and hold views outside the mainstream. However, that was shown not to be the case in Chapter 5. Heavy readers might also be expected to be more informed about the legal system (Table 5.3 shows that they are) and therefore less influenced by the distorted images of crime shows. Perhaps the most likely explanation for the relationship for heavy readers is that they may be more attentive to the messages of television crime shows and therefore more influenced by them.

To summarize, the cultivation of support for the legal system by crime shows appears to be generally strong regardless of individual characteristics. There were two conditions that produced a negative relationship, but the coefficients were quite small. In only one instance—the case of age—was the mainstreaming hypothesis explicitly supported. On the other hand, there was also just one instance—the case of school achievement—where the mainstream hypothesis failed to receive expected support. Perhaps the most interesting finding regarding individual characteristics was that students from working-class homes and those with low levels of achievement in school appeared to become less supportive of the law as a result of viewing crime shows.

FAMILY CHARACTERISTICS AND MAINSTREAMING SUPPORT FOR THE LEGAL SYSTEM

The structure of institutions such as the family play a major role in the development of compliance dispositions. Highly structured "authoritarian" families emphasize obedience of authority and conformity to norms; they produce offspring who are preoccupied with constraint by rules and established order. It is not surprising that respondents from families with a high socio-orientation are among the strongest supporters of the legal system; the data analysis presented in Chapter 5 showed that respondents from high socio-oriented families had significantly higher scores on the Index of Support for the Legal System than those from families who placed less emphasis on social conformity. Students from low socio-oriented families hold views that are outside of the mainstream with respect to support for compliance and should be more susceptible to cultivation by heavy viewing of crime dramas.

In Chapter 5 it was suggested that respondents from concept-oriented families should possess higher levels of information regarding the criminal justice system and a realistic, sophisticated view of compliance. Quite the opposite was found; high concept-oriented family members are significantly more supportive of the law than those from low concept-oriented families. Since most messages students receive about the criminal justice system reinforce the norm of compliance, it may be the case that those who are most "open" to communications develop mainstream views. The analysis undertaken in Chapter 5 suggests that students from low concept-oriented families hold views regarding the legal system that are outside of the mainstream; they should, according to the mainstream hypothesis, be more sensitive to the messages transmitted by crime dramas concerning compliance. The figures necessary to examine the conditioning effects of family communication patterns are found in Table 7.4.

The regression coefficients in Table 7.4 provide support for the cultivation hypothesis; none of the coefficients fall below the level

Table 7.4 The Effects of Crime Show Viewing on Support for the Legal System in Subgroups Defined by Family Communication Characteristics

Uncontrolled	.687[a]	
	(.024)[b]	
Family Socio-orientation		
Low	.805	
	(.042)	$p = $ ns[c]
High	.283	
	(.030)	
Family Concept-orientation		
Low	.361	
	(.037)	$p = $ ns
High	.843	
	(.033)	

[a] regression coefficient

[b] Standard errors of regression coefficients. If the regression coefficients are at least twice their standard errors, they are significantly different from zero.

[c] F-test of significance of difference between regression coefficients.

ns = not significant

of significance. Family communication patterns do not modify the original relationship significantly. However, the magnitudes of the regression coefficients are quite different for the varying values of the control variables. As expected, respondents from homes characterized by low socio-orientation are most likely to exhibit evidence of mainstreaming with regard to support for the law. Students from highly structured homes are predisposed to hold views that are in the mainstream, so crime show viewing has little influence on them.

Given the statistical results in Chapter 5, concept-orientation modifies the original relationship in a direction opposite of that expected; students from high concept-oriented families are most likely to be mainstreamed. Once again, the most likely reason for this conditioning effect is that those from high concept-oriented families are more open to the compliance reinforcing messages of television crime shows.

To summarize, the original cultivation relationship survives controls for family communication patterns. Neither control variable significantly modifies the influence of crime show viewing on support for the legal system. An examination of the magnitude of differences between regression coefficients for low and high socio-oriented family members provides some support for the hypothesis that television crime shows influence those who hold views outside of the mainstream. However, the coefficients for the two values of the concept-orientation variable fail to provide support for the mainstreaming hypothesis.

CONTEXTUAL FACTORS AND MAINSTREAMING SUPPORT FOR THE LEGAL SYSTEM

The structure of a student's school, like the structure of his or her family, may influence orientations toward the legal system and compliance. Authoritarian school structures are said to produce students who value the norm of conformity to rules. As noted in an earlier chapter private schools, especially parochial schools, are probably much more like socio-oriented families in that they both value discipline and conformity to explicit norms of behavior. In Chapter 5 it was shown that, as might be expected given earlier research, students who attend private schools are more supportive of the mainstream view regarding compliance with the legal system than attenders of public schools. The mainstream hypothesis would predict that students at public schools are likely to exhibit a greater influence of crime show viewing on attitudes toward compliance.

Where students live may have some influence on the crime show viewing-support for the legal system relationship. Suburban residence may be associated with middle class status, access to a high-quality education, and interaction with highly educated neighbors, all of which may produce "informed cynicism" regarding legal compliance. On the other hand conformity to middle class norms, including to compliance with the law, may be emphasized in the suburbs. City dwellers may, because of higher crime rates, have direct experience with the legal system and be skeptical of the messages transmitted by crime shows. Data analysis in Chapter 5 showed that students who live in urban areas are more supportive of the legal system; suburban residents have views on compliance that are relatively outside of the mainstream.

The conditioning effects of contextual factors on the relationship between crime show viewing and support for the legal system can be determined by an examination of the figures in Table 7.5. Once again there appears to be ample support for cultivation hypothesis, but little support for the mainstream hypothesis. While all of the regression coefficients in the table differ significantly from zero, the conditional variables do not contribute significantly to explaining the variance in

Table 7.5 The Effects of Crime Show Viewing on Support for the Legal System by Contextual Factors

Uncontrolled	.687[a]	
	(.024)[b]	
School Attended		
Public	.389	
	(.039)	p = ns[c]
Private	.711	
	(.032)	
Place of Residence		
Urban	.703	
	(.031)	p = ns
Suburban	.262	
	(.040)	

[a] Regression coefficients

[b] Standard errors of regression coefficients. If the regression coefficients are at least twice their standard errors, they are significantly different from zero.

[c] F-test of significance of difference between regression coefficients.

ns = not significant

support for the legal system. It appears that, given the magnitude of difference between coefficients, students who attend private schools are most likely to exhibit high scores on the Index of Support for the Legal System as a result of watching crime shows. This is the opposite of what the mainstream hypothesis predicts. Likewise, the figures regarding residence run counter to the mainstream hypothesis; urban dwellers demonstrate more evidence of cultivation of a television view of reality than suburban dwellers.

To summarize, the contextual factors examined in this study fail to be related to television's influence on legal system support in a way predicted by the mainstreaming hypothesis. Under some circumstances —in this case among private school attenders and urban residents—crime show viewing seems to reinforce the compliance attitudes of those who are predisposed to be in the mainstream.

THINKING ABOUT THE LAW: CRIME SHOW VIEWING AND LEVELS OF MORAL DEVELOPMENT

In Chapter 3 it was suggested that crime show viewing and perhaps television viewing in general does not encourage abstract thought about the dilemmas of legal obligation. Ethan Katsh pointed out that the law is best understood when conveyed in print because the print medium encourages abstract thinking.[10] Crime shows tend to offer simple, concrete, personal solutions to legal problems; they do not encourage the type of thinking about moral dilemmas that characterize Kohlberg's third, postconventional, level.

It is also reasonable to infer that, to the extent that television programming tends to contribute to the legitimacy of political authorities, viewers will be encouraged to think about the law as invariable; crime shows encourage preconventional and conventional modes of thinking about the legal system. In Chapter 4 an examination of sample distributions on a measure of moral development revealed that conventional thinking about the law is clearly in the mainstream. Both the television mainstream and the population mainstream appear to be characterized by conventional thinking.

In Chapter 5 a number of individual characteristics were found to be associated with conventional or mainstream thinking about the law. Consistent with earlier studies, there appeared to be a slight tendency for females, as opposed to males, to emphasize conventionalism. The differences were not statistically significant, but males appeared to be slightly outside of the mainstream. Grade in school had the greatest effect on the level of moral development; as expected, students in the higher grades were more sophisticated and hence more inclined to give postconventional responses when asked to give their views on compliance. Older students are outside of the mainstream with respect to thinking about the law. A similar relationship was found between parents' occupation and styles of reasoning; students from middle class homes were more likely to give postconventional responses.

The mainstreaming hypothesis predicts that crime show viewing should be most strongly associated with conventional and postconventional styles of reasoning among males, students in the higher grades, and students whose parents have professional or white-collar occupations. The figures necessary to test the hypothesis can be found in Table 7.6. The figures in the table are the percentage in each category who gave postconventional or nonmainstream answers to the open-ended question concerning compliance to the law. Generally, the figures show that there is a negative relationship between heavy viewing of crime shows and postconventional reasoning. As expected, the negative relationship is strongest among males and students from middle class households; both of these groups appear to be mainstreamed with respect to conventional thinking. The original relationship, while still

Table 7.6 Percentage Giving Postconventional Responses Regarding Compliance with the Law, by Crime Show Viewing, Controlling for Ten Variables

	Light Viewers	Medium Viewers	Heavy Viewers	Gamma
Overall	44.8	34.0	31.5	-.160*
Controlling for:				
Sex				
Male	55.8	37.5	35.1	-.234*
Female	38.5	31.1	26.0	-.134
Grade in School				
Lower grades (6th-8th)	38.3	29.0	24.7	-.083
Higher grades (9th-12th)	47.9	40.0	51.7	-.085
Head of Household Occupation				
Blue Collar	34.0	32.3	22.4	-.171
Professional/white-collar	52.3	35.4	40.3	-.160*
Grade Average				
Mostly C's or lower	40.5	43.4	41.7	-.023
Mostly A's and B's	46.5	31.4	29.0	-.203*
Reading Habits				
Light readers	50.0	31.2	32.7	-.236*
Heavy readers	39.4	35.8	31.0	-.095
Perception of TV Reality				
Low	33.9	25.8	20.6	-.173
High	51.2	39.2	42.4	-.121
Family Socio-orientation				
Low	56.1	38.7	38.2	-.263*
High	35.1	30.4	20.9	-.066
Family Concept-orientation				
Low	50.8	40.2	31.1	-.175*
High	42.5	27.7	33.3	-.154
School				
Public	48.1	32.1	25.6	-.266*
Private	40.6	36.5	42.9	-.001
Residence				
Urban	51.5	31.1	21.5	-.340*
Suburban	38.7	36.9	48.9	.070

*Significant at the .05 level using a Chi-square test of significance.

negative, seems to be substantially reduced when grade level is taken into account. Ultimately, grade in school is more strongly related to postconventional responses than crime show viewing.

Individual variables related to information-processing abilities should be related to both moral development and the influence of crime show viewing. An examination undertaken in Chapter 5 on the influence of these individual variables on conventional thinking revealed some surprises; grades in school and reading habits have little influence on the propensity to give postconventional responses. As expected, students who perceive entertainment television to be unrealistic hold views that are outside of the mainstream.

The figures in Table 7.6 show that crime show viewing is most negatively associated with postconventional styles of reasoning among students who receive high grades (A's and B's), light readers, and those who perceive television programming as unreal. The finding with regard to television reality is consistent with the mainstreaming hypothesis; television crime show viewing influences the style of reasoning of those who do not perceive programming as real. Light and heavy readers were not differentiated in terms of levels of moral development in Chapter 5, but Table 7.6 reveals that it is light readers who seem to be influenced most greatly by heavy television viewing; the combination of light reading and heavy television viewing seems to retard sophisticated thinking about the law. Students with high grades were found in Chapter 5 to be characterized by conventional-mainstream thinking, yet it is they and not the poorer students who are most influenced by heavy crime show viewing; this finding runs counter to the mainstream hypothesis.

Given earlier findings it is reasonable to expect that students from homes high in socio-orientation and low in concept-orientation would be characterized by their conventional thinking about the law. This expectation was only partially supported in Chapter 5; high socio-orientation and high concept-orientation were found to be associated with conventional styles of reasoning. The figures in Table 7.6 show that students from more permissive, low socio-oriented homes are mainstreamed by heavy viewing of crime shows; the figures provide some dramatic support for the mainstream hypothesis. The figures for concept-orientation also support the mainstream hypothesis; students from low-concept homes who are heavy viewers of crime shows are characterized by their conventional thinking about the law. The figures regarding concept-orientation are consistent with the mainstream hypothesis, but the fact that concept-oriented homes produce conventional thinking on the part of students is not consistent with previous findings.

The two contextual factors, place of residence and public/private school status, are not significantly related to conventional thinking about the law. There is no theoretical basis, derived from the mainstream hypothesis, to expect crime show viewing to influence one group any more than another. However, the figures in Table 7.6 show that contextual factors interact with television viewing habits in influencing styles of reasoning. The negative relationship between crime show viewing and postconventional responses is very strong among public school students and residents of urban areas. There is no relationship among private school students and only a weak one among suburbanites. Data presented in Chapter 5 showed a slight tendency for public school students to give postconventional responses, so the strong relationship shown in Table 7.6 may be viewed as support for the mainstream hypothesis. Private schools likely stress conventional thinking, so television has less of an influence among private school students. Urban residents are slightly more conventional in their thinking about the law, so television crime shows appear to enhance whatever influence living in a city has on styles of reasoning.

CONCLUSION

The findings of this chapter are clear with respect to the cultivation hypothesis. Heavy crime show viewing contributes to support for the legal system and the norm of compliance. Heavy viewing is also associated with unsophisticated preconventional or conventional styles of reasoning about legal compliance. In Table 7.7 the results of a multiple regression including 11 independent variables and support for the legal system are reported. The figures in the table show that while crime show viewing is a significant factor in influencing support for the legal system, it is not the most important. Grade in school (age), grade average, family socio-orientation, and concept-orientation all have a greater relative influence. Still, crime show viewing is an important contributor to the development of legal system support.

The influence of crime show viewing on support for the legal system and levels of reasoning about the law is mitigated by a number of control variables. The mainstream hypothesis on balance received support from the findings reported in this chapter. There were eleven instances where groups were expected to be mainstreamed. In seven

Table 7.7 The Relative Influence of 11 Variables on Support for the Legal System (Beta Weights)

	Beta	
Sex	.029*	
Grade in school	-.123	
Head of household occupation	.026	
Grade average	.077	
Reading habits	-.038	
Perception of TV reality	-.040	
Family socio-orientation	.146	
Family concept-orientation	.088	
Public/private school	-.035	
Residence	-.012	
TV crime show viewing	.060	
Final *df*	(554)	$R = .365$

*All of the beta weights are significantly different from zero.

instances the mainstreaming hypothesis received statistical support, while in two cases results were the opposite of those predicted and in two cases televison crime show viewing influenced orientations toward the law in a similar manner. It is important to note that certain groups appeared to be especially susceptible to the mainstreaming effects of heavy viewing. Respondents from middle class, low socio-oriented homes, and those who receive high grades in school were most responsive to the messages of crime shows. Crime show viewing appears to play a role in the inhibition of the natural growth of cynicism regarding the legal system that comes with cognitive maturation.

NOTES

1. George Gerbner and Larry Gross, "The Scary World of TV's Heavy Viewer," *Psychology Today* (April 1976): 89.

2. George Orwell, *1984* (San Diego: Harcourt, Brace, Jovanovich, 1977); Ray Bradbury, *Fahrenheit 451* (New York: Simon and Schuster, 1950).

3. Marie Winn, *The Plug-In Drug* (New York: Viking Press, 1977); Frank Mankiewicz and Joel Swerdlow, *Remote Control: Television and the Manipulation of American Life* (New York: Times Books, 1978).

4. George Gerbner et al., "Charting the Mainstream: Television's Contributions to Political Orientations," *Journal of Communication* 32 (Summer 1982): 100-27.

5. Ibid., p. 122.

6. David R. Berman and John A. Stookey, "Adolescents, Television and Support for Local Government," *Public Opinion Quarterly* 44 (1980): 330-40.

7. Joseph R. Dominick, "Children's Viewing of Crime Shows and Attitudes on Law Enforcement," *Journalism Quarterly* 51 (Spring 1974): 5-12.

8. See Russell H. Weigel and Richard Jessor, "Television and Adolescent Conventionality: An Exploratory Study," *Public Opinion Quarterly* 37 (Spring 1973): 76-90.

9. See Byron Reeves, "Perceived TV Reality as a Predictor of Children's Social Behavior," *Journalism Quarterly* 55 (Winter 1978): 682-95.

10. Ethan Katsh, "Is Television Anti-Law?: An Inquiry into the Relationship Between Law and Media," *The ALSA Forum* 7 (1983): 38.

8

SUPPORT FOR
CIVIL LIBERTIES

INTRODUCTION

In an earlier chapter the tension between laws protecting the rights of suspected criminals and the need for the political system to maintain order and stability was described in terms of a crime control model versus a due process model of the criminal justice process. According to Herbert Packer, who described the two value systems, those who support the due process model presume that suspects are innocent until proven guilty; they are concerned with protecting the individual from civil authority. Supporters of the crime control model implicitly assume that those who have been arrested are guilty because police make few mistakes. Legal procedures designed to protect suspected criminals are seen as obstacles to maintaining social order.

Information provided in Chapter 3 demonstrated that the television mainstream is characterized by a crime control point of view. Ethan Katsh argues persuasively that " . . . television has been projecting the desirability of an authoritarian legal order. . . . "[1] There are a number of reasons why viewers of crime shows might come to support a crime control point of view. Perhaps the most obvious is that there is a tremendous overrepresentation of violent crime on prime time television; the heavy crime show viewer can easily conclude the repressive measures are necessary to maintain order. Police are often shown as constrained by constitutional legal technicalities in situations where a suspect's guilt is known to the audience; the Constitution almost never protects the innocent in prime time crime dramas. On many crime shows the police systematically violate constitutional provisions that protect suspected criminals; these violations make it appear as though police are behaving legally. Arons and Katsh argue that all of these aspects of crime show programming have the effect of "softening up" the public's opinion regarding due process and making it more accepting of illegal police conduct.[2] The evidence from content analysis suggest the hypothesis that heavy crime show viewing cultivates a crime control point of view.

There is ample public opinion poll data to suggest that the public is more supportive of the crime control model than the due process model. A recent review of literature and data on the question of crime control versus due process concluded that

> there is a reservoir of support in the public for a tougher, less restrained role for the police and the courts. A harsh attitude toward "law and order" issues is supported by a substantial portion—a majority on some issues— of the population. This attitude may call for actions on the part of the police and courts which go beyond strict compliance with legal and constitutional rules.[3]

The mainstream of public opinion is characterized by a concern with crime and little sympathy for the rights of criminal suspects. Those who hold opinions outside of the mainstream regarding crime control are most likely to be influenced by the messages transmitted by crime dramas.

It is one matter to note that television transmits a crime control viewpoint and that the public shares that viewpoint, but quite another matter to demonstrate that there is an association between the two mainstreams. Given the fact that there has been so much systematic and unsystematic analysis of the content of crime shows regarding civil liberties and repressive police behavior, it is somewhat surprising that there is no published research that links crime show viewing to law and order attitudes. What evidence exists in support of a linkage is largely anecdotal and indirect.

Haney and Manzolati report an interesting piece of anecdotal evidence that viewers of crime shows are insensitive to illegal behavior on the part of prime time law enforcement officials. They trained some student assistants to view crime dramas and code various aspects of messages being transmitted. The student assistants failed to identify such illegal police behavior as assualting witnesses, breaking into suspects' homes, and stealing evidence. When quizzed about these omissions the students replied that, "They're not crimes, if the police do it."[4] In their analysis of a survey sample Haney and Manzolati found that heavy viewers of crime shows were less able to identify illegal police behavior than light viewers.

Only two pieces of evidence from survey data could be found that are related to a crime show viewing—anti-civil liberties linkage. In an analysis of television viewing habits and political orientations George Gerbner and his associates found that heavy viewers felt that the federal government was spending too little on crime control.[5] Haney and Manzolati reported that heavy television viewers (four hours or more per day) were more likely to endorse the statement, "police must often break the law to stop crime."[6]

The discussion of requirements of the political system in Chapter 4 emphasized the systemic need for social control. The system itself has little interest in encouraging attitudes consistent with the due process model of the criminal justice system. Inasmuch as television programmers have an interest in producing programs that are supportive of the status quo and mainstream viewpoints, the linkage between crime show viewing and low levels of support for civil liberties should be apparent in the data analyzed in this study.

The relationship between the Index of Crime Show Viewing and the Civil Liberties Support Scale is shown in Table 8.1. The figures in the table are partial regression coefficients accompanied by their standard errors. As expected, the regression coefficients in the table indicate a strong negative relationship between crime show viewing and support for civil liberties ($r = -.184, p < .001$). The original relationship is not greatly mitigated by any of the ten control variables; grade in school, when controlled, reduces the relationship more than any of the other control variables. The cultivation hypothesis with regard to support for civil liberties appears to be supported.

When crime show viewing is categorized as low, medium, and high and distributions of items related to support for civil liberties are examined, some interesting patterns are revealed.* Of the items included in the Civil Liberties Support Scale several stand out in their ability to distinguish heavy and light crime show viewers. The greatest difference occurs on the item concerning police brutality; 36 percent of

---

*The three categories for crime show viewing are low (16-24), medium (25-32), and high (33-57).

Table 8.1 The Effects of Crime Show Viewing on Support
for Civil Liberties by Selected Control Variables

Uncontrolled	-.958[a]
	(.023)[b]
Controlling For:	
Sex	-.921
	(.023)
Grade in school	-.749
	(.024)
Head of household occupation	-.943
	(.023)
Grade average	-.935
	(.023)
Reading habits	-.963
	(.023)
Perception of TV reality	-.916
	(.023)
Family socio-orientation	-.897
	(.023)
Family concept-orientation	-.992
	(.023)
School (public/private)	-.945
	(.023)
Residence (urban/suburban)	-.947
	(.023)
All controls	-.676
	(.025)
Final *df*	(554)

[a] regression coefficients

[b] Standard errors of regression coefficients. If the regression coefficients are at least twice their standard errors, they are significantly different from zero.

the heavy viewers compared to about 15 percent (14.8 percent) of the light viewers agree that, "Any man who insults a policeman has no complaint if he gets roughed up in return." Sixty-three percent of the heavy viewers compared to nearly 52 percent (51.7 percent) of the light viewers agreed that, "In order to protect the community from further crime, an arrested person should be kept in jail until his case comes to trial." Taking into account all six items included in the scale, the percentage difference between heavy viewers and light viewers of crime shows always exceeds 6 percent with the heavy viewers expressing an anti-civil libertarian viewpoint.

The Civil Liberties Support Scale was generated from an original pool of eleven items. The distributions for the five items not included in the scale for the three levels of crime show viewing are interesting. The most striking difference occurs on an item that states, "Some criminals are so evil that they don't deserve a trial;" 44 percent of the heavy crime show viewers agreed compared to about one-third (33.5 percent) of the light viewers. A substantial portion of the sample seemed to believe that evilness was to be considered in deciding whether a trial should be given. One additional item separated heavy viewers from light viewers; about 21 percent (21.3 percent) of the heavy viewers of crime shows compared with 12.5 percent of light viewers agreed that "If the courts stopped restricting the police, crime would not be a problem."

In general, crime show viewing cultivates a crime control view of the criminal justice system. Heavy viewers come to share the view promulgated by crime show programmers that the rights of individual suspects should give way to the need for social control.

INDIVIDUAL CHARACTERISTICS AND MAINSTREAMING AN ANTI-CIVIL LIBERTARIAN VIEW

Since the general population, as well as the sample examined in this study, is characterized by high support for the crime control model of the criminal justice system, those who indicate high support for civil liberties have views outside of the mainstream and should be most susceptible to cultivation by crime show viewing. Three individual demographic characteristics were related to support for civil liberties in an earlier chapter in order to identify which groups were outside of the mainstream. Previous studies suggested that males, students in the higher grades, and those with middle class backgrounds are generally more supportive of a due process point of view. An analysis undertaken in Chapter 5 revealed that only grade in school distinguished low and high support for civil liberties; students in the higher grades are more supportive and hold views outside of the mainstream. This finding is consistent with numerous other studies that have shown that concern for individual rights and concern about capricious government activity grows with age. The data necessary to determine whether three demographic characteristics mitigate the effects of crime show viewing on support for civil liberties can be found in Table 8.2.

Table 8.2 The Effects of Crime Show Viewing on Support for Civil Liberties in Subgroups Defined by Demographic Characteristics

Uncontrolled	-.958[a]	
	(.023)[b]	
Sex		
Male	-.117	
	(.031)	$p = ns$[c]
Female	-.366	
	(.036)	
Grade in School		
Lower grades (6th-8th)	-.371	
	(.030)	$p < .05$
Higher grades (9th-12th)	-.145	
	(.040)	
Head of Household Occupation		
Blue-collar	-.382	
	(.038)	$p = ns$
Professional/white-collar	-.116	
	(.031)	

  [a] regression coefficients

  [b] Standard errors of regression coefficients. If the regression coefficients are at least twice their standard errors, they are significantly different from zero.

  [c] F-tests for difference between regression coefficients.

ns = not significant

The figures in Table 8.2 serve to strengthen support for the cultivation hypothesis regarding nonsupport of civil liberties, but they offer no support for the mainstream hypothesis. Controls for sex and parents' occupation fail to contribute significantly to the explained variance in support for civil liberties. Crime show viewing appears to have a slightly greater influence on the views of females and students from working-class homes, but differences between regression coefficients are not significant.

Crime show viewing has a differential influence on the civil liberties attitudes of students in the higher and lower grades, but the difference is the opposite of that predicted by the mainstreaming hypothesis; students in grades six through eight are more likely to be "cultivated" through viewing crime shows than those in the higher grades. Crime show viewing appears to reinforce the anti-civil libertarian views of younger students, but does not pull older students into the mainstream. It is possible that crime show viewing retards development of a sophisticated view of the tension between individual rights and the needs for social control.

In Chapter 5 three individual level variables related to cognitive abilities and the processing of mass media messages were associated with support for civil liberties. Previous research led to the expectation that school achievement, measured by grades, would be positively associated with support for civil liberties; more intelligent, thoughtful individuals were thought to be more likely to recognize the tension between state authority and individual rights. However, what was found was that students who reported relatively low grades were more likely to support the due process model. It was suggested that high grades in school may reflect adherence to the norm of conformity. If that is the case, then students with high grades may be more supportive of authority as embodied in the police, as opposed to the rights of suspected criminals. Students with low grades held views outside of the mainstream.

It was hypothesized that students who reported that they were heavy readers would be more supportive of civil liberties; reading encourages abstract thinking and perhaps an appreciation for the need for due process. However, the data presented in Table 5.3 showed that reading habits have little influence on support for civil liberties.

The perceived reality of television programming does seem to have an influence on civil liberties attitudes. Students who feel that television presents an unreal image of the world are more supportive of the due process point of view. Students who see little distinction between the world of television and the real world have views that are in the mainstream. The perception of reality may have more to do with the processing of media messages than influencing civil liberties attitudes. However, those students who see television as especially credible may be those who have little access to alternative sources of information about the legal system. It was suggested in an earlier chapter that low levels of information may be associated with acceptance of the dictates of the system.

The figures necessary to examine the influence of individual information processing abilities on the crime show viewing/civil liberties support relationship can be found in Table 8.3. None of the regression coefficients in the table fall below the level of statistical significance, so the cultivation hypothesis is supported. There is no support in the table for the mainstreaming hypothesis. Crime show viewing has about

Table 8.3 The Effects of Crime Show Viewing on Support for Civil Liberties in Subgroups Defined by Individual Characteristics Related to Information Processing

Uncontrolled	-.958[a]	
	(.023)[b]	
Grade Average		
Mostly C's or lower	-.930	
	(.027)	$p = ns$[c]
Mostly A's and B's	-.952	
	(.044)	
Reading Habits		
Light reader	-.404	
	(.032)	$p = ns$
Heavy reader	-.142	
	(.034)	
Perception of TV Reality		
Low	-.156	
	(.033)	$p < .01$
High	-.355	
	(.033)	

[a] regression coefficients

[b] Standard errors of regression coefficients. If the regression coefficients are at least twice their standard errors, they are significantly different from zero.

[c] F-tests for difference between regression coefficients.

ns = not significant

the same negative effect on support for civil liberties on the groups with low and high grades; the mainstream hypothesis predicts greater influence on those with lower grades. As expected, reading habits do not significantly mitigate the original relationship. However, heavy crime show viewing appears to have a bit more influence on those who do not expose themselves to alternative sources of information.

The figures with respect to the perception of the reality of television run in a direction that is the opposite of what is expected; it is those who believe that the content of programming reflects reality who seem to exhibit low civil liberties support scores as a result of heavy viewing of crime shows. This finding is contrary to the prediction of the mainstream hypothesis. Perhaps those who are both heavy viewers of crime shows and believers in television's reality perceive that television police, like real police must engage in illegal behavior to maintain order. It is also possible that this group draws the conclusion that the behavior of television police is not illegal because real police cannot engage in illegal behavior. In either case it is clear that the perception of reality increases television's influence on attitudes in this instance.

To summarize, some unexpected findings resulted from an examination of the conditioning effects of individual variables on the crime show viewing-civil liberties support relationship. Regardless of the group considered, heavy crime show viewing is significantly associated with negative views of the due process model of the criminal justice system. The strength of the relationship varies significantly for values of two of the six individual characteristics considered. Contrary to predictions derived from the mainstreaming hypothesis, students in the lower grades and those who perceive that the content of television is real were significantly more likely to exhibit low support for civil liberties as a result of heavy viewing of crime dramas. A prediction that students with low grades in school would exhibit a stronger relationship between crime show viewing and support for crime control was not supported by the data.

FAMILY CHARACTERISTICS AND THE MAINSTREAMING OF CIVIL LIBERTIES SUPPORT

In an interesting article Meredith Watts argues that " . . . the predisposition to support severe treatment of criminals and to denigrate the structures of due process is related to a broad social attitude that might be called 'anti-heterodoxy'—a tendency to reject and punish those defined as deviant."[7] This broad social attitude—anti-heterodoxy —is highly related to socialization experiences in authoritarian structures such as the family and schools. Authoritarianism in the social environment may very likely contribute to support of a crime control point of view. It might also be argued that a broad range of social experience and exposure to a wide variety of information might as Watts argues " . . . de-reify the social and political structure and expose them as manipulable human processes."[8] The more diverse the sources of information individuals have at their disposal, the more likely a sensitivity to due process will be developed.

Two characteristics of families included as conditional variables in this study may reflect authoritarianism in the environment and exposure to diverse experiences and information. As noted earlier, the level of socio-orientation of family communication patterns may reflect an authoritarian structure in the family. If that is the case then it is reasonable to suggest that students from highly socio-oriented families may exhibit anti-heterodoxy and a crime control point of view. Data presented in Chapter 5 (Table 5.4) showed that this is in fact the case; students from families who are high in socio-orientation are less inclined to be supportive of civil liberties. Students from low socio-oriented homes hold views on civil liberties that are outside of the mainstream; they should, according to the mainstream hypothesis, be most influenced by the messages of television regarding crime control.

Concept-orientation may be related to the "openness" of family members to a wide variety of information and experiences. If exposure to diversity and encouragement to "think for one's self" is negatively associated with anti-heterodoxy, then high concept-oriented families should produce offspring who are sensitive to the democratic requirements of due process. However, the data presented in Chapter 5 do not support this line of reasoning; students from high concept-oriented homes are less supportive of civil liberties. Those from homes where the flow of information is restricted are more likely to hold views outside of the mainstream and therefore should be the most likely to be "cultivated" by heavy crime show viewing.

The statistics needed to determine the conditioning effects of the family communication pattern variables are shown in Table 8.4. Once again it must be noted that the cultivation hypothesis regarding civil liberties is supported because all of the coefficients in the table are significantly different from zero. Despite the finding that students from homes that are low in socio-orientation hold views regarding civil liberties that are outside of the mainstream, it is those from more authoritarian families who seem to be most greatly influenced by heavy viewing of crime shows; the difference between the two groups is statistically significant. Contrary to the mainstreaming hypothesis, crime show viewing seems to reinforce the predispositions of those who come from authoritarian families, but does not change those who view due process positively.

Family concept-orientation does not significantly modify the original relationship, but the difference in the magnitude of the regression coefficients tends to support the mainstreaming hypothesis; heavy crime show viewing is most strongly associated with an anti-civil libertarian view among those from low concept-oriented families. Generally, the statistics in Table 8.4 indicate that crime show viewing is most influential among those who come from the most constrictive families.

To summarize, the mainstream hypothesis leads to the expectation that crime show viewing is most negatively associated with support for

Table 8.4 The Effects of Crime Show Viewing on Support for Civil Liberties in Subgroups Defined by Family Communication Characteristics

Uncontrolled	-.958[a]	
	(.023)[b]	
Family Socio-orientation		
Low	-.173	
	(.040)	$p < .05$[c]
High	-.402	
	(.028)	
Family Concept-orientation		
Low	-.562	
	(.034)	p = ns
High	-.120	
	(.031)	

[a] regression coefficients
[b] Standard errors of regression coefficients. If the regression coefficients are at least twice their standard errors, they are significantly different from zero.
[c] F-tests for difference between regression coefficients.
ns = not significant

civil liberties for students from high socio-oriented and high concept-oriented families. Statistical support was not found for this expectation. It appears that crime show viewing encourages a crime control viewpoint among members of families who are authoritarian in that they stress conformity, and are constrictive in the sense that abstract thinking about information is discouraged.

CONTEXTUAL FACTORS: MEDIATING THE EFFECTS OF CRIME SHOW VIEWING ON CIVIL LIBERTIES ATTITUDES

As Watts points out the tendency to reject deviance and the desire to punish it severely may be linked to the social environment of the individual; anti-heterodoxy may be related positively to a narrowly constructed world view.[9] Where a person lives (especially a child or adolescent) and where one goes to school can be a major determinant of the diversity of social experiences. Private schools are usually seen as more homogeneous with respect to social background characteristics of students and social values. The probability of encountering people unlike one's self is greater in public schools. If exposure to deviant norms breeds tolerance, then public school students should be more supportive of civil liberties for "deviants." It may also be the case that the norm of social conformity is more highly valued in private schools. If that is the case, then the expectation that public school students will be low in anti-heterodoxy will be reinforced.

A similar argument can be made regarding place of residence. Urban living is often associated with exposure to a diversity of life styles and social values, while residents of suburbs live in close proximity to people much like themselves. Conformity is more valued in the suburbs, so it may be reasonable to expect that suburbanites would be less tolerant of deviants and more concerned with crime control than city residents. On the other hand urban residents may be more directly threatened by crime and hence less supportive of the rights of suspected criminals.

The statistical analysis in Table 5.5 in Chapter 5 shows that the two contextual factors fail to distinguish different levels of support for civil liberties. Urban and suburban dwellers, as well as public and private school attenders hold views on civil liberties that are squarely in the mainstream. There is no statistical basis for expecting any of

Table 8.5 The Effects of Crime Show Viewing on Support for Civil Liberties in Subgroups Defined by Contextual Factors

Uncontrolled	-.958[a]	
	(.023)[b]	
School Attended		
Public	-.826	
	(.036)	p = ns[c]
Private	-.898	
	(.030)	
Place of Residence		
Urban	-.939	
	(.030)	p = ns
Suburban	-.747	
	(.038)	

[a] regression coefficients

[b] Standard errors of regression coefficients. If the regression coefficients are at least twice their standard errors, they are significantly different from zero.

[c] F-tests for difference between regression coefficients.

ns = not significant

these four groups to demonstrate unusual sensitivity to the messages of crime shows regarding crime control.

The regression coefficients showing the strength of relationship between crime show viewing and support for civil liberties for each of the "contextual" groups are in Table 8.5. As expected, physical controls for school attended and place of residence do not mitigate the original relationship; heavy crime show viewing promotes support for crime control regardless of the condition. The only instance where there is a difference in coefficients of any magnitude is between urban and suburban residents; crime show viewing has slightly less influence on the level of support for civil liberties among suburban residents. Perhaps this finding reflects differences in the social status backgrounds of urban and suburban residents.

To summarize, the promising hypothesis that social environment affects perspectives on deviance and crime control and consequently the mainstreaming of views regarding civil liberties was not supported by the data. Perhaps more sensitive measures of context would have produced different results. However, it is clear that heavy crime show viewing influences perspectives on crime control regardless of place of residence or whether the school attended is private or public.

CONCLUSION

Television crime shows emphasize the crime control model of the criminal justice system and that emphasis influences conceptions of the heavy viewer. In every subgroup examined in this chapter those who spent the most time viewing crime shows were the least disposed to support civil liberties of those who are accused of crimes. The standardized partial regression coefficients (beta weights) displayed in Table 8.6 show that of 11 variables offered as explanations of support for civil liberties, heavy viewing of crime shows has the most influence. The data presented in this chapter suggest that crime show viewing does not explain a large proportion of the variance in attitudes toward civil liberties, but its contribution is significant and greater than many other factors which presumably are important in the socialization of democratic values such as social status, achievement in school, and family structure. Since television crime shows promote a crime control view that is squarely in the mainstream, their independent effects can only be expected to be small.

The mainstreaming hypothesis did not receive strong support in this chapter. Based on distributions of scores on the Civil Liberties

Table 8.6 The Relative Influence of 11 Variables on Support for Civil Liberties (Beta Weights)

	Beta	
Sex	.052	
Grade in school	.091	
Head of household occupation	-.030	
Grade average	-.100*	
Reading habits	.007	
Perception of TV reality	.069	
Family socio-orientation	-.062	
Family concept-orientation	-.115*	
Public/private school	-.022	
Residence	-.026	
TV crime show viewing	-.121*	
Final *df*	(554)	$R = .281$

*$p < .05$

Support Scale five groups were identified as holding views slightly outside of the mainstream. However, only one of the five groups (those from low-concept homes) was significantly more likely to be influenced by heavy viewing of crime shows.

Those who believe that cognitive maturation leads to more stable support for democratic values can take little comfort from the findings of this chapter. While it is true that students in the higher grades seem less "convinced" by the crime control messages purveyed by crime shows, even students who achieve high grades in school, are heavy readers, and are aware that television content is "unreal" learn to be nonsupportive of civil liberties.

NOTES

1. Ethan Katsh, "Is Television Anti-Law?: An Inquiry into the Relationship Between Law and Media," *The ALSA Forum* 7 (1983): 38.

2. Stephen Arons and Ethan Katsh, "How TV Cops Flout the Law," *Saturday Review*, March 19, 1977, pp. 11-19.

3. Michael Corbett, "Public Support for 'Law and Order': Interrelationships with System Affirmation and Attitudes Toward Minorities," *Criminology* 19 (November 1981): 339.

4. Craig Haney and John Manzolati, "Television Criminology: Network Illusions of Criminal Justice Realities," in *Readings About the Social Animal*, ed. E. Aronson (San Francisco: Freeman, 1980): 128.

5. George Gerbner et al., "Charting the Mainstream: Television's Contributions to Political Orientations," *Journal of Communication* 32 (Summer 1982): 100-27.

6. Haney and Manzolati, "Television Criminology," p. 128.

7. Meredith W. Watts, "Anti-heterodoxy and the Punishment of Deviance: An Explanation of Student Attitudes Toward 'Law and Order,'" *Western Political Quarterly* 30 (March 1977): 93-103.

8. Ibid., p. 95.

9. Ibid.

9

DEVELOPMENT OF IMAGES
OF POLICE

INTRODUCTION

As important as police are in a legal society, it is curious that social scientists have not given more attention to their role in maintaining the stability of political systems. Some credit can be given to David Easton, who articulated system-persistence theory, for directing research attention to the linkages between images of police and perceptions concerning the legitimacy of the political system.[1] As a result of the development of system-persistence theory, political socialization research has produced some interesting findings concerning images of police. A number of studies have shown that the authority of police is recognized by children at an early age and that images are generally positive; police are overall perceived to be powerful, helpful, competent, and honest.[2]

Unfortunately, since the original flurry of research activity by political scientists in the 1960s, there has been little progress made in determining the systemic relevance of police images or their sources. Most recent research, undertaken by criminologists, has focused on relationships of such variables as race, place of residence, victimization, and fear of crime with a generalized attitude toward police.[3] There have been a number of scholars who have suggested that police image may be multidimensional and that one source of images might be the mass media, but few have attempted to link media content and perceptions of police.

After reviewing content analyses and survey data in earlier chapters it became increasingly obvious that there is some difficulty in locating the mainstream regarding images of police. It appears likely that there is no single, clear, concrete image of police that is portrayed by television crime dramas or held in the minds of most citizens; both the images portrayed and the attitudes held are multidimensional.

If there is a single dimension of police image that seems pervasive on crime dramas it is the one concerning effectiveness and power. The review of content analyses in Chapter 3 provides ample support for the conclusion that television police are much more successful at catching criminals than real-life police. This general finding is consistent with the view that messages transmitted by television serve to maintain social control; the television industry and those who might regulate programming are very interested in transmitting the message that "crime does not pay." With regard to the basic message regarding compliance it is interesting to note that, while authorities are usually seen as benevolent by young children, the one aspect of police image that was most consistently held by the sample of children analyzed by Easton and Dennis was power and reliability.[4] It can be argued that from the perspective of those who are interested in system persistence, it is much more important that police are seen as effective than that they are seen as benevolent. The perception that police are extremely successful at catching criminals is likely to be cultivated by heavy viewing of crime shows.

The mainstream with regard to aspects of police image other than effectiveness is difficult to characterize. Content analyses show that on balance police are portrayed in a positive way, but a criminologist, John O'Brien, disagrees arguing that the mass media has developed its own model of police image that is not conducive to the development of positive police-community relations. According to O'Brien many crime dramas portray the average police officer as a Keystone Cop who plays a supporting role to private investigators and sometimes newsreporters; oftentimes television police are not up to the task of solving complicated crimes.[5] In sharp contrast programs that emphasize the "new realism" often portray police as brutal or corrupt.

The multidimensionality of police image can be seen in the way "Kojak" was portrayed in the popular series. Kojak, a New York City police detective, each week could be seen "solving" complex criminal schemes, kicking purse snatchers, stealing evidence, comforting victims, and giving lollipops to kids. While engaging in all these activities, Kojak was followed around by a cast of officers who Robert Alley described as " . . . buffoons, incapable of intelligent action save at the direction of the wise and intelligent leader."[6] Which of these aspects of image stand out so much that they affect perceptions of reality concerning police? Real police are neither Keystone Cops nor Kojaks, and for the most part the public seems predisposed to emphasize positive images; on balance the evidence shows that the public sees police as basically honest, hard-working, fair, and not overly violent. Still, cultivation analysis assumes that television drama presents coherent, consistent images of life and society; inconsistent portrayals of police characteristics and behavior may confuse the process of cultivation, since there does not seem to be a singular mainstream view.

Only one study could be found that makes a direct attempt to link crime show viewing to attitudes toward police. Joseph Dominick correlated his crime show viewing index with a six-item scale that measured "police evaluation" and a single item that asked, "Do criminals usually get caught?" He found no relationship at all between crime show viewing and evaluation of police; the attitudes of parents, friends, or actual contact with police were the only variables significantly correlated with the scale. There was, however, a strong relationship between viewing crime shows and the belief that police are effective; among both girls and boys Dominick found that 16 percent more heavy viewers than light viewers of crime shows believed that criminals usually get caught.[7] These data suggest that crime show viewing cultivates perceptions of police effectiveness, but has little influence on other aspects of police image.

It was reported in Chapter 2 that a factor analysis of ten survey items designed to measure police image produced two scales. The Police Effectiveness Scale consists of four of the items and the Police-Community Relations Scale was constructed from the remaining six. The relationships between the Index of Crime Show Viewing and the two police image scales are shown in Table 9.1.

The figures in Table 9.1 provide dramatic support for the idea that television presents multidimensional images of police. As expected, there is a strong significant relationship between heavy viewing of crime shows and the perception that police are effective. The relationship survives individual least squares controls for ten variables, though simultaneous controls reduce the size of the partial regression coefficient considerably. The finding that is perhaps surprising is that heavy crime show viewing has a significant negative influence on perceptions of police-community relations; the negative relationship is strong, as it is reduced little by controls for other variables.

Table 9.1 The Effects of Crime Show Viewing on Images of Police by Selected Control Variables

	Police-Community Relations	Police Effectiveness
Uncontrolled	-.400[a]	.365
	(.027)[b]	(.017)
Controlling For:		
Sex	-.373	.349
	(.028)	(.017)
Grade in school	-.698	.194
	(.028)	(.018)
Head of household occupation	-.405	.345
	(.028)	(.017)
Grade average	-.438	.350
	(.027)	(.017)
Reading habits	-.358	.372
	(.027)	(.017)
Perception of TV reality	-.411	.312
	(.027)	(.017)
Family socio-orientation	-.424	.325
	(.027)	(.017)
Family concept-orientation	-.351	.399
	(.027)	(.017)
School (public/private)	-.447	.356
	(.027)	(.017)
Residence (urban/suburban)	-.430	.381
	(.027)	(.017)
All controls	-.532	.174
	(.030)	(.019)
Final *df*	(554)	(554)

[a] regression coefficient

[b] Standard errors of regression coefficients. If the regression coefficients are at least twice their standard errors, they are significantly different from zero.

Sometimes exclusive analysis of additive scales can fail to reveal interesting relationships between individual items. Though the police image scales meet the criteria for scalability, it may be the case that crime show viewing is related to the individual items in different ways. It is instructive to examine the relationships of individual police image items with levels of crime show viewing. The distributions for the items concerning effectiveness of police are as expected; nearly 46 percent of the heavy crime show viewers agreed that "criminals usually get caught" while about 36 percent of the light viewers agreed.* Heavy viewers were also the most likely to agree that "police are doing an effective job" and that "policemen are generally more honest than most people." Though it appears that heavy viewers tend to see police as effective, they were less likely than light viewers to agree with the statement, "If I need help, I can rely on the police to come to my aid." Heavy viewers seem to see police as effective and honest, but not necessarily helpful or reliable. This attitude may not be surprising given the fact that many television police are busy chasing murderers and big-time criminals to help citizens. The response to the helpfulness item is indicative of the problem of trying to measure image with an additive scale; sometimes interesting relationships are hidden.

The negative influence of heavy crime show viewing on other aspects of police image is highlighted when the distributions for items included in the Police-Community Relations Scale are examined. Heavy viewers are much more likely than light viewers (27.5 percent versus 15.9 percent) to agree that, "The police are often too stupid to solve complicated crimes." Heavy viewers are also more likely to agree that police are too willing to use violence. In contrast, heavy viewers are more supportive of the police than light viewers in that they are less likely to agree that, "The police don't show proper respect for citizens" and "The police often enjoy pushing people around." Heavy viewers of crime shows indicate negative images of police on four of six Police-Community Relations items and positive images on two of them.

It is relatively easy to see how heavy crime show viewing might be related to the observed patterns of response to individual items. On crime dramas with a detective as a major character, police are often portrayed as stupid and, as noted earlier, television police are extremely violent. In contrast it may be argued that television police are respectful to citizens and do not "push people around" unnecessarily. The theoretical problem highlighted by these results arises from the multidimensionality of police image. It appears that crime show viewing cultivates multifaceted images of the police. The mainstream may very well be characterized by ambivalence as opposed to a consistent

------

*The three categories for crime show viewing are low (16-24), medium (25-32), and high (33-57).

system-supportive view. If that is the case then heavy crime show viewing likely interacts with other variables in ways that cannot be easily explained within the context of the mainstream hypothesis. If there is no consistent mainstream, how can mainstreaming take place?

INDIVIDUAL CHARACTERISTICS AND THE CULTIVATION OF IMAGES OF POLICE

Most recent research on the correlates of police image has given attention to the influence of such background characteristics as age, social status, race, ethnicity, and sex. A number of studies have found that women and middle class respondents have relatively positive images of police. However, an analysis of the survey data used for the present study showed that, of the social background characteristics considered, only grade in school differentiated those with positive and negative images of police; students in the higher grades (ninth through twelfth) have more negative images of police in that they see them as less effective and in less positive terms on the Police-Community Relations Scale. This finding is consistent with research on political socialization that has shown that older students have a more realistic, less positive view of police because they are more cognitively sophisticated. If the mainstream is described in terms of positive images of police, then of the social background characteristics only grade in school should mitigate relationships between crime show viewing and perceptions of police. The statistics necessary to examine the conditioning effects of social background variables on the crime show viewing-police attitudes relationship are shown in Table 9.2.

In five out of six groups defined by background characteristics crime show viewing cultivates negative images of police-community relations. Significant differences in the strength and/or direction of cultivation effects occur between males and females and between students from working-class and middle class families. The within group relationships revealed in the table are not consistent with the mainstream hypothesis, but post factum interpretations are possible. Heavy crime show viewing appears to have a greater influence on negative perceptions of police-community relations among males than females. This difference may be due to television program choice; females prefer programs such as "CHIPS," while males indicate a stronger preference for detective series such as "Rockford Files." As noted earlier, detective series often portray police as corrupt or incompetent.

Table 9.2 The Effects of Crime Show Viewing on Images of Police in Subgroups Defined by Demographic Characteristics

	Police-Community Relations		Police Effectiveness	
Uncontrolled	-.400[a]		.365	
	(.027)[b]		(.017)	
Sex				
Male	-.935		.454	
	(.036)	$p < .05$[c]	(.023)	p = ns
Female	-.378		.290	
	(.043)		(.027)	
Grade in School				
Lower grades (6th-8th)	-.844		-.500	
	(.036)	p = ns	(.023)	$p < .01$
Higher grades (9th-12th)	-.897		.251	
	(.047)		(.030)	
Head of Household Occupation				
Blue-collar	-.140		-.713	
	(.044)	$p < .01$	(.028)	$p < .01$
Professional/white-collar	.105		.407	
	(.037)		(.024)	

[a] regression coefficients
[b] Standard errors of regression coefficients. If the regression coefficients are at least twice their standard errors, they are significantly different from zero.
[c] F-tests for differences between regression coefficients.
ns = not significant

Another significant difference between groups regarding police-community relations indicates that heavy crime show viewing cultivates positive images of among middle class students and negative images among those from working-class families. This result may be indicative of differences in the likelihood of contact with police; because of a lack of direct experience with police, middle class students may be more disposed to accept as accurate the positive images of police portrayed on crime shows. Overall, there is no evidence of mainstreaming in the first column of Table 9.2; crime show viewing influences students of different grade levels in much the same way with regard to perceptions of police-community relations.

The pattern of results with regard to the conditioning effects of background variables on the cultivation of perceptions of police effectiveness demonstrate clearly that there is great variability within group

relationships. In two of the six groups defined by background characteristics, heavy crime show viewing cultivates an image of police effectiveness. Sex has no influence on the positive relationship, but controls
for the other two variables reveal dramatic differences; crime show
viewing cultivates negative images of police effectiveness among students in the lower grades and among those from working-class homes.
The results regarding grade in school may be viewed as consistent with
the mainstream hypothesis; students in higher grades who are predisposed to skepticism regarding police effectiveness are more likely to
develop positive views as a result of watching crime shows. Why would
crime show viewing produce negative images of police effectiveness
among younger students and those from working-class families? Perhaps younger students are more sensitive to the negative images of
police effectiveness portrayed on television because those images are
in such sharp contrast to preconceived views.

When attention is given to the relationships between crime show
viewing and responses to individual items in the Police Effectiveness
Scale among younger students some interesting patterns are revealed.
Young students are just as likely as older students to be responsive to
the effectiveness of television police in catching criminals. However,
unlike the sample as a whole, heavy crime show viewing by the youngest students tends to cultivate images of police dishonesty ($r = -.126$
for the relationship between crime show viewing and agreement that
"police are more honest than most people"). Crime shows appear to
have a dramatic impact on the idealistic images of police held by the
youngest students; students in the lower grades may resonate to negative images that are inconsistent with preconceived notions. The negative influence of crime show viewing on perceptions of police effectiveness among working-class students may be a reflection of that group's
preference for detective series, as opposed to programs where police
are major characters.

The patterns of results reported in Table 9.2 indicate that while
crime show viewing cultivates images of police, the aspects that are
influenced vary according to the group considered. In order to make
these patterns of results intelligible it was necessary to dig deeper to
try to find associations that were masked by simple relationships between additive scales.

It has been generally held that mass media influence is greatest
among those with the least amount of pre-existing knowledge and experience regarding the substance of the message. Variables related to
cognitive abilities and perception should condition the relationships
under examination because they are related to the quantity and quality
of information about police at the disposal of respondents.

In Chapter 5 variables reflecting information-processing abilities were related to the two measures of police image. It was found that adolescents who reported relatively low grades had significantly lower scores on the Police-Community Relations Scale and the Police Effectiveness Scale. It has been noted that grades may partially reflect student conformity to prevailing norms, so it should come as no surprise that school achievement is negatively associated with images of police. If the mainstream can be characterized as holding positive images of police, then those with low grades are outside of the mainstream.

Reading habits are related to the quantity of information held by adolescents, but also may be related to perception of police. Light readers were found in Chapter 5 to have significantly lower scores on the Police-Community Relations Scale. Reading may be related to school achievement and conformity; the same peer influences that discourage reading may also encourage negative images of police. Adolescents who perceive that television programming largely reflects reality were found to be significantly more likely to see police as effective as those who think programs are unreal. The mainstreaming hypothesis would predict that heavy viewers of crime shows among the "low reality" group would be most likely to be influenced by television's messages regarding police effectiveness. The statistics necessary to evaluate the conditioning influence of information processing variables are in Table 9.3.

In all six groups defined by the information processing variables crime show viewing cultivates negative perceptions of police-community relations. Grade average has no statistically significant conditional influence on the cultivation of negative images, but the negative regression coefficient is much larger for students with lower grades. This finding is consistent with the explanation that mass media influence is greatest among those who are least likely to acquire or comprehend information from other sources. Students with the lower grades were also the ones who were predisposed to hold negative images of police; if the mainstream contains positive images, then the mainstream hypothesis is not supported in this instance.

Light readers were found to be less positive about police-community relations than heavy readers, but reading habits appear to have little influence on the cultivation of police images; both light and heavy readers who are frequent crime show viewers hold negative views of police-community relations.

The perception of the reality of television drama mitigates the crime show viewing perception of police-community relations relationship; adolescents who believe that television portrayals are unreal are

Table 9.3 The Effects of Crime Show Viewing on Images of Police in Subgroups Defined by Individual Characteristics Related to Information Processing

	Police-Community Relations		Police Effectiveness	
Uncontrolled	-.400[a]		.365	
	(.027)[b]		(.017)	
Grade Average				
Mostly C's or lower	-.859		.844	
	(.031)	$p = $ ns[c]	(.033)	$p = $ ns
Mostly A's or B's	-.340		.302	
	(.031)		(.020)	
Reading Habits				
Light reader	-.404		.816	
	(.037)	$p = $ ns	(.023)	$p < .05$
Heavy reader	-.610		.294	
	(.040)		(.025)	
Perception of TV Reality				
Low	-.935		.372	
	(.040)	$p < .05$	(.025)	$p < .05$
High	-.143		-.819	
	(.040)		(.025)	

[a] regression coefficients

[b] Standard errors of regression coefficients. If the regression coefficients are at least twice their standard errors, they are significantly different from zero.

[c] F-tests for differences between regression coefficients.

ns = not significant

significantly more likely to have negative perceptions of police than those who believe in television reality. In other words the "low reality" group was influenced by the messages of crime dramas more than the "high reality" group, but the direction of influence was not toward more positive mainstream views of police-community relations. It is difficult to explain why those who see crime shows as unreal are more influenced by them. It may be the case that the perception of reality encourages involvement in the subject matter of crime programs and that low involvement or passive viewing facilitates cultivation.

In five out of the six groups defined by information processing variables, crime show viewing has a positive influence on the perception of police effectiveness. Grade average does not significantly mitigate the original relationship, but students with lower grades appear to be more susceptible to cultivation by crime shows. The difference in the magnitude of the regression coefficients lends some support to the mainstream hypothesis and the argument that media messages are most influential among those who exhibit fewer cognitive skills.

The reading habits of the adolescents in the sample interact with crime show viewing and perceptions of police effectiveness; light readers are more likely to come to see police as effective. This finding is consistent with the explanation that those who access a limited number of sources of information will be most likely to be influenced by the messages of television.

Perceptions of television reality appear to modify the influence of crime show viewing on perceptions of police effectiveness; those who believe television drama reflects reality and are also heavy viewers of crime shows have negative images of police effectiveness. The conditioning influence of the perception of reality in this instance is the opposite of what was found regarding police-community relations; adolescents who are "involved" in crime shows appear to be influenced by them. How can the differential conditioning effects be explained? It is possible that those who see television police as "real" perceive that real police simply do not measure up. For example, while most heavy viewers of crime shows are likely to view police as "more honest than most people," those who believe television drama is especially accurate view them as dishonest ($r = -.203$). This may be an example of what real police fear about television police shows—that they encourage unrealistic expectations about police honesty and effectiveness. The fact that those who perceive television as unreal are influenced in the positive direction supports the mainstream hypothesis.

The general pattern of results reported in Table 9.3 supports the cultivation hypothesis as it relates to police image. There is also some support in the table for the argument that cognitively uninvolved or unsophisticated adolescents are the most likely to be influenced by the crime show messages regarding police; four of the five largest regression coefficients in the table occur in groups defined by low grades, poor reading habits, or a perception that television content is unreal. With regard to perceptions of police effectiveness and community relations there is little support for the mainstream hypothesis in the table.

FAMILY COMMUNICATION PATTERNS AND CULTIVATION OF IMAGES OF POLICE

In earlier chapters family communication patterns were found to play a role in modifying the influence of crime show viewing. A great deal of research suggests that families play a major role in the development of orientations toward authorities. In fact it has been suggested that orientations toward the father are often directly generalized to such authority figures as police.[8] If it is the case that adolescents generalize from nonpolitical to political authority figures, then respondents from more authority-oriented highly structured families should display more positive orientations toward police. In Chapter 5 data were presented that provide some support for this supposition; subjects from high socio-oriented families believe that police are more effective than those from low socio-oriented families. It is also the case that respondents from high concept-oriented families have significantly higher scores on the Police-Community Relations Scale than those from low-concept families.

Families with a high concept-orientation are usually rich in information, they encourage openness and the use of a variety of sources of information. Adolescents from concept-oriented families may be more knowledgeable about police characteristics and behavior; it follows that they will be less likely to be influenced by the messages transmitted by crime dramas. The statistics necessary to determine whether family characteristics mitigate the influence crime show viewing on attitudes toward police are in Table 9.4.

The regression coefficients in Table 9.4 show that there is considerable intergroup variation in the influence of crime show viewing; adolescents from highly structured, conformity-oriented, socio-oriented families are significantly more likely to accept the negative messages of crime shows regarding police-community relations. Perhaps respondents from the more authority-oriented families resonate to images of police punishing deviance (pushing people around) and approve of this behavior; this interpretation is consistent with the view that people from authoritarian families tend to display anti-heterodoxy.

The figures pertaining to concept-orientation and the influence of crime show viewing on attitudes toward police-community relations support the mainstreaming hypothesis, assuming that the mainstream can be characterized by positive images of police. Adolescents from low concept-oriented homes were found in an earlier chapter to hold less positive views of police relations with the community, but the regression coefficients in Table 9.4 show that heavy viewing of crime shows tends to pull them back into the mainstream. The impact of crime show viewing on attitudes toward police-community relations among students from high concept-oriented homes is much weaker, as might be expected.

Table 9.4 The Effects of Crime Show Viewing on Images of Police in Subgroups Defined by Family Communication Characteristics

	Police-Community Relations		Police Effectiveness	
Uncontrolled	-.400[a]		.365	
	(.027)[b]		(.017)	
Family Socio-orientation				
Low	-.110		-.533	
	(.047)	$p < .05$[c]	(.030)	$p < .05$
High	-.293		.240	
	(.034)		(.021)	
Family Concept-orientation				
Low	.353		.645	
	(.040)	$p < .01$	(.025)	$p =$ ns
High	-.113		-.143	
	(.037)		(.023)	

[a] regression coefficients

[b] Standard errors of regression coefficients. If the regression coefficients are at least twice their standard errors, they are significantly different from zero.

[c] F-tests for differences between regression coefficients.

ns = not significant

Family socio-orientation mitigates the influence of heavy crime show viewing on views of the effectiveness of police. Adolescents from conformity-oriented homes are predisposed to view police as effective —they are squarely in the mainstream—and heavy crime show viewing encourages their predisposition; the mainstream hypothesis fails to receive support in this instance. The strongest regression coefficient is for the low socio-oriented group and it runs in the negative direction; students from less structured homes are less likely to see police as effective and crime show viewing encourages their perception of police ineffectiveness.

Family concept-orientation does not significantly mitigate the crime show viewing-police effectiveness relationship. However, the difference between regression coefficients for the two groups is quite large. Adolescents from low concept-oriented homes where the information environment may not be rich are encouraged to hold a positive view of police effectiveness by crime dramas. The relationship runs in the opposite direction for the high concept-oriented group. An inspection of relationships between crime show viewing and individual items in the Police Effectiveness Scale reveals that in the high concept-oriented group those who are heavy viewers are especially likely to disagree with the statement that, "If I need help, I can rely on the police to come to my aid." Adolescents from high-concept families are likely to be among the most knowledgeable concerning police effectiveness. Perhaps crime show information concerning the helpfulness of police conflicts sharply with information this group has acquired from other sources.

In summary, it appears that family communication patterns are important in conditioning the influence of crime show viewing on orientations toward police. While crime show viewing has a significant influence on the cultivation of negative images of police-community relations and positive perceptions of police effectiveness in most groups, there is little support for the mainstreaming hypothesis. Though the conditional relationships found with respect to family variables are not generally consistent with theoretical expectations, the influence of concept-orientation makes some theoretical sense; crime show viewing has the smallest influence on the images of police of those who are most likely to have alternative sources of information—adolescents from high-concept families.

CONTEXTUAL FACTORS AND CULTIVATION OF POLICE IMAGE

Previous research seems to indicate that place of residence and type of school attended influence images of police. Urban residents have been shown to have less positive images of police than suburban residents.[9] In his study of adolescents and police Bouma found that students who attended parochial schools were most likely to view police in positive terms.[10] Neither of these relationships can be found in the survey data analyzed in this study. In fact statistics presented in Chapter 5 indicated that suburbanites were more likely to have negative images of police-community relations than those who live in urban areas. It is reasonable to expect that contextual factors can modify the influence of television viewing on attitudes toward police; place of residence may be an indicator of actual experience with crime or police and the type of school a student attends may indicate the "value climate" of peers or predispositions toward authority. The statistics necessary to examine the mitigating effects of contextual factors on television's influence on police attitudes are found in Table 9.5.

The figures in Table 9.5 show that contextual factors do not mitigate the influence of crime show viewing on perceptions of police

Table 9.5 The Effects of Crime Show Viewing on Images of Police in Subgroups Defined by Contextual Factors

	Police-Community Relations		Police Effectiveness	
Uncontrolled	-.400[a]		.365	
	(.027)[b]		(.017)	
School Attended				
Public	-.141		-.102	
	(.042)	$p < .01$[c]	(.027)	p = ns
Private	-.360		.363	
	(.035)		(.022)	
Place of Residence				
Urban	-.322		.204	
	(.035)	$p < .05$	(.022)	p = ns
Suburban	-.958		.145	
	(.044)		(.028)	

[a] regression coefficients

[b] Standard errors of regression coefficients. If the regression coefficients are at least twice their standard errors, they are significantly different from zero.

[c] F-tests for differences between regression coefficients.

ns = not significant

effectiveness, but the relationship with perceptions of police-community relations is conditional. Students who attend private schools are not necessarily predisposed to have positive images of police, but they appear to be especially susceptible to cultivation of negative images of police-community relations by heavy viewing of crime shows. Why would private school students resonate to the negative images of police presented by crime dramas? Perhaps there are individual items in the Police-Community Relations Scale that are especially relevant to private school students. This is indeed the case; private school students as a group tend to disagree that, "The police don't show proper respect for students," but heavy viewers among private school students are much more likely to agree with the statement. With regard to police respect for citizens, private school students tend to have an idealized viewpoint that is tempered by crime shows.

Suburbanites tend to have negative images of police-community relations and heavy crime show viewing appears to encourage their predispositions. It is possible that urban residents have a more balanced view based on experience; since they have more firsthand knowledge of crime and law enforcement they are less likely to be influenced by the negative images of crime shows.

Contextual factors do not significantly mitigate the crime show viewing-police effectiveness relationship; but attendance at a public school does reverse the direction of the influence of television viewing. The difference between private and public school students is attributable to differential responses to the effectiveness item dealing with police honesty; crime show viewing appears to cultivate perceptions of police dishonesty among public school students. Private school students are predisposed to see police as "more honest than most people," and crime show viewing has little influence on their views.

CONCLUSION

The findings presented in this chapter point to some problems concerning testing the mainstreaming hypothesis. The major problem concerns the identification of a consistent and pervasive television mainstream regarding messages concerning police performance. Content analyses reviewed in Chapter 3 showed that crime shows generally portray police in positive terms. However, there were instances where the plot functions of police could be described as negative.[11] Images of police are multidimensional and messages transmitted by crime shows seem to reflect the many dimensions. Just what is the mainstream concerning images of police? It appears that there are several.

The fact that crime shows send conflicting messages regarding police was reflected in the findings of this chapter. In general negative images concerning police-community relations seem to be cultivated while at the same time crime shows induce perceptions of police effectiveness. Given the mixture of messages, it is not too surprising that there are large group variations in the magnitude and direction of effects. Different groups appear to attend and be cultivated by varying aspects of messages concerning police.

The relative influence of crime show viewing on images of police is indicated in Table 9.6. The beta weights in the table show that crime show viewing has a significant negative effect on police-community relations and a significant positive influence on perceptions of police effectiveness. However, the television consumption variable is not the most important influence on either perception. School grade, grade average, and family concept-orientation all have a greater impact on perceptions of police-community relations. There are three other variables that significantly influence perceptions of police effectiveness.

Table 9.6 The Relative Influence of 11 Variables on Images of Police (Beta Weights)

	Police-Community Relations	Police Effectiveness
Sex	.001	-.046
Grade in school	-.094*	-.103*
Head of household occupation	.018	.052
Grade average	.125*	.072
Reading habits	-.079	-.024
Perception of TV reality	-.026	-.119*
Family socio-orientation	-.015	.039
Family concept-orientation	.131*	.175*
Public/private school	-.074	-.001
Residence	.059	.081
TV crime show viewing	-.081*	.042*
Final *df*	(554)	(555)
	$R = .271$	$R = .283$

$*p < .05$

All in all the mixed messages concerning police transmitted by crime shows probably dilute television's influence in this case.

NOTES

1. David Easton, *A Systems Analysis of Political Life* (New York: Wiley, 1965).

2. See Fred I. Greenstein, *Children and Politics* (New Haven: Yale University Press, 1965), and David Easton and Jack Dennis, *Children and the Political System* (New York: McGraw-Hill, 1969).

3. See Scott H. Decker, "Citizen Attitudes Toward the Police: A Review of Past Findings and Suggestions for Future Policy," *Journal of Police Science and Administration* 9 (March 1981): 80-87.

4. Easton and Dennis, *Children in the Political System*.

5. John T. O'Brien, "Public Attitudes Toward Police," *Journal of Police Science and Administration* 6 (September 1978): 303-10.

6. Robert S. Alley, *Television: Ethics for Hire?* (Nashville: Abingdon Press, 1977): 108.

7. Joseph R. Dominick, "Children's Viewing of Crime Shows and Attitudes on Law Enforcement," *Journalism Quarterly* 51 (Spring 1974): 5-12.

8. Greenstein, *Children and Politics*.

9. Charles W. Thomas and Jeffrey M. Hyman, "Perceptions of Crime, Fear of Victimization, and Public Perceptions of Police Performance," *Journal of Police Science and Administration* 5 (Fall 1977): 305-17.

10. Donald Bouma, *Kids and Cops* (Grand Rapids: W. B. Erdman, 1969).

11. Linda S. Lichter and S. Robert Lichter, *Prime Time Crime* (Washington, D.C.: The Media Institute, 1983), p. 42.

10

PERCEPTIONS OF
A SCARY AND MEAN WORLD

INTRODUCTION

Beginning in 1967 with research conducted for the National Commission on the Causes and Prevention of Violence George Gerbner and his associates at the Annenberg School of Communications have each year reported on the results of a content analysis of portrayals of violence on television. Their research has consistently shown that the world of television is many times more violent than the real world. In a recent report they indicated that eight out of ten programs and six out of every ten characters are involved in violence.[1] This heavy barrage of violent programming means that " . . . by the time an American child graduates from high school he or she will have seen more than 13,000 violent deaths on television."[2]

In Chapter 3 ample evidence was provided that showed that television crime shows teach some important lessons concerning criminal victimization. Television characters have a high probability of falling victim to a violent crime. Criminal aggressors are likely to be strangers, so one lesson of crime shows is that one must always be cautious in dealing with people and always be on the lookout for threats to personal safety. There is little doubt that the television mainstream urges concern for victimization and pessimism regarding human nature.

The effects of television violence have been a subject of debate since the early 1950s. Most of the debate has centered on the fear that viewing televised violence will make people more aggressive and more likely to engage in antisocial behavior.[3] A few have argued that viewing

170

violence on television dissipates the need to be aggressive through catharsis.[4] At the very least the massive amount of evidence on the question seems to indicate that the more television people watch the more desensitized they become to aggressive behavior. While early research was dominated by concern with the antisocial effects of television, in recent years increasing attention has been given to the influence of televised violence on conceptions of social behavior.

The greatest amount of research on cultivation theory has been concerned with the hypothesis advanced by George Gerbner and his associates that the overrepresentation of violence on television leads to impressions that society is dangerous and threatening; what is cultivated is fear of victimization and distrust of fellow citizens. The research on television's influence on conceptions of social reality is becoming voluminous; a recent review by Hawkins and Pingee included 48 studies based on 24 different samples.[5] A substantial portion of the research was reported by Gerbner, his associates, and students, but there have been a number of interesting studies undertaken by other scholars that have both challenged and confirmed the basic argument.

In a long series of studies using a variety of samples, but primarily samples taken by the National Opinion Research Corporation, Gerbner and his associates have examined the cultivation of distorted perceptions of reality resulting from heavy viewing of television. A number of areas of social reality have been investigated, but there are three sets of findings that are especially relevant to the concerns of this chapter. The first has to do with television's influence on perceptions of the extent of crime and law enforcement. Gerbner and his associates have found that heavy viewers of television overestimate the amount of crime in society and the proportion of the national work force employed in law enforcement. For example, in reality about 10 percent of all crimes are violent, while on television 77 percent of all major characters who commit crimes also commit violence. When asked to indicate whether 15 percent or 25 percent of crimes are violent, survey respondents who are heavy viewers of television estimate the higher figure. A consistent finding of the research on cultivation effects indicates that heavy viewers perceive that crime is more pervasive than it is in reality.[6]

It follows that heavy viewers would demonstrate greater fear of victimization than light viewers. A second set of findings by the Gerbner group confirms this expectation. Heavy viewers are more likely than light viewers to say they are afraid to walk alone at night.[7] They are also likely to overestimate their personal probability of getting involved in violence. Research supports the view that heavy television viewers see society as threatening and victimization likely.

Finally, a set of findings has been produced that indicate that heavy viewers of television develop a pessimistic view of human nature. Those who watch a great deal of television tend to believe that people cannot be trusted, that they generally are not helpful, and that they "take advantage" given the opportunity. Gerbner and his associates have employed the same Mean World Index used in the present study to show that heavy viewing of television breeds interpersonal mistrust.[8]

A large number of studies conducted in the past decade have confirmed that television cultivates the perception that the world is scary and mean. However, cultivation analysis has not been without its critics; some negative findings have been produced. Perhaps the most important challenge has come from several researchers who argue that cultivation effects are an artifact of uncontrolled or improperly controlled third variables. In two separate critiques researchers found that the relationship between heavy viewing and television-biased conceptions of reality disappear when simultaneous controls for demographic characteristics are imposed.[9] Doob and McDonald reported that in several instances the correlation between television viewing and fear of crime is reduced to insignificance when the area in which respondents reside is controlled.[10] Others have suggested that a control for psychological withdrawal would explain cultivation effects.[11]

Both Paul Hirsh and Michael Hughes have argued that Gerbner's results could be attributed to measurement and choice of variables. Hughes analyzed several items from the NORC data sets that appear to be relevant to cultivation analysis, but have been ignored by Gerbner and his colleagues; he failed to find evidence of a cultivation effect.[12] Hirsh recoded the television consumption variable to discriminate nonviewers and extreme viewers; he found that nonviewers perceived the world as more scary than extreme viewers. Additionally, Hirsh argued that much of the non-NORC data used by Gerbner to support hypotheses concerning cultivation were derived from nonrandom surveys that lacked representativeness.[13]

Gerbner and his associates have answered most of the criticisms of their research. In their most recent reports television viewing has been treated as a continuous variable and simultaneous controls for as many as six background variables have been imposed on television viewing-perception of reality relationships.[14] The basic hypothesis that television viewing cultivates fear of crime and interpersonal mistrust has been reconfirmed in analyses of a variety of data sets including one based on a sample of children from Australia.[15] So, despite some dissent the bulk of the evidence indicates that there is a small, but reliable and consistent, relationship between heavy television viewing and perceptions of a scary world.[16]

To account for findings that cultivation effects are subject to influence by third variables, Gerbner and his associates developed the concepts of "mainstreaming" and "resonance." Mainstreaming has been discussed at length in earlier chapters. It is offered as an explanation for findings that indicate that groups who hold views that are deviant from the mainstream are more likely to be influenced by television viewing than those who are predisposed to hold a television viewpoint. The refinement of the cultivation hypothesis termed "resonance" asserts that television may be most influential in groups where real-life situations parallel situations portrayed on television. Resonance may account for the finding by Doob and McDonald that television viewing produced greater fear of victimization among respondents who lived in high-crime neighborhoods.[17] Those who live in high-crime neighborhoods and are heavy viewers of television may get a "double dose" of messages that produce fear of victimization.

Most of the studies concerned with television's cultivation of fear of victimization and interpersonal mistrust have used some measure of the overall quantity of television viewed as the independent variable. There is, however, some evidence that the types of programs viewed differentially influence the perceptions of a scary and mean world. In their study of Australian school children Hawkins and Pingee found that heavy viewing of crime adventures was most strongly associated with perceptions of a Mean World and Violence in Society. No other program types were correlated significantly with perceptions of a Mean World. Viewing television news was unrelated to both dependent variables.[18] In the present study the cultivation hypothesis predicts that crime show viewing is positively associated with Fear of Crime and perceptions of a Mean World. The statistics necessary to test these hypotheses can be found in Table 10.1

The regression coefficients in Table 10.1 show that crime show viewing does in fact cultivate fear of crime and interpersonal mistrust. The relationships survive controls for ten variables, providing strong support for findings reported by Gerbner and his associates. The control for grade in school reduces the size of the partial regression coefficients for both dependent variables, but they still differ significantly from zero. The correlation for Fear of Crime ($r = .12$) and Perception

Table 10.1 The Effects of Crime Show Viewing on Fear of Crime and Perceptions of a Mean World by Selected Control Variables

	Fear of Crime	Mean World
Uncontrolled	.551[a]	.126
	(.023)[b]	(.005)
Controlling for:		
Sex	.947	.135
	(.022)	(.005)
Grade in school	.425	.107
	(.024)	(.005)
Head of household occupation	.555	.126
	(.023)	(.005)
Grade average	.543	.128
	(.023)	(.005)
Reading habits	.532	.123
	(.023)	(.005)
Perception of TV reality	.463	.131
	(.023)	(.005)
Family socio-orientation	.508	.120
	(.023)	(.005)
Family concept-orientation	.563	.125
	(.023)	(.005)
School (public/private)	.556	.126
	(.023)	(.005)
Residence (urban/suburban)	.552	.134
	(.023)	(.005)
All controls	.793	.120
	(.024)	(.005)
Final *df*	(554)	(554)

[a] regression coefficients

[b] Standard errors of regression coefficients. If the regression coefficients are at least twice their standard errors, they are significantly different from zero.

of a Mean World ($r = .11$) are small, but persistent, which is consistent with previous findings.

When the Index of Crime Show Viewing is trichotomized and distributions for items included in the Fear of Crime and Mean World measures examined, some interesting patterns are revealed.* Hawkins and Pingee suggested that heavy television viewing may lead to the percep-

---

*The three categories for crime show viewing are low (16-24), medium (25-32), and high (33-57).

tion that crime is a problem, but not necessarily to a concern for personal safety.[19] The data from this study indicate that this is not the case; about 30 percent of heavy viewers compared to about 15 percent of light viewers agreed that, "Crime is such a problem that this city is not a safe place to raise children." About 40 percent of the heavy viewers compared to 31 percent of light viewers indicated concern for their personal safety by agreeing that, "Crime is such a problem that I am afraid to go out alone at night." Clearly heavy viewing is associated with a perception that crime is a major problem *and* a concern for personal safety.

The greatest difference between light and heavy viewers of crime shows on the Mean World items occurs on the one dealing with trust in people; 64 percent of the heavy viewers compared to about 52 percent of the light viewers felt that, "Generally speaking . . . you can't be too careful in dealing with people." Contrary to findings reported by Gerbner and his associates equal proportions (about 45 percent) of heavy and light viewers felt that, " . . . most people would take advantage of you if they get the chance."[20]

With respect to fear of crime and interpersonal mistrust the data set examined in this study provides strong support for the cultivation hypothesis; the violent content of crime shows appears to cultivate a distorted view of reality. The mainstreaming hypothesis predicts that certain groups are most likely to be influenced by crime shows, and it is subgroup differences in cultivation that receive attention next.

INDIVIDUAL CHARACTERISTICS AND CULTIVATION OF PERCEPTIONS OF A SCARY WORLD

Like the television mainstream, the mainstream of the sample of adolescents analyzed in this study reflects fear of victimization and interpersonal mistrust. In Chapter 4 it was shown that few disagreed that crime is a major concern and that caution is necessary to avoid criminal victimization. A majority of the student sample indicated pessimism concerning human nature on all three items included in the Mean World Index. It is clear that respondents who exhibit relatively low levels of fear of crime and relatively high levels of interpersonal trust have views that are outside of the mainstream.

In Chapter 5 demographic characteristics were associated with Fear of Crime and perceptions of a Mean World in order to determine which groups have views that are outside of the mainstream. On the Fear of Crime scale males and students in the higher grades (9th to 12th) exhibited less fear than females and younger respondents. Students from middle class homes exhibited a relatively high degree of interpersonal trust.

In recent reports Gerbner and his associates have given attention to the influence of television on fear and mistrust in various demographic groups. The evidence for mainstreaming of fear of victimization and perceptions of a Mean World has not always been consistent. For example, in their 1978 report Gerbner and his associates reported that male school children were more likely than females to be cultivated to fear of walking alone at night.[21] In the 1979 report females exhibited greater cultivation effects.[22] Yet in the 1980 report the fact that females who were heavy viewers said that "fear of crime is a very serious problem" was offered as evidence of resonance.[23] While fear may be most salient to female respondents, males exhibit less fear and are candidates for mainstreaming.

Older students exhibit lower levels of fear of crime in Chapter 5; the mainstreaming hypothesis indicates that they would be most influenced by the messages of crime shows. The 1978 report by Gerbner and his associates indicates that older students who are heavy television viewers are most likely to agree that they are "afraid to walk alone at night."[24] However, the 1979 report shows that students in the lower grades are most likely to respond to the scary aspects of television.[25] The same pattern of inconsistent results has been reported with respect to interpersonal trust. In the 1979 report by Gerbner and his associates heavy viewing was associated with saying, "you must be careful in dealing with people" among seventh graders, but not eighth graders. The opposite results were obtained for the Mean World item dealing with the helpfulness of people.[26] Hawkins and Pingee reported that television viewing was strongly associated with perception of a Mean World among students in higher grades, but not lower grades.[27] The mainstream hypothesis predicts that students in the higher grades are most likely to be "cultivated" with regard to Fear of Crime.

Gerbner and his associates have found that high-status individuals are most likely to hold views that are outside of the mainstream. This finding is confirmed in the present study with respect to perceptions of a Mean World; statistics presented in Chapter 5 show that students from middle class homes display relatively high levels of interpersonal trust. It would appear that high-status individuals are likely to hold views outside of the mainstream, but in several studies reported by Gerbner and his associates the cultivation effect with regard to fear of walking alone at night is greatest in low-status groups. Hawkins and Pingee found that social class has no effect on cultivation of perceptions of a Mean World.[28] In a more recent report Gerbner and his

Table 10.2 The Effects of Crime Show Viewing on Fear of Crime and Perceptions of a Mean World in Subgroups Defined by Demographic Characteristics

	Fear of Crime		Mean World	
Uncontrolled	.551[a]		.126	
	(.023)[b]		(.005)	
Sex				
Male	.707		.194	
	(.029)	$p < .05$[c]	(.007)	p = ns
Female	.134		.606	
	(.034)		(.008)	
Grade in School				
Lower grades (6th-8th)	-.109		-.239	
	(.030)	$p < .01$	(.006)	$p < .05$
Higher grades (9th-12th)	.162		.237	
	(.039)		(.008)	
Head of Household Occupation				
Blue-collar	.981		.121	
	(.037)	$p < .05$	(.007)	p = ns
White-collar	.515		.129	
	(.031)		(.006)	

[a] regression coefficients
[b] Standard errors of regression coefficients. If the regression coefficients are at least twice their standard errors, they are significantly different from zero.
[c] F-tests for differences between regression coefficients.
ns = not significant

associates offered as evidence for mainstreaming the finding that heavy television viewing is most strongly associated with saying "fear of crime is a very serious personal problem" among high- and medium-income respondents.[29] The prevailing evidence leads to the hypothesis that heavy television viewing is most likely to cultivate fear of crime and perceptions of a Mean World among higher status respondents, who are outside of the mainstream. The statistics necessary to determine the mitigating influence of individual demographic characteristics on the cultivation of fear of crime and interpersonal mistrust are found in Table 10.2.

The regression coefficients in Table 10.2 provide some strong support for the cultivation and mainstreaming hypotheses. Male students, who are inclined to be less fearful of crime than females, become more fearful as a result of heavy crime show viewing. Sex does not significantly mitigate the relationship between crime show viewing and perceptions of a Mean World. However, the coefficient for females is substantially larger indicating that they are most likely to be cultivated to feel interpersonal mistrust. This result is consistent with findings reported by Gerbner in 1979.[30]

The regression coefficients for the two grade levels also provide support for the mainstream hypothesis; students in the higher grades are significantly more likely to be mainstreamed with respect to fear of crime and interpersonal mistrust. As students mature they become less anxious about crime and victimization, but heavy crime show viewing appears to retard this process. The interesting finding with respect to grade in school is that there are negative relationships for students in the lower grades between crime show viewing and perceptions of a mean and scary world. How does crime show viewing reduce fear and increase interpersonal trust in this group? A possible explanation has been suggested by some recent research; Wakshlag, Vial, and Tamborini suggest that the fact that "justice is served" in most crime shows may provide some reassurance regarding the probability of victimization.[31]

Contrary to expectations, students from working-class homes are more likely to be cultivated with respect to Fear of Crime than those from middle class families. Head of household occupation does not mitigate the relationship with interpersonal trust. This finding may be consistent with the idea of resonance; students from working-class families may live in high-crime neighborhoods and receive a "double dose" of fear by heavy viewing of crime shows. Generally the figures in Table 10.2 provide support for the mainstream hypothesis.

Gerbner and others have examined cultivation of fear of crime and interpersonal mistrust in subgroups defined by individual characteristics related to information-processing abilities, but have not related their analyses to the mainstreaming hypothesis. Cultivation of "fear of walking alone at night" was greatest among school children with low school achievement and those who did not regularly read a newspaper in a New Jersey sample examined by Gerbner and his associates.[32] However, regular readers of newspapers who were heavy television viewers were most likely to say that "you can't be too careful in dealing with people." In their study of Australian school children Hawkins and Pingee found cultivation effects greatest among children who had not had a course on mass media and among those who did not perceive that television reflects reality.[33] It appears that crime show viewing may cultivate fear and interpersonal mistrust among those respondents

Table 10.3 The Effects of Crime Show Viewing on Fear of Crime and Perceptions of a Mean World in Subgroups Defined by Individual Characteristics Related to Information Processing

	Fear of Crime		Mean World	
Uncontrolled	.551[a]		.126	
	(.023)[b]		(.005)	
Grade Average				
Mostly C's or lower	.324		.335	
	(.044)	p = ns[c]	(.010)	p = ns
Mostly A's and B's	.629		.158	
	(.026)		(.006)	
Reading Habits				
Light reader	.797		.103	
	(.031)	p = ns	(.007)	p = ns
Heavy reader	.394		.143	
	(.033)		(.007)	
Perceptions of TV Reality				
Low	.651		.201	
	(.033)	$p < .05$	(.007)	p = ns
High	.644		.594	
	(.033)		(.007)	

[a] regression coefficients
[b] Standard errors of regression coefficients. If the regression coefficients are at least twice their standard errors, they are significantly different from zero.
[c] F-tests for differences between regression coefficients.
ns = not significant

who are not cognitively sophisticated and those who are not "involved" in the content of crime dramas. In Chapter 5 the group that feels television is unreal was shown to have relatively low levels of fear of crime. Of all the groups defined by information-processing abilities, it is the "low TV reality" group that is predicted to be most influenced by heavy crime show viewing. Table 10.3 contains the statistics necessary to determine the mitigating effects of information-processing variables.

In only one instance in Table 10.3 is there evidence that information-processing variables significantly mitigate the cultivation of fear of crime or interpersonal mistrust. As expected, students who perceive that television does not reflect reality are significantly more likely to indicate a fear of crime as a result of heavy viewing of crime shows; the differences between the regression coefficients for the two TV reality groups is small, but statistically significant. This finding is consistent with the argument that cultivation is most likely when involvement in television content is low.

There are some other sizable intergroup differences in cultivation in the table, but none are statistically significant. It appears that students with relatively high grades are more likely to come to fear crime as a result of heavy viewing. The same appears to be true of light readers. The only large difference in cultivation of perception of a Mean World is between TV reality groups; the regression coefficient is larger for the group that believes that television reflects reality. For the most part the statistics in Table 10.3 are inconsistent with those reported by George Gerbner and his associates concerning similar variables. However, the relationship between crime show viewing and perceptions of a scary and mean world survives controls for individual characteristics; the cultivation hypothesis receives general support.

FAMILY COMMUNICATION PATTERNS
AND THE CULTIVATION OF FEAR AND MISTRUST

Family characteristics have been related to fear and interpersonal mistrust in the literature on socialization.[34] Families who are overprotective tend to transmit the message that there is something to fear outside of the family. Consequently, children from overprotective families are often anxious about threats from their social environment. If previous findings are a guide then it is reasonable to expect that adolescents from highly socio-oriented families will be fearful of crime and exhibit low levels of interpersonal trust. The statistics reported in Chapter 5 showed that there is in fact a tendency for socio-oriented families to produce offspring who fear crime and are pessimistic about human nature, but differences are not significant.

It might be argued that families who are open and encourage the use of a variety of sources of information will produce offspring who are confident and less anxious about their environment. Students from high concept-oriented families may also be in possession of information that competes with messages transmitted by television concerning the frequency of crime and the trustworthiness of people. In Chapter 5 it was reported that students from concept-oriented families tend to be more trustful of people than students from families where information seeking is not encouraged. With respect to perceptions of a Mean World, television viewing should be most influential among concept-oriented families. The statistics necessary to examine the miti-

Table 10.4 The Effects of Crime Show Viewing on Fear of Crime and Perceptions of a Mean World in Subgroups Defined by Family Communication Characteristics

	Fear of Crime		Mean World	
Uncontrolled	.551[a]		.126	
	(.023)[b]		(.005)	
Family Socio-orientation				
Low	.177		.213	
	(.040)	$p < .001$[c]	(.008)	p = ns
High	-.380		.710	
	(.028)		(.006)	
Family Concept-orientation				
Low	.856		.180	
	(.034)	p = ns	(.007)	p = ns
High	.291		.824	
	(.031)		(.007)	

[a] regression coefficients
[b] Standard errors of regression coefficients. If the regression coefficients are at least twice their standard errors, they are significantly different from zero.
[c] F-tests for differences between regression coefficients.
ns = not significant

gating effects of family communication patterns on the relationships of interest in this chapter are in Table 10.4

The regression coefficients in Table 10.4 provide support for the cultivation hypothesis; regardless of the structure of family communications, crime show viewing significantly influences fear of crime and perceptions of a Mean World. However, there is only one instance in the table where family structure significantly mitigates the original relationship. For students from highly socio-oriented homes crime show viewing appears to reduce fear of crime. It was suggested earlier that highly structured or protective families may produce offspring who fear the world outside of the family. It may be the case that the fact that "crime does not pay" in crime shows may be reassuring to this group. Students from families who are not overly protective are not predisposed to fear the social environment and are therefore more influenced by crime shows.

Family characteristics do not significantly mitigate any of the other relationships in the table, but there are some large differences between regression coefficients. It appears that adolescents from highly socio-oriented families are more likely to accept the messages of crime shows concerning interpersonal mistrust. This finding appears to be inconsistent with the one concerning fear of crime, but it is important to point out that fear of crime and perceptions of a Mean World are conceptually distinct. It is quite possible that students who watch crime shows could have some of their fears concerning victimization reduced and still come to hold a pessimistic view regarding human nature. After all, it is usually law enforcers who solve crimes on television while "citizens" are often uncooperative with television police.

The statistics concerning concept-orientation also seem contradictory. Students from low concept-oriented homes are most likely to be cultivated to interpersonal mistrust. The findings with respect to mistrust are consistent with the mainstream hypothesis; products of high-concept families are predisposed to be trustful and are therefore most likely to be mainstreamed by crime show viewing. Students from homes that are low in concept-orientation are most likely to come to fear victimization as a result of viewing crime shows. It is this group that is least likely to have access to a variety of sources of information concerning the extent of crime. Lacking alternative sources of information it makes sense that this group is most influenced by crime shows.

In summary, it appears that family characteristics have little significant influence on the cultivation of fear of crime and interpersonal mistrust. There is no statistically significant support for the mainstreaming hypothesis in Table 10.4.

CONTEXTUAL FACTORS AND THE CULTIVATION OF FEAR OF CRIME AND INTERPERSONAL MISTRUST

In recent years a great deal of attention has been given to the mitigating effects of contextual factors on the influence of television viewing. The attention can be partially attributed to the finding by Doob and McDonald that controls for crime rate and place of residence explain the television viewing-fear of crime relationship. Their findings showed that television viewing was correlated with fear of crime only among residents of urban high-crime neighborhoods.[35] Gerbner and his associates report similar findings—cultivation of fear of crime is greatest among urban dwellers—and have argued that they provide evidence of resonance. City dwellers who are heavy viewers receive a double dose of fear-producing stimuli and show stronger correlations between viewing and fear of victimization.[36] In the present study the statistics reported in Chapter 5 did not indicate that urban dwellers have a greater fear of crime or interpersonal mistrust. Still, previous research would seem to indicate that crime show viewing would be most influential among urban dwellers.

There is no previous research dealing with the possible effects of attending a private or a public school on the cultivation of fear of crime or interpersonal mistrust. However, it can probably be assumed that one reason parents send their children to private schools is fear for their safety. Private schools are noted for their discipline and their exclusion of students who "cause trouble." It is possible that private school students are "protected" and their protection justified in terms of perceived threats from the social environment. If that is the case, then private school students should exhibit greater fear of crime than public school students. Statistics reported in Chapter 5 showed that, though the relationship is in the expected direction, there are no significant differences between private and public school students with respect to fear of crime. Private school students are slightly more trusting of people than public school students, but the differences are not significant. If private school students are overprotected and fearful, then the mainstreaming hypothesis predicts that public school students would most likely be cultivated to fear crime. It may also be the case that the protective environment of a private school generates interpersonal trust. If that is true, then private school students may be the most susceptible to television's messages regarding trust in people. The statistics necessary to examine the mitigating effects of contextual factors are in Table 10.5.

The regression coefficients in Table 10.5 provide additional support for the cultivation hypothesis; regardless of the control, crime show viewing has a significant influence on fear of crime and perceptions of a Mean World. As in the previous section, there is one instance where crime show viewing appears to reduce fear of crime; among private school students it may be the case that crime show viewing leads to reassurance that criminal victimization is not a threat. Public school students are mainstreamed. While the difference is not significant, the regression coefficient for private school students indicates that they are most likely to exhibit interpersonal mistrust as a result of watching crime shows. If private school students are protected on a day-to-day basis from people who would take advantage of them, then they may be most responsive to television's messages regarding interpersonal trust.

Table 10.5 The Effects of Crime Show Viewing on Fear of Crime and Perceptions of a Mean World by Contextual Factors

	Fear of Crime		Mean World	
Uncontrolled	.551[a]		.126	
	(.023)[b]		(.005)	
School Attended				
Public	.199		.171	
	(.035)	$p < .001$[c]	(.007)	$p = $ ns
Private	-.317		.952	
	(.030)		(.006)	
Place of Residence				
Urban	.274		.926	
	(.029)	$p < .01$	(.007)	$p = $ ns
Suburban	.147		.188	
	(.037)		(.008)	

[a] regression coefficients

[b] Standard errors of regression coefficients. If the regression coefficients are at least twice their standard errors, they are significantly different from zero.

[c] F-tests for differences between regression coefficients.

ns = not significant

The statistics regarding place of residence are consistent with earlier findings. Urban residents are significantly more likely to resonate to television crime show messages concerning victimization. The size of the regression coefficient for Mean World perception among urban dwellers indicates that Gerbner's argument concerning resonance is plausible.

To summarize, cultivation of fear of crime and perceptions of a Mean World takes place in three of four groups defined by contextual variables. Only among private school students does the relationship run in the opposite direction. There is some support in the data for Gerbner's argument that urban dwellers resonate to television's messages concerning fear of crime and interpersonal mistrust.

CONCLUSION

There is strong support in this chapter for the general hypothesis that crime show viewing cultivates a perception of a scary and mean world. For the most part findings were consistent with previous research. However, in several groups viewing crime shows seemed to

Table 10.6 The Relative Influence of 11 Variables on Fear of Crime and Perceptions of a Mean World (Beta Weights)

	Fear of Crime	Mean World
Sex	.319*	-.027*
Grade in school	-.026	-.047*
Head of household occupation	-.033	.001
Grade average	.039	.060*
Reading habits	.053	.068
Perception of TV reality	-.108	.056*
Family socio-orientation	.039	.046*
Family concept-orientation	.061	-.022*
Public/private school	.067	-.016
Residence	-.030	.056*
TV crime show viewing	.144*	.106*
Final *df*	(554)	(554)
	$R = .350$	$R = .169$

*$p < .05$

reduce fear of crime. It is possible that the message that "criminals always get caught" serves to reduce apprehension and anxiety in some groups. There is some evidence that those who fear crime seek out programming where criminals are caught and punished.

The standardized regression coefficients displayed in Table 10.6 show that of 11 variables offered as explanations of interpersonal mistrust crime show viewing has the greatest influence. The "cognitive" variables, grade average and reading habits, are second and third in importance. Only sex has more influence on fear of crime than crime show viewing. All in all the findings of this chapter strongly confirm the results reported in the series of articles by Gerbner and his colleagues.

NOTES

1. George Gerbner et al., "The Demonstration of Power: Violence Profile No. 10," *Journal of Communication* 29 (Spring 1979): 177-96.

2. Ibid., p. 178.

3. For a good review of the debate see Robert M. Liebert, Joyce N. Sprafkin, and Emily S. Davidson, *The Early Window: Effects of Television on Children and Youth* (New York: Pergamon Press, 1982).

4. L. Rowell Huesmann, "Television Violence and Aggressive Behavior" in *Television and Behavior: Ten Years of Scientific Progress and Implications for*

the Eighties, vol. 2 of *Technical Reviews*, ed. David Pearl, Lorraine Bouthilet, and Joyce Lazar (Washington, D.C.: National Institute of Mental Health, 1982).

5. Robert P. Hawkins and Suzanne Pingee, "Television's Influence on Social Reality," in *Television and Behavior: Ten Years of Scientific Progress and Implications for the Eighties*, vol. 2 of *Technical Reviews*, ed. David Pearl, Lorraine Bouthilet, and Joyce Lazar (Washington, D.C.: National Institute of Mental Health, 1982).

6. George Gerbner et al., "TV Violence Profile No. 8: The Highlights," *Journal of Communication* 27 (Spring 1977): 171-80.

7. George Gerbner et al., "Cultural Indicators: Violence Profile No. 9," *Journal of Communication* 28 (Summer 1978): 176-207.

8. Gerbner et al., "TV Violence Profile No. 8"; Gerbner et al., "The Demonstration of Power."

9. See Paul M. Hirsh, "The 'Scary World' of the Nonviewer and Other Anomalies," *Communication Research* 7 (October 1980): 403-56; Michael Hughes, "The Fruits of Cultivation Analysis: A Reexamination of Some Effects of Television Watching," *Public Opinion Quarterly* 44 (Spring 1980): 287-302.

10. Anthony N. Doob and Glenn E. McDonald, "Television and Fear of Victimization: Is the Relationship Causal?" *Journal of Personality and Social Psychology* 37 (1979): 170-79.

11. Thomas D. Cook, Deborah A. Kendzierski, and Stephen Thomas, "The Implicit Assumptions of Television Research: An Analysis of the 1982 NIMH Report on Television and Behavior," *Public Opinion Quarterly* 44 (Spring 1983): 161-201.

12. Hughes, "The Fruits of Cultivation Analysis."

13. Hirsh, "The Scary World."

14. George Gerbner, Larry Gross, Michael Morgan, and Nancy Signorielli, "The 'Mainstreaming' of America: Violence Profile 11," *Journal of Communication* 30 (Summer 1980): 10-29.

15. Robert P. Hawkins and Suzanne Pingee, "Some Processes in the Cultivation Effect," *Communication Research* 7 (April 1980): 193-226.

16. For a thorough review see Hawkins and Pingee, "Television's Influence on Social Reality."

17. Doob and McDonald, "Television and Fear of Victimization."

18. Hawkins and Pingee, "Some Processes in Cultivation Effect."

19. Hawkins and Pingee, "Television's Influence on Social Reality."

20. Gerbner et al., "TV Violence Profile No. 8."

21. Gerbner et al., "Cultural Indicators."

22. Gerbner et al., "The Demonstration of Power."

23. Gerbner et al., "The 'Mainstreaming' of America."

24. Gerbner et al., "Cultural Indicators."

25. Gerbner et al., "The Demonstration of Power."

26. Ibid.

27. Hawkins and Pingee, "Some Processes in Cultivation Effects."

28. Ibid.

29. Gerbner et al., "The 'Mainstreaming' of America."

30. Gerbner et al., "The Demonstration of Power."

31. Jacob Wakshlag, Virginia Vial, and Ronald Tamborini, "Selecting Crime Show Drama and Apprehension About Crime," *Human Communication Research* 10 (Winter 1983): 227-42.

32. Gerbner et al., "The Demonstration of Power," p. 191.

33. Hawkins and Pingee, "Some Processes in Cultivation Effects," p. 211.

34. Frank A. Pinner, "Parental Overprotection and Political Distrust," *The Annals* 361 (September 1965): 58-70.

35. Doob and McDonald, "Television and Fear of Victimization," p. 177.

36. Gerbner et al., "The 'Mainstreaming' of America," p. 15.

II

SUMMARY AND CONCLUSIONS

The previous chapters have provided a great deal of information about the influence of television entertainment on attitudes that are relevant to social control and the stability of the political system. I believe that the significance of this book lies in its emphasis on entertainment programming, as opposed to news programming, and its consequences for political socialization. The mass media have been largely ignored in research on political socialization, but in recent years increasing attention has been given to the possible effects of news programming on political information acquisition, political attitudes, and electoral behavior. The "limited effects" explanation of media influence is being revised and this book represents a natural extension of research in this area to a concern with entertainment programming and pre-adults.

The research reported in earlier chapters benefited from theoretical formulations developed by George Gerbner and his associates at the Annenberg School. It goes without saying that other theories might have been utilized. However, at the present time cultivation theory is the most promising available for helping us understand the complexities of television's influence on social attitudes. The analysis reported in this study could have included a wider variety of variables and more extensive statistical controls for third variables, but despite obvious limitations, in my judgment the most important variables have been included and controls were adequate. In this final chapter I summarize the major findings of the study, discuss linkages between system-relevant variables, and suggest some implications of the research.

SUMMARY OF FINDINGS: CULTIVATION

Cultivation analysis required an analysis of the content of television crime shows to determine whether or not they reflect the real world of crime and law enforcement. A review of a number of studies revealed that crime shows are highly unrealistic. Television unreality is reflected in the perceptions of crime and law enforcement of heavy crime show viewers. A brief review of the most important findings concerning cultivation of a television point of view gives us the following observations.

First, television crime shows omit a great deal of information about criminal legal processes. What information is presented is often distorted or simply incorrect. The poor information level of crime shows is reflected in information holding by heavy viewers; adolescents who are heavy viewers of crime shows compared to light viewers actually have lower scores on the scale that measures knowledge of criminal justice processes. Crime shows do not "teach" adolescents about the legal system and their constitutional rights.

Second, crime shows are morality plays that transmit the simple message that legal compliance is an important norm and that violations of the law are always punished. On crime shows there are never any mitigating circumstances that might justify illegal behavior. Not surprisingly, heavy viewers of crime shows are disposed to support the legal system; they value the norm of compliance to a greater degree than light viewers. Furthermore, heavy viewers tend to exhibit preconventional or conventional thinking when responding to open-ended questions concerning legal compliance. Critics of television crime shows have expressed concern that heavy viewing might produce antisocial behavior. The evidence presented in this book suggests that the opposite may be the case; heavy crime show viewing promotes conventionality and social control.

Third, a review of content analyses of crime shows revealed that the constitutional rights of criminal suspects were seldom treated with sympathy. In most cases civil liberties are treated as "technicalities" that hinder the apprehension, conviction, and punishment of truly nasty criminals. Television police often complain about the constraints placed on law enforcement by the Constitution. Analysis of the survey data revealed that heavy crime show viewers are likely to hold a "crime control," as opposed to a "due process," point of view concerning law enforcement. Television crime shows contribute little to the support for procedural guarantees. In fact, crime shows appear to promote antiheterodoxy—the desire to punish those who deviate from accepted norms.

Fourth, the images of police projected by crime shows are multifarious. To be sure, television police are much more effective than in reality; TV criminals rarely get away. However, detective shows in particular often portray police as incompetent, dishonest, or misdirected. Almost all shows portray police as more violent than they are in reality. While the evidence indicates that crime shows for the most part project positive images of police, it is possible to see how attention to some programs might produce an emphasis on negative traits. The cultivation analysis undertaken earlier showed that heavy crime show viewing has a varying influence on police images. Heavy viewers, compared to light viewers, tend to see police as very effective. However, crime show viewing seems to cultivate the perception of some negative traits of law enforcers; heavy viewers are most likely to see police as stupid and too willing to use violence. The cultivation of police effectiveness is probably most important; social control requires that police are seen as effective, but does not require that they are liked.

Finally, the television world is a dangerous place where every citizen must use caution to avoid becoming a victim of a terrible crime. Numerous content analyses have confirmed that violence is overrepresented on television. Most studies of cultivation theory have given attention to television's influence on perceptions of a scary world. The basic findings of earlier studies were confirmed in this book; heavy viewers of crime shows exhibit an exaggerated fear of victimization and a perception that people cannot be trusted. The influence of television viewing on the widely used Mean World Index, while statistically significant, is not as strong in this study as in those reported by Gerbner and his associates. A long series of reports including the present one instills confidence in the conclusion that crime show viewing is associated with fear of victimization.

In general cultivation theory received strong support in the previous chapters. In all but a very few instances the measures of association between television consumption and the dependent variables examined were statistically significant. Crime show viewing has a small, but remarkably persistent influence on perceptions of crime and the legal system.

SUMMARY OF FINDINGS: MAINSTREAMING

The concept of mainstreaming, introduced by Gerbner and his associates, would appear to offer a very promising theoretical explanation for subgroup variations in cultivation. In this book an attempt was made to examine the theoretical construct within a hypothesis testing framework. An examination based on several categories of variables identified subgroups that appeared to hold views outside of the television and public opinion mainstream. Once identified, it was possible to determine whether these "deviant" groups were significantly more likely to come to share television's view of society as a result of heavy crime show viewing.

The results with regard to mainstreaming were disappointing. There were 39 instances where a group was identified as holding nonmainstream views on one of the eight dependent variables. In only 12 cases (30.8 percent) was there statistically supported evidence of mainstreaming. In many instances differences between groups in cultivation effect ran in the opposite direction predicted.

When individual groups were examined to determine whether there are any that are especially susceptible to cultivation only one interesting pattern emerged. On six of the eight dependent variables examined adolescents from families where the head of the household had a blue-collar occupation were significantly more likely to be cultivated to a television viewpoint. This finding is remarkable in light of the fact that blue-collar adolescents were well within the mainstream on all eight dependent measures. This would seem to be evidence in support of the argument that crime show viewing reinforces support for the status quo.

Heavy crime show viewing obviously does not have the same influence on all groups. More attention needs to be given to the development of theoretical explanations for conditional relationships. The concepts of mainstreaming, and perhaps resonance, may still be of some utility. However, as Cook, Kendzierski, and Thomas point out, "Until there is an exact theoretical analysis of the conditions under which mainstreaming and resonance occur, it will not be possible to falsify either construct."[1]

THE SPILLOVER HYPOTHESIS

In previous chapters attention was given to the influence of crime show viewing on variables concerning the criminal justice system. Each of the variables can be seen as indicators of orientations toward levels of the political system; fear of crime and perceptions of a mean world may tell us something about political community, perceptions of police about authority, and attitudes concerning compliance and civil liberties about the constitutional regime. The literature on political socialization leads to a theoretical expectation that there is a developmental sequence among orientations toward the political system. The most common assertion is that orientations toward political authorities tend to "spillover" and influence orientations toward the political regime.[2] Orientations toward police have been found to be associated with the disposition to comply with the law and with a generalized sense of political trust.[3] If that is the case, then it is possible that crime show viewing influences support for the legal system, support for civil liberties, and political cynicism (all measures of regime orientations) indirectly. By extrapolation of earlier findings it is reasonable to expect that orientations toward the community, measured in terms of fear of crime and perceptions of a mean world, might also influence regime orientations.

To test for the possibility of a developmental sequence between variables, a series of three variable models was constructed. The dependent or endogenous variables in the models included the scales that measure support for the legal system and support for civil liberties. In addition the Political Cynicism Scale described in Chapter 2 is included as an indicator of overall affect for the political system. The Index of Crime Show Viewing is the independent variable in the models. Measures of fear of crime, perception of a mean world, perception of police effectiveness, and perception of police-community relations are intervening variables. The variables combine to form twelve different three-variable models that can be examined to test the spillover hypothesis. For example, the spillover hypothesis predicts that heavy crime show viewing influences perceptions of police effectiveness, which in turn influences support for the legal system.

The test of the hypothesis that there is a developmental sequence involves two steps.[4] First, the relationships between intervening variables and the dependent variables or endogenous variables in the models are examined and controls for crime show viewing are imposed. This establishes the presence of a "spillover" and provides a test for spuriousness. The statistics necessary to determine whether orientations toward authorities and community influence regime orientations are in Table 11.1.

The figures in Table 11.1 are simple and partial unstandardized regression coefficients. In general there is strong support in the table for the spillover hypothesis. Fear of crime is negatively associated with political cynicism and support for civil liberties, and positively associated with support for the legal system. Perceptions of a mean world are not significantly associated with the regime orientation variables.

Table 11.1 Regression Coefficients: Authority and Community Variables with Regime Variables by Crime Show Viewing

Dependent Variable	Fear of Crime	Mean World	Police-Community Relations	Police Effectiveness
Political Cynicism				
Simple *b*	-.214*	.196	-.128*	-.219*
Partial *b*	-.230*	.204	-.129*	-.219*
Support for Civil Liberties				
Simple *b*	-.249*	-.171	-.134*	-.214*
Partial *b*	-.232*	-.175	-.230*	-.196*
Support for the Legal System				
Simple *b*	.316*	-.420	.293*	.533*
Partial *b*	.307*	-.494	.302*	.522*

*$p < .05$

Both measures of police image are negatively associated with political cynicism and support for civil liberties, while they are positively related to support for the legal system. Political cynicism can be viewed as a reverse indicator of political trust. That being the case, it is interesting to note that those who fear victimization the most are most supportive of the political system and least supportive of constitutional rights for those accused of crimes. Support for police also leads to support for the political system, but not civil liberties. The second step in the test for developmental sequence involves the examination of relationships between crime show viewing and the regime orientations, controlling for authority and community orientations. The statistics necessary for the second step are in Table 11.2.

The partial regression coefficients in Table 11.2 provide little support for a pure developmental sequence between variables. A hybrid model seems most appropriate. Regardless of the control the influence of crime show viewing remains significant. The figures suggest that there may be a developmental sequence in three models. It appears that crime show viewing may cultivate perceptions of a mean world, and that those who perceive the world as "mean" may oppose extension of civil liberties to those accused of crimes. Perceptions of police-community relations intervene between crime show viewing and political cynicism and support for civil liberties. The indirect effect of crime

Table 11.2 Regression Coefficients: Television Crime Show Viewing with Regime Variables by Authority and Community Variables

Dependent Variable	Controlling for				
	Crime Show Viewing	Fear of Crime	Mean World	Police-Community Relations	Police Effectiveness
Political Cynicism	-.651*	-.784*	-.874*	-.118*	-.587*
Support for Civil Liberties	-.958*	-.864*	-.101*	-.100*	-.930*
Support for the Legal System	.687*	.543*	.714*	.801*	.543*

*p < .05

show viewing in these instances is to increase cynicism and support for civil liberties. However, the direct effects are much stronger.

To summarize, the spillover hypothesis receives support from the data analyzed in this study, but there is little evidence of a developmental sequence. Crime show viewing, authority orientations, and community orientations all have largely independent effects on regime orientations. In each instance the relationship is in a direction that serves to affirm the legitimacy of the political regime.

IMPLICATIONS

Despite the complaints of parents, educators, the PTA, and television critics that the violence on television contributes to aggressiveness and antisocial behavior, this study supports the conclusion drawn by Gerbner and Gross that, "Instead of threatening the social order television may have become our chief intrument of social control."[5] The most important impact of television may be its role in the socialization of acceptance of the legitimacy of the American political system.

Some more specific implications are suggested by the conclusion that crime show viewing promotes anxiety about victimization, ignorance of the procedural guarantees found in the Constitution, and rigid adherence to the dictates of authority. Most theories of democracy emphasize the need for an informed, tolerant citizenry that is willing to question authority. Crime shows, it appears, contribute little to the socialization of support for the democratic creed. In fact an argument can be made that heavy viewers are most likely to support an increase in repressive behavior on the part of police. Despite the fact that television criminals are not distinctive in terms of population groups, heavy crime show viewing likely promotes acceptance of punishment of groups that are outside of the mainstream and are associated with crime in the public mind; what is promoted is intolerance rather than tolerance of outgroups.

The messages transmitted by crime shows may have important implications for the operation of the criminal justice system. Because of increased fear of victimization there may be an increase in demand for police protection. Since television police are portrayed as being particularly effective the public may develop unrealistic expectations concerning police performance. The combination of increased demand for protection and the perceived "inability" of police to deal with the problem of crime may lead to a deterioration of police-community relations.

Several commentators have suggested that crime shows could influence the behavior of juries. Jurors who watch a great deal of television may be more likely to presume that defendants are guilty and their assessment of evidence may be influenced by their distorted perceptions of police procedure. These factors in addition to ignorance of the law may lead to juries that are prone to vote for conviction.

The basic findings of this study have some implications for future research. It is clear that television deserves more attention in studies of political socialization. In the future a larger proportion of research efforts should be given to the influence of entertainment television on political orientations. Future studies should be longitudinal, to clarify questions of causality, and should include measures of the influence of other agents of socialization such as the family, school, and peer group so that questions concerning spuriousness can be clarified. The examination of television's influence on system relevant attitudes and behavior has just begun.

NOTES

1. Thomas D. Cook, Deborah A. Kendzierski, and Stephen Thomas, "The Implicit Assumptions of Television Research: An Analysis of the 1982 NIMH Report on Television and Behavior," *Public Opinion Quarterly* 44 (Spring 1983): 178.

2. See Richard A. Joslyn and Peter F. Galderisi, "The Impact of Adolescent Perceptions of the President: A Test of the 'Spillover' Hypothesis," *Youth and Society* 9 (December 1977): 151-70.

3. Harrell Rodgers, Jr. and George Taylor, "The Policeman as an Agent of Regime Legitimation," *Midwest Journal of Political Science* 15 (February 1971): 72-86.

4. See Hubert B. Blalock, "Controlling for Background Factors: Spuriousness versus Developmental Sequence," *Sociological Inquiry* 34 (September 1964): 28-39.

5. George Gerbner and Larry Gross, "The Scary World of TV's Heavy Viewer," *Psychology Today* (April 1976): 89.

APPENDIX

Providence College
Political Science Department

A professor of political science at Providence College is conducting a study of children in Rhode Island. We are interested in how you feel about a number of things. *THIS IS NOT A TEST*. No one in this school will ever see any of your answers, and the results will not be put into your records.

Please answer the questions as *frankly* and *quickly* as you can. In most cases you only need to place a check mark before the answer you want. *Disregard* the numbers beside the answers; these numbers are for tabulating purposes only.

Thank you for your help.

Case number _____ _____ _____ _____   Card number __1__
           1   2   3   4   5

_____ 6. What is your sex?
      _____ 1. Male   _____ 2. Female

_____ 7. Is your religious preference Protestant, Catholic, Jewish, or something else?
      _____ 1. Protestant   _____ 3. Jewish
      _____ 2. Catholic   _____ 4. Other _____

_____ 8-9. How old are you? _____

_____ 10-11. What grade in school are you in? _____

_____ 12. What is your race?
      _____ 1. White   _____ 2. Negro   _____ 3. Other _____

_____ 13. What social class do you think that you belong to?
      _____ 1. Don't understand what social class means
      _____ 2. Upper class
      _____ 3. Middle class
      _____ 4. Working class
      _____ 5. Lower class

_____ 14. What is your father's job? If he is retired or no longer living, write this in. (Be specific and tell exactly what he does.)

_____
_____
_____

_____ 15. What is your mother's job? If she is retired or no longer living, write this in. (Be specific and tell exactly what she does.)

_____

_____

_____

_____ 16. Other than the United States, what *one* country did most of your relatives come from? _____

_____ 17. About how many hours a week do you watch television?

    _____ 1. None   _____ 4. 11-15 hours

    _____ 2. 1-5 hours   _____ 5. 16-20 hours

    _____ 3. 6-10 hours   _____ 6. 21 or over

_____ 18. What is your favorite television program?

_____

_____ 19. What one person on TV would you most like to be? _____

_____ 20. Do you read any newspapers regularly? _____ 1. yes _____ 2. no

_____ 21. Do you read any magazines? _____ 1. yes _____ 2. no

_____ 22. If you read magazines, which ones?

_____

_____

_____ 23. Have you read any books not required in school lately?

    _____ 1. yes _____ 2. no

_____ 24. Do you think that quite a few of the people running the government are a little crooked, not very many are, or do you think hardly any of them are?

    _____ 1. Quite a few are crooked

    _____ 2. Not very many are crooked

    _____ 3. Hardly any are crooked

_____ 25. Do you think that people in the government waste a lot of the money paid in taxes, waste some of it, or don't waste very much of it?

    _____ 1. Waste a lot

    _____ 2. Waste some

    _____ 3. Don't waste very much of it

_____ 26. How much of the time do you think you can trust the government in Washington to do what is right—just about always, most of the time, or only some of the time?

    _____ 1. Just about always

    _____ 2. Most of the time

    _____ 3. Some of the time

_____ 27. Generally speaking, would you say that most people can be trusted or that you can't be too careful in dealing with people?

    _____ 1. Most people can be trusted

    _____ 2. Can't be too careful

_____ 28. Do you feel that almost all of the people running the government are smart people who usually know what they are doing, or do you think that quite a few of them don't seem to know what they are doing?

     _____ 1. Almost all know what they are doing.

     _____ 2. Quite a few don't seem to know what they are doing.

_____ 29. Would you say that most of the time, people try to be helpful or that they are mostly just looking out for themselves?

     _____ 1. Try to be helpful

     _____ 2. Look out for themselves

_____ 30. Would you say the government is pretty much run by a few big interests looking out for themselves or that it is run for the benefit of all the people?

     _____ 1. Run by a few big interests looking out for themselves.

     _____ 2. Run for the benefit of all.

_____ 31. Do you think that most people would try to take advantage of you if they get a chance or would they try to be fair?

     _____ 1. Take advantage of me

     _____ 2. Try to be fair

     Do you belong to any of the following organizations?

_____ 32. Boy Scouts or Cub Scouts   _____ 1. yes   _____ 2. no

_____ 33. Girl Scouts or Brownies   _____ 1. yes   _____ 2. no

_____ 34. Other Organizations (please name them) _____

_____ 35. Do you know a policeman or policewoman personally?

     _____ 1. yes

     _____ 2. no

Listed below are some things that parents may do with their children. For each one check how often your parents do it with you.

_____ 36. Say you shouldn't show anger in a group.

     _____ 1. never _____ 2. rarely _____ 3. sometimes _____ 4. often

_____ 37. Say that parents' ideas are correct and shouldn't be challenged by children.

     _____ 1. never _____ 2. rarely _____ 3. sometimes _____ 4. often

_____ 38. Make it clear that you should not argue with adults.

     _____ 1. never _____ 2. rarely _____ 3. sometimes _____ 4. often

_____ 39. Say the best way to keep out of trouble is to stay away from it.

     _____ 1. never _____ 2. rarely _____ 3. sometimes _____ 4. often

_____ 40. Encourage you to give in on arguments, rather than risk making people mad.

     _____ 1. never _____ 2. rarely _____ 3. sometimes _____ 4. often

_____ 41. Say that getting your ideas across is important even if others don't like it.

     _____ 1. never _____ 2. rarely _____ 3. sometimes _____ 4. often

_____42. Say that you should look at both sides of issues.

_____ 1. never _____ 2. rarely _____ 3. sometimes _____ 4. often

_____43. Hold family talks about politics or religion, where some people take different sides from others.

_____ 1. never _____ 2. rarely _____ 3. sometimes _____ 4. often

_____44. Visit people who take the other side in arguments about politics or religion.

_____ 1. never _____ 2. rarely _____ 3. sometimes _____ 4. often

_____45. Take a side they don't believe in, just for the sake of argument.

_____ 1. never _____ 2. rarely _____ 3. sometimes _____ 4. often

_____46. What is your father's favorite television program? _____

_____47. What is your mother's favorite television program? _____

In this part of the questionnaire we would like to determine some of the television programs you watch and how often you watch them. Please place a check to the right of each program listed indicating how often you watch each program.

		Never	Sometimes	Often	Almost Always
_____48.	Little House on the Prairie	_____	_____	_____	_____
_____49.	Happy Days	_____	_____	_____	_____
_____50.	Paris	_____	_____	_____	_____
_____51.	Mork and Mindy	_____	_____	_____	_____
_____52.	Hawaii Five-O	_____	_____	_____	_____
_____53.	Hart to Hart	_____	_____	_____	_____
_____54.	The Waltons	_____	_____	_____	_____
_____55.	Charlie's Angels	_____	_____	_____	_____
_____56.	Vegas	_____	_____	_____	_____
_____57.	Different Strokes	_____	_____	_____	_____
_____58.	Barney Miller	_____	_____	_____	_____
_____59.	Quincy	_____	_____	_____	_____
_____60.	Eight is Enough	_____	_____	_____	_____
_____61.	Barnaby Jones	_____	_____	_____	_____
_____62.	Chips	_____	_____	_____	_____
_____63.	Eishied	_____	_____	_____	_____
_____64.	Rockford Files	_____	_____	_____	_____
_____65.	B.J. and the Bear	_____	_____	_____	_____
_____66.	The Incredible Hulk	_____	_____	_____	_____
_____67.	B.A.D. Cats	_____	_____	_____	_____
_____68.	Stone	_____	_____	_____	_____
_____69.	Misadventures of Sherriff Lobo	_____	_____	_____	_____
_____70.	The World's Greatest Superfriends	_____	_____	_____	_____

	Never	Sometimes	Often	Almost Always
_____71. Spiderwoman				
_____72. Tarzan and the Super Seven				
_____73. Plasticman Show				
_____74. Mighty Mouse				
_____75. Scooby and Scrappy Doo				
_____76. Godzilla/Globetrotters				
_____77. Daffy Duck Show				
_____78. Bugs Bunny				
_____79. The Jetsons				
_____80. Fred and Barney				

Case number _____ _____ _____ _____   Card number __1__
              1   2   3   4   5

These questions cover briefly many different topics. Indicate whether you agree or disagree with each statement by checking the appropriate response.

_____ 6. American political institutions are the best in the world.
         _____1. strongly agree
         _____2. agree
         _____3. undecided
         _____4. disagree
         _____5. strongly disagree

_____ 7. If I need help, I can rely on the police to come to my aid.
         _____1. strongly agree
         _____2. agree
         _____3. undecided
         _____4. disagree
         _____5. strongly disagree

_____ 8. Criminals usually get caught.
         _____1. strongly agree
         _____2. agree
         _____3. undecided
         _____4. disagree
         _____5. strongly disagree

_____ 9. Americans are more democratic than any other people.
         _____1. strongly agree
         _____2. agree
         _____3. undecided
         _____4. disagree
         _____5. strongly disagree

_____10. People on TV shows are just like people in the real world.
         _____1. strongly agree
         _____2. agree
         _____3. undecided
         _____4. disagree
         _____5. strongly disagree

_____ 11. The American political system is a model that foreigners would do well to copy.

_____ 1. strong agree
_____ 2. agree
_____ 3. undecided
_____ 4. disagree
_____ 5. strongly disagree

_____ 12. The criminals on TV are just like the criminals in real life.

_____ 1. strongly agree
_____ 2. agree
_____ 3. undecided
_____ 4. disagree
_____ 5. strongly disagree

_____ 13. Crime is such a problem that this city is not a safe place to raise children.

_____ 1. strongly agree
_____ 2. agree
_____ 3. undecided
_____ 4. disagree
_____ 5. strongly disagree

_____ 14. The founding fathers gave us a blessed and unique republic when they gave us the Constitution.

_____ 1. strongly agree
_____ 2. agree
_____ 3. undecided
_____ 4. disagree
_____ 5. strongly disagree

_____ 15. TV shows tell about life the way it really is.

_____ 1. strongly agree
_____ 2. agree
_____ 3. undecided
_____ 4. disagree
_____ 5. strongly disagree

_____ 16. The programs on TV show policemen just the way they are in real life.

_____ 1. strongly agree
_____ 2. agree
_____ 3. undecided
_____ 4. disagree
_____ 5. strongly disagree

_____ 17. It just is not safe to go downtown at night in Providence anymore.

_____ 1. strongly agree
_____ 2. agree
_____ 3. undecided
_____ 4. disagree
_____ 5. strongly disagree

_____ 18. The extent of crime is one of my major concerns.

_____ 1. strongly agree
_____ 2. agree
_____ 3. undecided
_____ 4. disagree
_____ 5. strongly disagree

_____ 19. Crime is such a problem that I am afraid to go out alone at night.

_____ 1. strongly agree
_____ 2. agree
_____ 3. undecided
_____ 4. disagree
_____ 5. strongly disagree

_____ 20. Policemen are generally more honest than most people.

_____ 1. strongly agree
_____ 2. agree
_____ 3. undecided
_____ 4. disagree
_____ 5. strongly disagree

_____ 21. The individual who refuses to obey the law is a menace to society.

_____ 1. strongly agree
_____ 2. agree
_____ 3. undecided
_____ 4. disagree
_____ 5. strongly disagree

_____ 22. People with money and contacts can often avoid problems with the police.

_____ 1. strongly agree
_____ 2. agree
_____ 3. undecided
_____ 4. disagree
_____ 5. strongly disagree

_____ 23. The police spend most of their time going after people who do little things and ignore most of the really bad things going on.

_____ 1. strongly agree
_____ 2. agree
_____ 3. undecided
_____ 4. disagree
_____ 5. strongly disagree

_____ 24. Police often enjoy pushing people around.

_____ 1. strongly agree
_____ 2. agree
_____ 3. undecided
_____ 4. disagree
_____ 5. strongly disagree

_____ 25. I must always obey the law.

_____ 1. strongly agree
_____ 2. agree
_____ 3. undecided
_____ 4. disagree
_____ 5. strongly disagree

_____ 26. The police don't show proper respect for citizens.

_____ 1. strongly agree
_____ 2. agree
_____ 3. undecided
_____ 4. disagree
_____ 5. strongly disagree

_____ 27. The crime rate in the area where I live seems to be rapidly increasing.

_____ 1. strongly agree
_____ 2. agree
_____ 3. undecided
_____ 4. disagree
_____ 5. strongly disagree

_____ 28. The police are too willing to use force and violence.

_____ 1. strongly agree
_____ 2. agree
_____ 3. undecided
_____ 4. disagree
_____ 5. strongly disagree

_____29. Personal circumstances should never be considered an excuse for lawbreaking.

_____1. strongly agree
_____2. agree
_____3. undecided
_____4. disagree
_____5. strongly disagree

_____30. The police in this community are guilty of discrimination against people like the poor and minority groups.

_____1. strongly agree
_____2. agree
_____3. undecided
_____4. disagree
_____5. strongly disagree

_____31. The police are often too stupid to solve complicated crimes.

_____1. strongly agree
_____2. agree
_____3. undecided
_____4. disagree
_____5. strongly disagree

_____32. The police or F.B.I. may sometimes be right in giving a man the "third degree" to make him talk.

_____1. strongly agree
_____2. agree
_____3. undecided
_____4. disagree
_____5. strongly disagree

_____33. Some criminals are so evil that they don't deserve a trial.

_____1. strongly agree
_____2. agree
_____3. undecided
_____4. disagree
_____5. strongly disagree

_____34. The police in our city are doing an effective job and deserve our thanks.

_____1. strongly agree
_____2. agree
_____3. undecided
_____4. disagree
_____5. strongly disagree

_____35. A person should obey the law even if it goes against what he thinks is right.

_____1. strongly agree
_____2. agree
_____3. undecided
_____4. disagree
_____5. strongly disagree

_____36. Judges should punish criminals more severely.

_____1. strongly agree
_____2. agree
_____3. undecided
_____4. disagree
_____5. strongly disagree

_____37. The threat of crime is so great that nobody can feel safe in his own home anymore.

_____1. strongly agree
_____2. agree
_____3. undecided
_____4. disagree
_____5. strongly disagree

_____ 38. There are too many restrictions on what the police can do.

_____ 1. strongly agree
_____ 2. agree
_____ 3. undecided
_____ 4. disagree
_____ 5. strongly disagree

_____ 39. The government should have the right to listen in on private telephone conversations in order to fight organized crime and subversives.

_____ 1. strongly agree
_____ 2. agree
_____ 3. undecided
_____ 4. disagree
_____ 5. strongly disagree

_____ 40. In order to protect the community from further crime, an arrested person should be kept in jail until his case comes to trial.

_____ 1. strongly agree
_____ 2. agree
_____ 3. undecided
_____ 4. disagree
_____ 5. strongly disagree

_____ 41. In some cases police should be allowed to search a person or his home even if they do not have a warrant.

_____ 1. strongly agree
_____ 2. agree
_____ 3. undecided
_____ 4. disagree
_____ 5. strongly disagree

_____ 42. Any man who insults a policeman has no complaint if he gets roughed up in return.

_____ 1. strongly agree
_____ 2. agree
_____ 3. undecided
_____ 4. disagree
_____ 5. strongly disagree

_____ 43. Disobedience of the law can never be tolerated.

_____ 1. strongly agree
_____ 2. agree
_____ 3. undecided
_____ 4. disagree
_____ 5. strongly disagree

_____ 44. Evidence which shows that a defendant did commit a crime should be used at his trial regardless of how the police got that evidence.

_____ 1. strongly agree
_____ 2. agree
_____ 3. undecided
_____ 4. disagree
_____ 5. strongly disagree

_____ 45. It would be difficult for me to break the law and keep my self-respect.

_____ 1. strongly agree
_____ 2. agree
_____ 3. undecided
_____ 4. disagree
_____ 5. strongly disagree

_____ 46. The police should have the authority to stop anyone on the street and ask the person for his name, address, and an explanation for his presence in the neighborhood.

_____ 1. strongly agree
_____ 2. agree
_____ 3. undecided
_____ 4. disagree
_____ 5. strongly disagree

_____47. If the courts stopped restricting the police, crime would not be a problem.

_____1. strongly agree
_____2. agree
_____3. undecided
_____4. disagree
_____5. strongly disagree

Please indicate whether the following statements are true or false:

_____48. If an innocent man is arrested it is up to him to prove that he is not guilty.

_____1. True
_____2. False
_____3. Don't know

_____49. Criminal trials in the United States are usually secret.

_____1. True
_____2. False
_____3. Don't know

_____50. A man who has committed a crime can be made to answer questions about the crime in court.

_____1. True
_____2. False
_____3. Don't know

_____51. When a person is arrested, police have to tell him he has a right to have a lawyer with him before he is questioned.

_____1. True
_____2. False
_____3. Don't know

_____52. It is the job of a judge to prove that a man accused of a crime is guilty.

_____1. True
_____2. False
_____3. Don't know

_____53. The amendment to the U.S. Constitution that says a person does not have to testify against himself is the Sixth Amendment.

_____1. True
_____2. False
_____3. Don't know

_____54. About how many comic books do you read each week? _____

_____55. What are your three favorite comic books?
1. _____
2. _____
3. _____

_____56. Do you think people should always obey laws?
_____1. yes   _____2. no

_____57. If you answered yes, why would you obey a law you disagree with?

_____58. If you answered no, why wouldn't you obey a law?

_____59. Generally, what grades do you get in school?
_____1. Above average (A's and B's)
_____2. About average (Mostly C's)
_____3. Below average

BIBLIOGRAPHY

Abramson, Paul R. *Political Attitudes in America: Formation and Change.* San Francisco: W. H. Freeman, 1983.

Acuri, Alan F. "You Can't Take Fingerprints Off Water: Police Officers' Views Toward 'Cop' Television Shows." *Human Relations* 30 (Summer 1977): 237-47.

Adelson, Joseph, and Robert O'Neill. "The Growth of Political Ideas in Adolescence: The Sense of Community." *Journal of Personality and Social Psychology* 4 (July 1966): 295-306.

Alley, Robert S. *Television: Ethics for Hire?* Nashville: Abingdon Press, 1977.

Arons, Stephen, and Ethan Katsh. "How TV Cops Flout the Law." *Saturday Review*, March 19, 1977, pp. 11-19.

Bayley, David H., and Harold Mendelsohn. *Minorities and Police.* New York: Free Press, 1969.

Blalock, Hubert B. "Controlling for Background Factors: Spuriousness versus Developmental Sequence." *Sociological Inquiry* 34 (September 1964): 28-39.

Block, Richard. "Support for Civil Liberties and Support for the Police." *American Behavioral Scientist* (July 1970): 781-96.

Blumler, Jay, and Elihu Katz. *The Uses of Mass Communications.* Beverly Hills: Sage, 1973.

Bouma, Donald. *Kids and Cops.* Grand Rapids: W. B. Erdman, 1969.

Bradbury, Ray. *Fahrenheit 451.* New York: Simon and Schuster, 1950.

Brown, Ben. "A New Semester of 'Paper Chase' on Showtime." *USA Today*, May 21, 1984, p. 50.

Cantor, Muriel G. *Prime-Time Television: Content and Control.* Beverly Hills: Sage, 1980.

Carlson, James M. "Crime Show Viewing by Preadults: The Impact on Attitudes Toward Civil Liberties." *Communication Research* 10 (1983): 540.

Chaffee, Stephen, with Marilyn Jackson-Beeck, Jean Durall, and Donna Wilson. "Mass Communication in Political Socialization." In *Handbook of Political Socialization*, edited by Stanley Renshon, pp. 223-58. New York: Free Press, 1977.

Chaffee, Stephen, Jack McLeod, and Daniel Wackman. "Family Communication Patterns and Adolescent Political Participation." In *Socialization to Politics*, edited by Jack Dennis, pp. 349-64. New York: Wiley, 1973.

Citrin, Jack. "Comment: The Political Relevance of Trust in Government." *American Political Science Review* 68 (December 1974): 973-88.

Comstock, George, Steven Chaffee, Nathan Katzman, Maxwell McCombs, and Donald Roberts. *Television and Human Behavior.* New York: Columbia University Press, 1978.

Cook, Thomas D., Deborah A. Kendzierski, and Stephen Thomas. "The Implicit Assumptions of Television Research: An Analysis of the 1982 NIMH Report on Television and Behavior." *Public Opinion Quarterly* 44 (Spring 1983): 161-201.

Corbett, Michael. "Public Support for 'Law and Order': Interrelationships with System Affirmation and Attitudes Toward Minorities." *Criminology* 19 (November 1981): 328-43.

Daley, Robert J. "Police Report on the TV Cop Shows." *New York Times Magazine*, November 19, 1972, pp. 39-40.

Decker, Scott H. "Citizen Attitudes Toward the Police: A Review of Past Findings and Suggestions for Future Policy." *Journal of Police Science and Administration* 9 (March 1981): 80-87.

Dominick, Joseph R. "Children's Viewing of Crime Shows and Attitudes on Law Enforcement." *Journalism Quarterly* 51 (Spring 1974): 5-12.

_____. "Crime and Law Enforcement in the Mass Media." In *Deviance and Mass Media*, edited by Charles Winick, pp. 105-27. Beverly Hills: Sage, 1978.

_____. "Crime and Law Enforcement on Prime Time Television." *Public Opinion Quarterly* 37 (Spring 1973): 241-50.

Doob, Anthony N., and Glenn E. McDonald. "Television and Fear of Victimization: Is the Relationship Causal?" *Journal of Personality and Social Psychology* 37 (1979): 170-79.

Easton, David. *A Systems Analysis of Political Life.* New York: Wiley, 1965.

Easton, David, and Jack Dennis, *Children in the Political System.* New York: McGraw-Hill, 1969.

Gerbner, George. "Violence and Television Drama: Trends and Symbolic Functions." In *Television and Social Behavior, vol. 1: Content and Control,* edited by G. A. Comstock and E. A. Rubinstein. Washington: U.S. Government Printing Office, 1972.

Gerbner, George, and Larry Gross. "The Scary World of TV's Heavy Viewer." *Psychology Today* (April 1976): 89-91.

_____. "Living with Television: The Violence Profile," *Journal of Communication* 26 (Spring 1976): 172-99.

Gerbner, George, Larry Gross, Michael Eleey, Marilyn Jackson-Beeck, Suzanne Jeffries-Fox, and Nancy Signorielli. "TV Violence Profile No. 8: The Highlights." *Journal of Communication* 27 (Spring 1977): 171-80.

Gerbner, George, Larry Gross, Marilyn Jackson-Beeck, Suzanne Jeffries-Fox, and Nancy Signorielli. "Cultural Indicators: Violence Profile No. 9." *Journal of Communication* 28 (Summer 1978): 176-207.

Gerbner, George, Larry Gross, Nancy Signorielli, Michael Morgan, and Marilyn Jackson-Beeck. "The Demonstration of Power: Violence Profile No. 10." *Journal of Communication* 29 (Spring 1979): 177-96.

Gerbner, George, Larry Gross, Michael Morgan, and Nancy Signorielli. "A Curious Journey Into the World of Paul Hirsh." *Communication Research* 8 (January 1981): 39-72.

————. "Charting the Mainstream: Television's Contributions to Political Orientations." *Journal of Communication* 32 (Summer 1982): 100-27.

Gerstein, Robert. "The Practice of Fidelity to Law." *Law and Society Review* 4 (May 1970): 479-94.

Greenstein, Fred I. *Children and Politics.* New Haven: Yale University Press, 1965.

Gunther, Max. "You Have the Right to Remain Silent," *TV Guide*, December 18, 1971, pp. 7-9.

Hawkins, Robert P., and Suzanne Pingee. "Some Processes in the Cultivation Effect." *Communication Research* 7 (April 1980): 193-226.

————. "Television's Influence on Social Reality." In *Television and Behavior: Ten Years of Scientific Progress and Implications for the Eighties, vol. 2: Technical Reviews*, edited by David Pearl, Lorraine Bouthilet, and Joyce Lazar, pp. 224-47. Washington: National Institute of Mental Health, 1982.

Hess, Robert, and Judith Torney. *The Development of Political Attitudes in Children.* Garden City, N.Y.: Doubleday, 1967.

Himmelweit, Hilde T. "Social Influence and Television." In *Television and Social Behavior: Beyond Violence and Children*, edited by S. B. Withey and R. P. Abeles, pp. 136-60. Hillsdale, N.J.: Erlbaum, 1980.

Hirsh, Paul M. "The 'Scary World' of the Nonviewer and Other Anomalies." *Communication Research* 7 (October 1980): 403-56.

Huesmann, L. Rowell. "Television Violence and Aggressive Behavior." In *Television and Behavior: Ten Years of Scientific Progress and Implications for the Eighties, vol. 2: Technical Reviews*, edited by David Pearl, Lorraine Bouthilet, and Joyce Lazar, pp. 126-57. Washington: National Institute of Mental Health, 1982.

Hughes, Michael. "The Fruits of Cultivation Analysis: A Reexamination of Some Effects of Television Watching." *Public Opinion Quarterly* 44 (Spring 1980): 287-302.

Jennings, M. Kent, and Lawrence E. Fox. "The Conduct of Socio-Political Research in Schools: Strategies and Problems of Access." *The School Review* 76 (December 1968): 428-44.

Jennings, M. Kent, and Richard G. Niemi. *The Political Character of Adolescence: The Influence of Families and Schools*. Princeton: Princeton University Press, 1974.

Joslyn, Richard A., and Peter F. Galderisi. "The Impact of Adolescent Perceptions of the President: A Test of the 'Spillover' Hypothesis." *Youth and Society* 9 (December 1977): 151-70.

Katsh, Ethan. "Is Television Anti-Law?: An Inquiry into the Relationship Between Law and Media." *The ALSA Forum* 7 (1983): 26-40.

_____. "Television: The Message, The Medium, and Legal Values." In *Law and Society*, edited by R. Vicylesteke, pp. 241-58. Honolulu: East-West Center, 1977.

Kirscht, J. P., and R. C. Dillehay. *Dimensions of Authoritarianism: A Review of Theory and Research*. Lexington, Kentucky: University of Kentucky Press, 1967.

Klapper, Joseph. *The Effects of Mass Communications*. Glencoe, Ill.: Free Press, 1960.

Koeppen, Sheilah. "Children and Compliance: A Comparative Analysis of Socialization Studies." *Law and Society Review* 4 (May 1970): 545-64.

Krugman, Herbert E. "The Impact of Television Advertising: Learning Without Involvement." *Public Opinion Quarterly* 29 (Fall 1965): 349-56.

Krugman, Herbert E., and Eugene L. Hartley. "Passive Learning from Television." *Public Opinion Quarterly* 34 (Winter 1970): 184-90.

Lewis, W. H. "Witness for the Prosecution." *TV Guide*, November 30, 1974, pp. 5-7.

Lichter, Linda S., and S. Robert Lichter. *Prime Time Crime*. Washington, D.C.: The Media Institute, 1983.

Liebert, Robert M., Joyce N. Sprafkin, and Emily S. Davidson. *The Early Window: Effects of Television on Children and Youth*. New York: Pergamon Press, 1982.

Litt, Edgar. "Civic Education, Norms, and Political Indoctrination." *American Sociological Review* 28 (February 1963): 69-75.

Mankiewicz, Frank, and Joel Swerdlow. *Remote Control: Television and the Manipulation of American Life.* New York: Times Books, 1978.

McLeod, Jack M., and Byron Reeves. "On the Nature of Mass Media Effects." In *Television and Social Behavior: Beyond Violence and Children,* edited by S. B. Withey and R. P. Abeles, pp. 17-54. Hillsdale, N.J.: Erlbaum, 1980.

Miller, Arthur. "Political Issues and Trust in Government: 1964-1970." *American Political Science Review* 68 (December 1974): 951-72.

O'Brien, John T. "Public Attitudes Toward Police." *Journal of Police Science and Administration* 6 (September 1978): 303-10.

Orwell, George. *1984.* San Diego: Harcourt, Brace, Jovanovich, 1977.

Packer, Herbert. *The Limits of Criminal Sanction.* Stanford: Stanford University Press, 1968.

Peek, Charles W., Jon P. Alston, and George Lowe, "Comparative Evaluation of Local Police." *Public Opinion Quarterly* 42 (Fall 1978): 370-79.

Pinner, Frank A. "Parental Overprotection and Political Distrust." *The Annals* 361 (September 1965): 58-70.

Prothro, James W., and Charles M. Grigg. "Fundamental Principles of Democracy: Bases of Agreement and Disagreement." *Journal of Politics* 23 (May 1960): 276-84.

Reeves, Byron. "Perceived TV Reality as a Predictor of Children's Social Behavior." *Journalism Quarterly* 55 (Winter 1978): 682-95.

Rodgers, Harrell, Jr., and Edward B. Lewis. "Political Support and Compliance Attitudes: A Study of Adolescents." *American Politics Quarterly* 2 (January 1974): 61-77.

Rodgers, Harrell, Jr., and George Taylor. "Pre-adult Attitudes Toward Legal Compliance: Notes Toward a Theory." *Social Science Quarterly* 51 (December 1970): 539-51.

————. "The Policeman as an Agent of Regime Legitimation," *Midwest Journal of Political Science* 15 (February 1971): 72-86.

Rosenberg, Morris. *Occupations and Values.* Glencoe, Ill.: Free Press, 1957.

Rubin, Alan M. "Child and Adolescent Television Use and Political Socialization." *Journalism Quarterly* 55 (Winter 1978): 125-29.

Sarat, Austin. "Support for the Legal System." *American Politics Quarterly* 3 (February 1975): 3-24.

Searing, Donald D., Joel T. Schwartz, and Oldin E. Lind. "The Structuring Principle: Political Socialization and Belief Systems." *American Political Science Review* 67 (June 1973): 415-32.

Schuman, David. *A Preface to Politics.* Lexington, Mass.: D. C. Heath, 1973.

Smith, Paul, and Richard O. Hawkins. "Victimization, Types of Citizen-Police Contacts, and Attitudes Toward Police." *Law and Society* (Fall 1973): 135-52.

Stein, Benjamin. "The Social Value of TV Thrillers." *Wall Street Journal*, May 28, 1975, p. 8.

Stinchcombe, Arthur L., Rebecca Adams, Carol A. Heimer, Kim Lane Scheppele, Tom W. Smith, and D. Garth Taylor. *Crime and Punishment—Changing Attitudes in America.* San Francisco: Jossey-Boss, 1980.

Thomas, Charles W., and Jeffrey M. Hyman. "Perceptions of Crime, Fear of Victimization, and Public Perceptions of Police Performance." *Journal of Police Science and Administration* 5 (Fall 1977): 305-17.

Volgy, Thomas J., and John E. Schwarz. "TV Entertainment Programming and Sociopolitical Attitudes." *Journalism Quarterly* 57 (January 1980): 150-55.

Wakshlag, Jacob, Virginia Vial, and Ronald Tamborini. "Selecting Crime Show Drama and Apprehension About Crime." *Human Communication Research* 10 (Winter 1983): 227-42.

Watts, Meredith W. "Anti-Heterodoxy and the Punishment of Deviance: An Explanation of Student Attitudes Toward Law and Order." *Western Political Quarterly* 30 (March 1977): 93-103.

Weigel, Russell H., and Richard Jessor. "Television and Adolescent Conventionality: An Exploratory Study." *Public Opinion Quarterly* 37 (Spring 1973): 76-90.

Weissberg, Robert. *Political Learning, Political Choice and Democratic Citizenship.* Englewood Cliffs, N.J.: Prentice-Hall, 1974.

Winn, Marie. *The Plug-In Drug.* New York: Viking Press, 1977.

Wright, Gerald C., Jr. "Linear Models for Evaluating Conditional Relationships." *American Journal of Political Science* 20 (May 1976): 349-73.

INDEX

ABOUT THE AUTHOR

JAMES M. CARLSON is an associate professor of Political Science at Providence College. He received his Ph.D. from Kent State University. Professor Carlson's research on political socialization, political psychology, political parties, and elections has appeared in *American Politics Quarterly, Micropolitics, Polity, International Political Science Review,* and *Communication Research,* among other professional journals.